"Dawn Lerman grew up Jewish in
Might sound different, but for the m
when it comes to food. The philoso
Fat Dad hilariously and poignantly
you're Italian, Jewish, or anything else, you can relate to how family,
food, and the love of both affect how we grow up and live our life.
Mangia!"
—Ray Romano, Emmy award–winning actor

"Everything you want in a book about food: thoughtful, moving,
funny, and, of course, delicious (see the recipe on sweet potato latkes).
Dawn reminds us that eating is about much more than protein and
carbs and nutrients—it's about family, history, and identity. Dawn's
grandmother put it best: 'I can find my heritage in a bowl of soup.'"
—A. J. Jacobs, journalist and *New York Times*
bestselling author of *Drop Dead Healthy*

"Dawn Lerman takes the reader along on one of life's important
journeys—to find true nourishment. Her discoveries about the powerful ways that food connects us to our families, our heritage, and,
ultimately, to ourselves are profound and beautiful."
—Andie Mitchell, *New York Times* bestselling author
of *It Was Me All Along*

"Dawn Lerman's love letter to her father is a big, funny, welcome
embrace to all of us fat dads out there."
—David Sax, James Beard Award–winning author of *Save the Deli*

"Told with no fear, some surprises, and much humor, punctuated
with delightful and delicious recipes from both the old and the new
world of cooking, the best dishes being those made with love. We can
all relate to a life obsessed with food; and Dawn shows that food
often does equal love, and that being fed well equates to being nur-
tured as well as nourished . . . A truly wonderful journey!"
—Lisa Goldberg, cofounder of Monday Morning Cooking Club

"[Lerman's] passion for cooking and good food, a constant joy during a challenging childhood, shines throughout this touching memoir."
—Martha Rose Shulman, cookbook author, cooking teacher, and food columnist for *The New York Times*

"Some of Dawn Lerman's vivid childhood food memories made me smile; others brought tears to my eyes. I particularly enjoyed reading about her inspiring grandmother, who, with her love and her delicious cooking, saved Dawn Lerman's life 'spoonful by spoonful,' patiently teaching her to taste and to cook."
—Faye Levy, author of *1,000 Jewish Recipes*

My Fat Dad

A Memoir of Food, Love, and Family,
with Recipes

Dawn Lerman

BERKLEY BOOKS, NEW YORK

BERKLEY

An imprint of Penguin Random House LLC
375 Hudson Street, New York, New York 10014

This book is an original publication of Penguin Random House LLC.

Library of Congress Cataloging-in-Publication Data

Lerman, Dawn.
My fat dad : a memoir of food, love, and family, with recipes / Dawn Lerman.—
Berkley trade paperback edition.
p. cm.
ISBN 978-0-425-27223-7
1. Lerman, Dawn—Family.   2. Cooks—United States—Biography.
3. Cooking, American.   I. Title.
TX649.L478A3 2015
641.5092—dc23
[B]
2015016904

PUBLISHING HISTORY
Berkley trade paperback edition / September 2015

PRINTED IN THE UNITED STATES OF AMERICA

10 9 8 7 6 5 4 3 2 1

Cover design by Daniel Rembert.
Cover photo © Tim Platt / Getty Images.

Penguin is committed to publishing works of quality and integrity.
In that spirit, we are proud to offer this book to our readers;
however, the story, the experiences, and the words
are the author's alone.

To my family:
My dad, my mom, my sister April, my grandmother Beauty—
without you, there would be no story.
And to Dylan and Sofia, you are my world and my heart.

Contents

My Fat Dad

PART ONE

Always Hungry

As far back as I can remember, there was an invisible wall that separated me from my dad, a distance that I could never completely penetrate. His closest relationship was with the bathroom scale—his first stop every morning and his last stop every evening. It controlled his moods, our days, what we were going to eat, and basically ruled our family life.

My father, a brilliant copywriter in the *Mad Men* era of advertising, was known for his witty ad campaigns—he was responsible for such iconic slogans as "Fly the Friendly Skies of United," "Coke Is It," "This Bud's for You," and "Leggo My Eggo"—and being able to solve any image problem that was thrown his way. Unfortunately, he was not able to use the same problem-solving skills when it came to his weight. My dad was fat while I was growing up—450 pounds at his heaviest. His weight would go up and down like an elevator, depending on what diet he was on or not on that month. For six months, he ate only white rice; another time, he drank only shakes; and another time he had only Special K—hoping that after a week of eating the cereal, there would be only an inch to pinch. What was most vivid to me about those early years with my parents was the constant feeling of hunger that consumed me as my obese father rotated from diet to diet.

Each week he would discover a new miracle plan, and my mom and I were forced to eat whatever freeze-dried, saccharin-loaded concoction he was testing, so as not to tempt him by eating "normal" food. Before I entered grade school, I was an expert on Atkins, Weight Watchers, the Barbie Diet, the Grapefruit Diet, the Cabbage Soup Diet, the Drinking Man's Diet, and the Sleeping Beauty Diet, able to recite their rules and agreeing with my dad that the world would be a better place if food did not have calories. Of course, I had no idea what a calorie was, but I knew it was something that was really upsetting to my father, and he would be happier without them.

My mother, on the other hand, never understood what the big deal was with food and ate only one small meal a day—usually a can of StarKist light tuna right out of the can with a plastic fork—while standing up and chatting on the phone. She had no interest in preparing meals. Mostly what I ate consisted of my dad's diet foods, a meal replacement shake, or on a good day a bagel or pizza in the car. We never ate meals together as a family. In fact, we never ate sitting down, which was really troubling to my pediatrician, Dr. Levy, who shook his head each time he weighed and measured me at my checkups. He would constantly tell my mom to put some meat on my bones, scolding her as he handed me an extra sucker, telling her she must feed me if she wanted me to grow.

Despite Dr. Levy's recommendations, my dad lined the

shelves of our kitchen with mystery powders, shakes, and basically anything that had the word "NO" on it. No Sugar, No Starch, No Fat, No Calories, No Taste! With each new diet came an elaborate array of rules, until he could not take the boredom of the routine anymore—justifying the chips, the Mallomar cookies, the fried chicken, and fast-food burgers as market research for his ad campaigns. My dad felt that in order to create a good campaign, you needed to believe in the product you were selling. And he was always the best customer for the products he advertised, testing them excessively—especially when he was working on Kentucky Fried Chicken, Schlitz Beer, Sprite, and Pringles Potato Chips.

"Regardless of what it looks like, I am eating to further my career," my dad would proclaim, as he gobbled every morsel without sharing any with me. "My campaigns are nothing if they are not authentic," he declared, closing his bedroom door behind him as he went in there to work, taking his "research" with him. Sometimes, I would sit at the door listening to him peck away at the typewriter, imagining that each potato chip he ate inspired him to come up with a witty slogan.

While the diets came and went, the feeling of loneliness and the constant uncertainty lingered in the air. My only glimpse into a nourishing, normal environment, my only model of healthy eating, was the weekends I spent with my beloved grandmother. It was in her kitchen where I learned what love and happiness were—one recipe at a time.

1

All It Takes Is a Spoonful of Soup

....

Beauty's Chicken Soup with Fluffy Matzo Balls,
Sweet Potato Latkes, Mohn Kichlach

....

M y maternal grandmother always told me if just one person loves you, that is enough to make you feel good inside and grow up strong. For me, that person was my grandmother Beauty.

I spent most weekends with my grandmother because my parents liked to go out and stay out late, and my mother hated to pay good money for a babysitter only to find her asleep on the couch with Tinker Toys and Mr. Potato Heads sprawled all over the plush white, blue, and green patterned shag carpet in the living room when she returned home. It infuriated her that her Moroccan ashtrays on the side tables would inevitably be filled to the brim with menthol cigarettes and Juicy Fruit gum, and my dad would expect her to empty them while he would gleefully offer to drive the babysitter home—taking way longer than the five minutes the drive normally took.

He insisted that he needed to stop at the Jewel for a case of Diet Black Cherry Shasta and a carton of Salem Menthol Lights, so he could make it through the night without snacking. "You do not want me to blow my diet, do you?" he would repeatedly say to my mom. "I only ate shrimp cocktail and iceberg lettuce all evening. I need support, not criticism."

My dad, an ambitious copywriter, recently hired by the Leo Burnett Company in Chicago, was invited out pretty much every night, either to the Playboy Club for a members' only dinner or to one of the new nightclubs on Rush Street for cocktails with his creative team. "It's a job requirement," he would tell my mom, returning home to our third-floor walk-up apartment as the sun was coming up.

While many nights during the week my father went out solo, my mom would not let him go without her on the weekends. "Why should I stay home while you are having all the fun?" He would try to convince her that wives weren't allowed, and that Hugh Hefner, for whom my dad used to work as a columnist reviewing modern jazz albums, had many good connections that would further his career.

"In order to achieve real success, I need to be able to socialize freely and not be held back. It's about image. All the other wives seem to get it." My dad, a VIP key holder at the Playboy Club, was very proud of his status—prominently dangling the key with the raised bunny ears while rolling his eyes back and forth to charm his way out of not having my mom tag along.

My mom, usually swayed by his devilish brown eyes, refused to give in when it came to going out. She was an aspiring actress and wanted to be discovered. "I have no interest in being the kind of wife my mother is. It is 1966, not 1950. You are not the only one in this house who graduated from Northwestern and has career plans."

But my father would constantly remind her that she was the one who wanted to start a family, and now it was time for her to act like a proper mother and wife—especially since she was only teaching high school English part-time and it was his salary supporting them.

I would spend most mornings, when I was not at my grandmother's house, outside my parents' door listening to them have the same argument over and over again.

"Taking Dawn to the sandbox once a day does not make you a good mother."

"Putting a roof over our heads does not make you a good father or husband."

Often, they would forget I was even in the house, raising their voices behind their closed bedroom door, and no matter how many times I knocked, they never seemed to hear. Hoping someone would remember I had not yet had breakfast, I would write a note, with pictures instead of actual words, and slip it under the door before I rushed into my room and packed my little paisley suitcase. I didn't really want to run away; I just wanted to be found. No matter how long I hid in my closet, my parents never seemed to search for me; nor were they ever thrilled when I magically reappeared. Even though I was only three and a half, I was consistently consumed with an overwhelming feeling of sadness and pain in my stomach that would linger from Sunday till Friday. I knew the days of the week because my grandmother showed me how to check them off on a calendar. "There are only four checks between visits."

Each and every Friday night, when I arrived at my grandparents' house, my grandmother would run down her front porch stairs in her lacey matching nightgown and robe set and scream in excitement, "My little beauty, my little beauty!" I thought when I heard her say "beauty" over and over again, she was trying to tell me her name—so Beauty is what I called her. The name stuck, and soon everyone in her small neighborhood of West Rogers Park in Chicago knew my grandmother as Beauty—including my grandfather Papa, my mother, and all the neighbors.

The cooking aromas coming from her kitchen made my mouth water. Beauty always had a pot of something cooking on the stove, a freshly drawn bath, and a fluffy, lavender-smelling nightgown waiting for me. She would bathe me before we ate, softening my skin with cream and rose talcum powder that she dusted on my back with a big powder puff.

For meals, she would lift me up and sit me in a special chair, which she piled high with several phone books—both the White and Yellow Pages—and an overstuffed round corduroy pillow. She wanted to make sure I could see above the table, which was set with silverware that she polished every week and an embroidered tablecloth that my Papa brought back from New Orleans, where he would go to visit his race horses, Glen and Phyllis, named after my mother and her brother Glen.

Beauty would tease Papa, saying he had three wives: his restaurant supply store, the track, and her. Papa would say it was a tough decision to decide whom he loved the most, tying the thick cream-colored napkin around my neck so I wouldn't soak my pj's when I sipped the warm pea soup that had been simmering for hours.

"There is no competition really," he would exclaim. "No matter where I am, I can taste the love that Beauty puts into her food."

Before we even finished our meal, Papa would ask Beauty what she would be preparing the next evening, telling me to pay careful attention to all the details as we shopped and cooked. "Katchkala," my grandfather would say, calling me by the pet name he had for me, "there is nothing like Beauty's soups and roasts to make all the problems of the world go away." Before I even had words to describe the delicious, thick-as-fog split pea soup flavored with bone marrow, I knew what he was saying to be true. No matter what I felt during the rest of the week, the anticipation of Beauty's food and of time spent with her lifted my spirits. Little Beauty is what she called me, and beautiful and special is how she always made me feel.

I loved strolling hand in hand with her up and down Devon Avenue. As we walked by each shop that she frequented daily, the owners would run out and say, "Beauty is here." They would hug her and she would hug me, saying, "Look who I brought with me today. I am so lucky to have my little beauty with me, my precious Dawn." Everyone seemed so happy to see us, gifting us with all sorts of goodies. Gittel at Levinson's Bakery would give us cinnamon and chocolate babkas to taste— flaky and buttery, filled with chocolate almost as gooey as raw brownie dough. Robert at Robert's Kosher Fish Market would give us lox tails to suck on—smoky, greasy, and a little too salty for my taste. And Golda, the woman at the fruit stand would always give me a couple pieces of dried apricot—naturally sweet as candy—to enjoy while my grandmother filled her basket with the freshest produce. They would all tell me what a nice, good girl I was, and Beauty would say there was no better girl than me, making sure to compliment them as well.

Beauty was the perfect name for my grandmother. She was like a shiny star that radiated light on the top of a Chanukah bush. Everywhere she went, she made people smile. She would jokingly say she was Jackie Mason's real wife—he just didn't know it. But it was not what my grandmother said that was so funny, but that she would just laugh so hard after she said something that everyone else couldn't help but join in. "Laugh and people will laugh with you, cry and you will cry alone. The closest distance between two people is a good laugh"—a saying she got from a fortune cookie that she saved and kept in her pocketbook. Beauty emphasized how important it was to make others happy, even if it sometimes meant putting your own feelings aside.

"We do not know what goes on in anyone else's house, but we can change their day by just saying hello and offering a kind gesture."

Beauty always carried a batch of mohn cookies when we went shopping. There were always some of these poppy seed treats for the pharmacist at Rosen's Drug Store; the women at the hair salon who forever admired her decorative, big-brimmed hats, telling her she was a dead ringer for Ruth Gordon—both standing just about five feet—and the eight kids that lived across the street, who would call her Grandma Beauty, lining up youngest to oldest to get a cookie, a coin, and a hug since their own grandma lived in Cleveland, and they rarely saw her.

I thought how lucky I was as I helped Beauty hand out her weekly bag of treats. I asked her if she did that with my mom when she was a little girl.

"Your mom was born during the Great Depression. We were so poor that she had to sleep in a wooden drawer with some old clothes for blankets. At the time, I was working with Papa. We had a small soda shop, and I worked all day making home-cut French fries and hot dogs that I sliced open and grilled instead of just boiling like many of the other places in town. Many famous gangsters were customers—they would walk out without paying their five-cent check. I kept your mom near me in the shop, but I didn't really have time to teach her anything. But your mother, like your Papa, was smart as a whip. She taught herself to read and add and subtract before she even went to first grade, by deciphering the names and number combinations off Papa's racing sheets."

I loved listening to Beauty tell the stories about my mom and my uncle Glen—who was now a Sufi living in a commune in Oregon—when they were kids, and the romantic story of how she met Papa. She loved to tell it often. "Papa was a boarder in my parents' boardinghouse, where he was renting a room after he crossed the Canadian border. He had no money, but he had the bluest eyes I had ever seen and was the best salesman. A year after we met, he convinced me to elope with him to Detroit. I never had a real wedding, so we rented some clothes to take a picture to send to my parents, hoping they would forgive me when they saw how happy I looked in the photograph."

My grandmother always spoke about my Papa with great pride. She wanted me to know about his history because, like my mother, he was not one to sit down and share about his life or feelings. "Your Papa is a great man and a very hard worker with a spirit as wild as the horses he loves."

My grandmother was very proud of Papa's work ethic and his successful business, the Sidney Supply Company, which sold cutlery and bar supplies to all the big restaurants in Chicago. Beauty just wished he had a little more time for her. She fondly recalled how romantic he was when they first met. But my grandmother never took him for granted. No matter what time my Papa returned home—and most of the time it was late, except Saturdays, when he walked in the door at five o'clock sharp—Beauty was ready for his entrance. Her hair was done up in a perfect beehive, and warm, delicious, homemade food was on the table—potato latkes, or a cholent, or chicken soup with matzo balls—which I always helped make.

Changing our clothes and putting our special aprons on before we cooked was almost as important as what we were cooking. While Beauty liked everything immaculate, she wanted us to be able to be covered in flour, chocolate, or whatever, and not worry about stains, no matter what we were cooking. If we did dirty our garments, we would scrub them on a washboard down in the basement before we ate. Sometimes, when we were doing chores, my grandmother would put egg masks on our faces—she said it would make us look young forever. Beauty made everything fun, even when we realized how much of the day had passed, and we had to hurry to get dinner on the table for Papa.

I loved helping her chop, dice, mix, fry, and stew. If I asked her how much celery to chop for her famous chicken soup, she'd wave off the question. "Just use your creativity," she'd say. "You can't go wrong when you use fresh ingredients." She'd throw in a few parsnips, sweet potatoes, garlic, chicken legs, chicken bones, even chicken feet, and two hours later it was the most delicious thing I'd ever tasted.

The matzo balls were a little trickier. They required a little more precision. Usually, Beauty was a little-bit-of-this, little-bit-of-that, taste-as-you-go-along cook, but matzo balls were not included in this repertoire. "I used to just mix the matzo meal with oil, eggs, salt, and throw them into some boiling water. But then when your mother became engaged to your dad and I went to your Bubbe Mary's for Rosh Hashanah, I was transformed. Who knew a matzo ball could be so fluffy, not hard like a baseball!"

"Did you ask her how to make them?"

"I did. She told me it was her little secret. But on your parents' wedding day, she whispered to me, 'Schmaltz and ginger ale!'

"It took me a lot of experimenting before they stopped sinking to the bottom of the pot. But I think I have come close."

Beauty held her hand over mine as we cracked and separated the eggs, and added seltzer instead of ginger ale to the wooden bowl. She reached for the small jam jar that contained the schmaltz that she stored in her refrigerator—instructing me to take just two spoonfuls and no more. "I save the drippings when I roast a chicken. You don't want to cook with schmaltz every day, but everything in moderation is okay. And a little bit, here and there, adds flavor."

Once the mixture was chilled, we'd coat our damp hands with crumbled fresh matzo so they wouldn't stick to the mixture when we rolled the balls. One by one, I'd hand them to her, and she'd place them into the stock—never water.

When Papa would rave about the meal, she'd say that everything tasted so good because I helped. I paid careful attention to Beauty's directions—never over-salting. "You could always add more," she said, "but it is hard to take the salt out."

During the summer months, while my grandfather was preoccupied after dinner with counting his S&H Green Stamps to redeem for prizes, my grandmother would put on a pair of pedal pushers, a freshly pressed blouse, and matching shoes, and we would play outside with a red rubber ball, taking turns bouncing the ball under our knee, seeing who could last the longest without the ball rolling away. With each bounce, we had to name a food that corresponded to the next letter in the alphabet, trying our hardest to make it from A to Z. "A is for apple, B is for banana, C is for cherry . . ." When it started getting really dark, we would head inside for dessert. My grandmother loved making oatmeal cookies, fruit compote, or a seasonal crumble that she topped with Cool Whip or homemade whipped cream that we would beat by hand until it was nice and fluffy.

During the winter, when it was too cold to play outside, we would go into the living room—which she would turn into a little hotel for me when I would stay over. She would pull out old photo albums; some were filled with pictures and others were filled with poems. My grandmother wrote a poem about everyone she ever met. She would write them all out by hand, and then her sister Jeannie would type them up so she could save them nicely in her album. "This is my favorite one," she would say before reading the poem aloud.

My Darling Dawn,

Painting is art.
Dancing and singing and making people
laugh and cry—that is art.
Making children feel that they are
loved and wanted—that is art.
And when a child looks at a grandmother
with shining eyes of love—that is art.
Art is many things to different people,
Feelings for others is one of the greatest
arts which we can all have.
Never change.
You are my treasure
And being with you always gives me pleasure.

Love,
Beauty

As I lay on her lap, she would stroke my hair, and I would ask her why she liked spending time with me and my mother did not. "Your mom loves you very much; she just has a funny way of showing it. You shouldn't take it personally."

But no matter what my grandmother said, I often felt uneasy

around my mother, knowing I could do something wrong at any minute—even if I was just sitting and reading. "Why are you watching me put on my makeup?" "I know how to make a liverwurst sandwich. Stop inspecting every little thing I do." "You do not need to follow me around. Look at a book or play in your room with your imaginary friend."

My mom was not very affectionate and she would constantly yell, "You're invading my space!" when I got too close or tried to give her a hug. But Beauty was the opposite. She liked to spend time with me as much as I liked to spend time with her. We could sit around the table cooking and talking about our feelings for hours.

Beauty would say, "G-d is in my kitchen, not in temple"— which was really upsetting to her very good friend and neighbor the rabbi next door. My grandmother lived in a neighborhood with many religious families, although Beauty never believed in organized religion or going to temple herself. "I am a culinary Jew," she'd proclaim. "I honor tradition and those who came before me, and I want to pass the history of the food on to you. I can find my heritage in a bowl of soup. I believe in the power of sweet-and-sour meatballs. I believe that when I combine eggs, raisins, cottage cheese, yogurt, and baby shells into a kugel, I honor my own grandmother. I believe that stuffed cabbage connects me to my father, whom I miss. My bible is recipes that fill your soul and will keep you healthy and nourished for years to come."

Beauty knew my father was always dieting and eating "food-like" products instead of real food, and this upset her because she knew that during the week, when I was home with my parents, this was the food they would give me. "Food needs to have a delicious fresh taste and smell," she would tell me, and she would always make me smell and taste things to guess the ingredients, whether it was vanilla in cookies, strawberries in freshly baked muffins, or dill in a barrel of pickles. "It needs to be made in nature and not in a factory." While my grandmother sympathized with my father's weight struggles, she thought his approach to eating was all wrong. Beauty never openly criticized my father's eating habits, because he was college-educated and she was not, but she constantly reminded me about the importance of fresh foods and going to the market every day. "Bread gets moldy, fruit gets soggy, and vegetables get wilted. If it lasts for months on the shelf, imagine what it does to your body."

From the time I could hold a spoon, my grandmother involved me in the cooking process, allowing me to mix the onions, green peppers, and bread crumbs for the salmon patties and decide what kind of soup we were going to prepare. And Beauty always made sure I was the one who tasted whatever we were making first. In her arms, I was never hungry for food, love, or affection. She was my mentor and my savior—saving my life, spoonful by spoonful.

Beauty's Chicken Soup

Yield: 8–10 servings

32 ounces water (plus at least 10 more cups to add as the broth
    absorbs)
1 (3½-pound) chicken, cut into 8 pieces, most of the skin removed
4 medium carrots, peeled and cut into ¼-inch pieces
4 ribs celery, cut into ¼-inch pieces
2 medium parsnips, peeled and cut into ¼-inch pieces
1 large sweet potato, peeled and cubed
1 medium yellow onion, quartered
Handful of fresh dill, chopped
Salt and pepper, to taste
Garlic powder or a couple of cloves of fresh garlic, to taste

Place the 32 ounces of cold water in an 8-quart stockpot set over
high heat and bring to a boil. Add the chicken and cook until foam
comes to the top. Spoon off the foam, reduce the heat, and add the
carrots, celery, parsnips, sweet potato, onion, and dill. Simmer the
soup for at least 2 hours and add the 10 cups of cold water, 1 cup
at a time, as needed. As the soup cooks, the liquid will evaporate
and the soup will thicken.

Check the soup every 30 minutes to remove any film that rises
to the top. Make sure not too much liquid has absorbed. If there
is less than half a pot of water, add a little more. Stir in the salt,
pepper, and garlic powder to taste, and remove the pot from the
heat. Remove the chicken and the vegetables from the soup, and
pull the chicken meat off the bones. Ladle the broth into bowls
and add the desired amount of chicken and vegetables to each
bowl.

Fluffy Matzo Balls

....

Yield: 8–10, depending on the size of the balls

4 eggs
1 cup matzo meal
Salt and pepper, to taste
½ teaspoon baking powder
2 tablespoons schmaltz (see note)
¼ cup club soda

Beat eggs. Fold in the matzo meal, salt, pepper, and baking powder. Mix in the schmaltz and club soda. The mixture should be moist. Refrigerate for 1 hour. The consistency should look like wet porridge. Wet hands and form into small balls. Do not form them too tight; otherwise they will be too dense. Drop into boiling chicken broth. Cover and cook for 20 minutes

Note: *To make your own schmaltz, just scrape off the fat that rises to the surface of stock. You will see an obvious layer of it after refrigerating the broth overnight—it becomes solid when it's cold.*

Sweet Potato Latkes

Yield: 8 pancakes

2 medium sweet potatoes, peeled and quartered
½ medium yellow onion, peeled and quartered
2 large eggs, beaten (plus 1 more, as needed, for thinning)
3 tablespoons all-purpose flour (plus more, as needed, for thickening)
1 tablespoon fresh lemon juice
1 teaspoon brown sugar
1 teaspoon ground cinnamon
1 teaspoon salt
½ cup oil for frying
Applesauce, plain yogurt, or sour cream for topping (optional)

Using the fine side of a grater or a food processor, grate the potatoes and onions. Transfer them to a large bowl and thoroughly combine with the eggs, flour, lemon juice, sugar, cinnamon, and salt. Set aside.

In a large skillet set over high heat, warm the oil to cover the bottom of the pan. (If it smokes it is too hot.) Using a large spoon, add dollops of the latke batter to the pan. Use a spatula to shape and flatten the batter into pancakes. Do not overcrowd the pan; you may need to do this in batches. Immediately decrease the heat to medium and cook the latkes until golden brown on each side, approximately 4 minutes on one side and 3 minutes on the other side. Flip the latke only when it is halfway cooked through; otherwise it will break apart. If you're working in batches, repeat with the remaining batter.

Serve the latkes topped with applesauce, yogurt, or sour cream (if desired).

Note: *If the latke batter is too watery, add a bit more flour; if it is too thick, add a little more beaten egg yolk.*

Mohn Kichlach/Poppy Seed Cookies

Yield: approximately 48 cookies

3 eggs, beaten
1 cup granulated sugar
1 cup unsalted butter, softened, or vegetable oil
1 teaspoon vanilla
3 cups all-purpose flour
4 tablespoons poppy seeds
1 teaspoon baking powder
¼ teaspoon salt
Parchment paper for rolling out the dough and lining the baking sheet
1 egg yolk thinned with 2 tablespoons of water for a thin egg wash

In a large bowl beat the eggs and sugar with an electric mixer until the mixture is a light yellow color. Continue beating while adding the softened butter and vanilla. Mix well.

Combine the remaining dry ingredients in a bowl, and with a fork mix so that the poppy seeds are evenly distributed throughout. Then add the dry ingredients into the egg mixture until the dough just comes together. Form it in a ball and roll out the dough between 2 parchment papers about an inch thick. Place on a sheet pan and refrigerate the dough until it hardens, about 20 minutes.

Preheat oven to 350 degrees and cover a baking sheet with parchment paper.

Take the dough out of the fridge and peel off the parchment paper. Cut into desired shapes using a knife or pizza cutter. Place squares on the prepared baking sheet and brush on the egg wash. Bake in the middle of the oven for 10 to 12 minutes, or until slightly puffed and golden.

Cool on a wire rack. The cookies will harden as they cool.

2

My New Baby Sister

....

Aunt Jeannie's Apple Strudel, Chocolate Chip
Mandel Bread, Russian Borscht, Sure to Make You
Feel Special Shirley Temple

....

I was the only person in Miss Duckler's kindergarten class
without a sibling. I had wished so long for a sister. But I
had also wished on a star for a Baby Alive doll, and that wish
never came true. So when my aunt Jeannie woke me early on a
freezing-cold winter morning a week before Valentine's Day
to tell me that my parents and grandparents had left to go to
the hospital to deliver my new baby sister or brother, I couldn't
really believe it.

I knew my mom had been pregnant for nine months, but I
didn't know what nine months meant. And most of my friends'
mothers had big bellies and ate a lot of ice cream when they
were about to have a new baby. My mom bragged that she
gained only twelve pounds, and her belly was barely noticeable,
so it was hard to believe this special day was really here.

Jeannie, Beauty's younger sister, famous in our family for

her blond wavy hair and her talent for playing the piano by ear, but mostly for her delicious cookies and strudels—that my dad said could make a grown man cry with joy—comforted me that morning with a warm breakfast of scrambled eggs with lox and sweet onions, and the rare and wonderful sight of a full refrigerator, which she had stocked with white fish salad, an applesauce meatloaf, and carrot coins swimming in a honey sauce.

I didn't want to go to school for fear of missing the call from the hospital, but my aunt assured me I didn't need to hover by the phone, that she would notify my teacher if there was any news. She then zipped my coat, adjusted my earmuffs, and off we went to my elementary school, Anshe Emet on the North Side of Chicago, where I spent my morning learning Hebrew and waiting for news about my mom. I was so nervous I couldn't tell the letter *Gimel* from the letter *Bet*.

Finally, during my favorite school lunch of broiled kosher chicken with stewed tomatoes and black-and-white cookies for dessert, they announced over the loudspeaker, "Dawn Lerman has a new baby sister." I just couldn't believe it. I screamed so loudly, so gutturally, that I was sent to the back of the line and lost my star for the day. I always received a gold star for being a good girl—standing in line quietly, raising my hand, and never talking out of turn. But on this day, I couldn't stop jumping up and down and screaming in my loudest, happiest voice, "I have a sister, I have a sister!"

At three o'clock, when the lineup bell rang, I dashed for the door where my aunt was waiting for me in her long, black mink coat. She was trying to meet my friends and see my classroom, but I was so excited I rushed her out the door, dashing as fast as I could toward her silver El Dorado Cadillac with crushed velvet interiors. It was so cold outside that I could see my breath. Aunt Jeannie kept trying to hold my hand with hers in a leather glove, but the glove was slippery and I managed to wiggle free, chanting, "I have a sister, I have a sister!" As we drove off, the song "Aquarius" from the musical *Hair* was playing on the radio. My sister April was born in February, and my mom had told me her astrological sign would be Aquarius (mine was Gemini). I remember thinking how appropriate the song was, but how inappropriate the name April was, given the current weather conditions.

I asked my aunt how long it would take to get to the hospital, as every second was a second too long.

"We need to wait till morning before we can see your mom and sister," she said, rattling off all the things we needed to buy before my mom and my precious little baby sister came home. "Diapers, bibs, bottles, laundry detergent, maybe even one of those cute mobiles that go above the crib. I hear they stimulate brain activity."

"But I want to see her now," I whimpered, trying as hard as I could to hold back the salty tears.

"No time for long faces. We have some serious work to do, and I need you to be my big girl helper."

I was disappointed, but I knew she was right. My dad's home office, which was now going to be my new baby sister's nursery, looked nothing like any baby's room I had seen in my dad's commercials. There were no baby murals, or painted clouds on the wall, no fancy baby furniture, or stuffed animals sitting on a dresser. It had old movie posters that my dad collected, a big metal desk, a gray filing cabinet secured with a metal combination lock, where my dad stuffed and secured emergency stashes of Yodels, Twinkies, and Devil Dogs, and a mini fridge with a sign posted on the front that said in big red letters, "Keep Out." There were also lots of unpacked cartons of books, and records, and stacks of *Playboy* magazines. My father saved every publication to which he contributed. He wrote close to a hundred reviews in his three years at that magazine—so there were several stacks of the naked lady booklets.

In the center of the room stood my old mahogany crib that my grandmother had retrieved from her basement and a space heater that you had to sit close to if you didn't want to freeze, since the room was a converted porch. Beauty always feared that the sleeves of my nightgown would catch on fire. But my mom thought she was a worrywart and scolded her for instilling fear in me.

Sitting in the backseat of the car watching all the cars speed past us, I became lost in thought—daydreaming about finally having someone with whom I could share my thoughts. April would be the only person in the world with the exact same life as me. She would understand our shared reality without words or explanation. My aunt glanced at me, and asked if I would like to stop and buy a giant poster board to make a welcome home sign for April's room.

Normally, I loved doing crafts with Aunt Jeannie. She knew how to paint, crochet, knit, and do origami, but today the thought of sitting still was extremely painful. I was fixated on the fact that Beauty, Papa, and my dad were all at the hospital, and I was being driven thirty-five minutes in the opposite direction. It would be a whole day before I could meet my new baby sister and I was dying with anticipation. I wanted to see what April looked like, hold her, and be one of the first voices she heard. At the stoplight, my aunt pulled out a bag of her just baked chocolate chip mandel bread.

"They're still warm," she said in her usual enticing tone.

Biting into one of the heavenly biscuits, still somewhat moist in the middle, with puddles of melted chocolate, I remembered how Beauty admired her so. "If you could grow up and be like

Jeannie, that wouldn't be such a bad thing." Beauty loved to brag and talk about her sister Jeannie. In fact, my mother thought it was a bit of an obsession, and that she should focus less on Jeannie and develop some more of her own interests.

Beauty would lament that she had had to leave school after the eighth grade to help care for her younger siblings. She said she didn't mind because she never thought she was very smart. "But your aunt Jeannie went all the way through high school, often making the honor roll for math."

Beauty admired Jeannie's talents and believed there was no better way to spend an afternoon than to watch her sister roll out the strudel dough so thin that you could read through the dough the many love letters she had received from men, or to dance to "Hava Nagila" in her living room while Jeannie played the Jewish melody on the piano. Even though they were in their fifties, when they interacted, they seemed like giggly little girls—laughing and gossiping. I imagined that was what April and I would be like when we were older.

Arriving at my aunt's house, which Beauty always called the Enchanted Cottage because once you arrived you never wanted to leave, my mood lifted. The house was warm and cheery, decorated with beautiful French furniture, my aunt's original paintings, antique dolls, a player piano, and an organ. But best of all were the many mirrors that somehow made everyone look beautiful and happy as the light reflected from the velvet curtains. Even my father thought his diet was working when he caught his reflection in those mirrors.

Jeannie gave me special slippers, which she called peds, and we tiptoed down her carpeted stairs to her newly finished basement, which had been under construction for the last two years. Uncle Louie, who was a general contractor and an artist, had turned what was a regular basement into a miniature city. He had re-created Bourbon Street in the French Quarter of New Orleans, where he had imagined taking my aunt Jeannie for their honeymoon. But they were married in the winter, and were snowed in, which is why nine months later my cousin Linda was born.

One of the walls housed a three-dimensional, twelve-foot-long mural that went from floor to ceiling. The mural featured wood carvings and a neon sign that flashed "Bourbon Street." There were also cafes, gift shops, old apartment buildings, seafood restaurants, and street performers. Every structure and character was hand-carved and carefully painted by my uncle, and individually decorated with multicolored Christmas lights that were continuously twinkling.

On the other side of the basement, there was a real bar covered in hand-painted mosaics, a jukebox, a real movie screen, a big popcorn machine, and a mini kitchen where Jeannie combined butter and brown sugar to coat the popcorn. We sat at the bar drinking Shirley Temples with pink paper umbrellas, clinking glasses and toasting April's birth. The bubbles tickled my throat when I drank the fizzy drink. Listening to Ella Fitzgerald and Louis Armstrong play on the jukebox, my aunt shared tales about Beauty and her when they were kids. I always found it intriguing how Beauty's and Jeannie's stories were so different, and how I learned about each of them through the other.

"Growing up, Beauty and I lived with a bunch of boarders in addition to our parents and our siblings: Nooti, Hymie, Billy, Harry, and Bevy. Our house was on the West Side of Chicago, directly across from Kim Novak's home before she became a movie star. We didn't have the biggest house on Springfield Avenue, but we had the grandest cherry tree in the neighborhood.

"During the early summer months, we'd spend all day in the hot sun picking the cherries off the trees. They were so sour they would make your mouth pucker. Around sunset, my dad, the big goof, would show up with his big hose and spray us down. 'This should clean you guys up a little,' aiming the freezing water at each of us, till our feet showed no traces of dirt. With clean feet we gathered in the cramped tub, jumping up and down, as hard and as fast as we could, until the cherries were smashed and the pits popped out. My dad used the extracted juice for wine. And my mom used the pitted cherries to make preserves for the wintertime. Sometimes even a pie with a perfect lattice crust."

Imagining the tartness of those cherries, the crispiness of that crust, entertained me enough to quiet my discomfort about not being with my mom and sister. Keeping me busy, Jeannie pulled out crayons and markers from a Folgers coffee can. We started decorating the pastel-pink poster board that Jeannie had laid out for my masterpiece. She showed me how to write "Welcome Home April" in bubble letters, and I drew little hearts all over the sign, which I then decorated with purple and gold glitter—making my words look extra special.

Jeannie soon began making the dough for our strudel. Whenever there was a special occasion, you could count on my aunt Jeannie for her baked goods and lavish spreads. When it was someone's birthday, an anniversary, or a holiday, she would often spend weeks baking and coming up with ways to outdo herself from the previous year. She even had an extra freezer that she called "Just In Case"—just in case she was invited somewhere or someone just popped in unexpectedly. There was never a shortage of strudels, hamantaschen, cakes, and challah breads in my aunt's freezer.

While Beauty relied on her instincts when cooking and the

power of fresh ingredients, Jeannie was very precise with her measurements and presentation, and entertaining was very important to her. A whiz at math, she could double and triple recipes without even using a piece of scratch paper, and she could make chopped liver look like fresh strawberries by shaping it with bread crumbs, adding a touch of food coloring, and inserting parsley. Everybody thought it was real fruit until they bit into the liver.

Aunt Jeannie handed me a bowl of peeled and cored apples to slice with a butter knife for the filling. She made me wear gloves so if the knife slipped, even though it wasn't too sharp, I wouldn't cut myself. Working on the apples, I watched my aunt pour the measured flour, water, eggs, and melted butter into the bowl before she mixed the dough. She began throwing the dough against the table—kneading it and rolling it, and kneading it and rolling it.

"You have to beat the dough hard if you want to get rid of all the air bubbles," she said.

She then made a ball of dough and placed it into a buttered bowl to rest. Next, it was time to chop the nuts.

"This is your job; it is a trick you should never forget," she instructed, filling two Ziploc bags, one with walnuts and one with pecans. "Always leave a little space for air to escape; otherwise, the bag will explode." Once the bags were filled and properly sealed, she showed me how to crush the nuts with a rolling pin.

It was now time to perfect the dough. Jeannie took the dough and began stretching it across her worn, wooden kitchen table, which was lightly covered with flour. She pulled the dough from all sides, stretching it as if she were making a bed, making sure all sides were equal.

"This is the most important step," she said, making me

stretch the dough until it was hanging down the sides of the table. Helping her knead and pull the dough until it was paper-thin, I had to stop to shake out my hands. They were beginning to cramp.

"The more you practice, just like the more you play the piano, the better and quicker you will be at making dough. At your age, Beauty and I would make two hundred varenikas at one time. When we would run out of room on the table to cut the dough and fill them with the mashed potatoes and onion mixture, we would spread a large sheet across our parents' bed to hold the finished varenikas."

I kept my eyes on Jeannie, concentrating as she demonstrated how to make a sample varenika with the scraps from the strudel bowl. "Your turn," she said enthusiastically, placing my palm on the bottom of a tall glass and adjusting my wrist just hard enough to cut the dough. But before I had the chance to perfect the art of using the glass as a cookie cutter, or figured out how to make my hands stop shaking when working so hard, my uncle burst in the door with a bunch of shopping bags.

"Do you know what's inside?"

I shook my head no, secretly hoping there was something for me. My uncle let me open two bags. One bag contained a set of bumpers with little puppies and kittens on them; the other bag held a set with a moon and stars. "Pick your favorite."

"I pick the one with the bright yellow stars. I love it. April will think she is a star every time she looks at it." Uncle Louie let out a hearty laugh at my answer and gave me a big hug, throwing me in the air in the process. Then he performed his usual trick of pulling coins out of my ears. I loved Uncle Louie, and I loved the way he smelled, like fresh-cut lumber and lemon-lime aftershave, his beard always a little scratchy when he held me close.

Jeannie took off his coat, then fed him a taste of our sweet apple filling. Savoring the bite, Uncle Louie made me guess how many guys he had to fight off to win my aunt as his bride. "Many," he announced, watching Jeannie finish the strudel by rolling it up and placing more butter, cinnamon, and sugar on top before pinching it closed and placing it in the oven.

While the strudel was baking, Jeannie worked on dinner— hot Russian borscht with shredded beets, pureed tomatoes topped with sour cream, and trout with a pecan crust. I helped Jeannie dip the fillets first in the eggs, then the flour, then the eggs again, and then into a Ziploc bag of pecans. Jeannie had me shake the plastic bag with the fish fillets like a maraca, to coat them evenly, while Uncle Louie relayed the story of how they met at the Veterans Hospital after he returned from World War II.

He had been a paratrooper. She was a secretary and was engaged to another army man. He bet her two dollars that after a cup of coffee with him, she would break off her engagement. They married six weeks later. The two-dollar bill was framed and proudly hung above the kitchen table where we enjoyed our dinner.

I struggled to keep my eyes open during supper, so Uncle Louie fed me a couple bites of borscht and carried me into bed. It had been a long day—my last day as an only child. I slept in my cousin Linda's room. She had already moved to California to pursue her dreams of being in film, but Jeannie had saved every Barbie, every puzzle, every piece of Linda's dress-up clothes, and her wooden dollhouse with the spiral staircases and flowered window boxes from when she was a little girl. She had even saved one of her flannel nightgowns, which she gave me to put on. It was snuggly and warm, and I slept peacefully through the night dreaming of my little sister.

As soon as it was light, I leaped out of bed and ran into the kitchen hoping we would be leaving for the hospital soon. Uncle Louie pointed to the window—the ground was covered in snow, and the flakes were large and thick. The snow was coming down fast and heavy, accumulating quickly, and the Chicago winds were fiercely cold and sharp. The weather conditions appeared on the news, warning people to stay off the roads.

"I'm so sorry. I think we are snowed in," Uncle Louie said, trying his hardest to push the front door open. "I think too much snow has settled."

Aunt Jeannie put her arms around me. "We will go to the hospital as soon as the roads are safe. Meanwhile, you and I have some baking to do." With each foot of snow that fell, we made another batch of cookies—round cookies, oval cookies, bow-shaped cookies, cookies with anise extract, cookies with almond extract, and cookies flavored with fresh orange juice when we ran out of vanilla.

What started out as a one-night sleepover, when my parents and grandparents were in the hospital, turned into a three-day bake-a-thon with Aunt Jeannie. I learned how to measure, whip, and separate eggs. She also taught me the magic of transforming recipes using swaps from her bag of tricks. If you were missing a couple of ingredients and couldn't get to the store— or in our case could not even open the door because the snow was so high—or if you wanted to lighten the sugar, butter, or dairy content in a recipe to make it a little healthier and a little more waistline friendly, my aunt had the all the tricks. When I left her house, I had not only a new baby sister but several baking secrets—many of which were top secret—including Land O'Lakes Margarine, which Jeannie said tasted like butter in baked goods but was much better for your heart and figure.

When we finally made it to the hospital and I saw my

precious baby sister, the feeling was indescribable. She was swaddled in a blanket and was wearing a little beanie. I was so excited to hold her. I remember having to wash my hands up to my elbows before I could touch her, but my hands were too cold, so the nurse put a towel over them and then laid my sister in my arms. I was a little frightened at first. She was smaller and more perfect than I had imagined. From the first second I held her, I was never the same. I loved her instantly, and my life was forever transformed.

Aunt Jeannie's Apple Strudel

Yield: 8–10 servings

FOR THE DOUGH:

    2½ cups all-purpose flour (plus more for dusting the work space)

    ½ tablespoon salt

    1 teaspoon baking powder

    2 large eggs, beaten

    1⅓ cups warm water

    4 tablespoons oil

FOR THE FILLING:

    ¼ cup white sugar

    ⅛ cup brown sugar

    1 teaspoon ground cinnamon

    Pinch of salt

    4 apples, chopped, peeled, and cored (Aunt Jeannie always preferred tart apples)

    1 tablespoon fresh lemon juice

    1 tablespoon fresh lemon rind

    ½ cup dried fine bread crumbs

    ¼ cup ground walnuts (optional)

    ¼ cup raisins

    Parchment paper or vegetable oil for the baking sheet

    ½ stick of melted unsalted butter, for brushing the dough

    Powdered sugar, for dusting

Sift the flour, salt, and baking powder into a bowl. Make a well in the center and drop in the beaten eggs, water, and oil. Mix until a dough forms. Transfer the dough to a lightly floured work space and knead the dough until smooth. Place the dough ball in a bowl and let sit for 30 minutes.

    Meanwhile, begin to prepare the filling by combining the sugars, cinnamon, and salt in a large bowl. Set aside 3 tablespoons of the above mixture. Mix the chopped apples with the lemon juice and lemon rind; stir into the sugar mixture and add the bread crumbs, nuts, if using, and raisins.

Preheat oven to 350 degrees and line a baking sheet with parchment paper or oil.

Cover a table with a lint-free tablecloth or tea towels and lightly dust with flour. Place the dough on the floured work space and roll it out. Gently stretch it until it is paper thin.

Brush the dough with melted butter. Spread the filling across the rolled dough, leaving a ½-inch border. Starting with a long end, roll up the dough to enclose the filling; place the strudel, seam side down, on the baking sheet. Brush the top with butter and sprinkle with the reserved sugar and cinnamon. Bake until golden brown and cooked through, 45 to 50 minutes. Let cool on a wire rack 10 minutes. Sprinkle with powdered sugar before slicing.

Note: *Depending on apple sizes, there should be a little extra filling for nibbling.*

Chocolate Chip Mandel Bread

Yield: 28 biscuits

3 cups flour (plus more for kneading)
1½ teaspoons baking powder
¼ teaspoon of salt
3 eggs, beaten
1 cup sugar
1 cup unsalted butter, melted, or oil
2 teaspoons vanilla extract
1 teaspoon almond extract or orange juice
½ cup semi-sweet chocolate chips
Butter, oil, or parchment paper for the baking sheet

In a large bowl, mix together the flour, baking powder, and salt and set aside. In another bowl combine the beaten eggs and sugar until smooth. Whisk in the butter, the vanilla extract, and the almond extract and then pour into the dry ingredients until it turns into dough. Then stir in the chocolate chips. Form into a large ball and chill in a glass bowl covered with plastic wrap in the refrigerator for 2 hours.

Grease a baking sheet or cover with parchment paper and preheat oven to 350 degrees.

Remove the dough from the refrigerator and wait 5 minutes so the dough is more pliable. Coat your hands with flour and remove the dough from the bowl. Knead the dough, and divide into two pieces. Form each piece into a roll about 3 inches wide. Place the rolls side by side on the prepared baking sheet. They should stretch the length of the sheet. Bake 20 minutes until the rolls have started to turn brown. Then reduce the heat to 250 degrees and bake for another 15 minutes.

Remove the rolls from the oven onto a rack. Let cool about 10 minutes, until cool enough to handle. Then slice them diagonally about every ½ inch. Return the cookies to the baking sheet and lay them flat. Return to the oven and bake until lightly golden, about 30 minutes at 250 degrees. Allow to cool completely on a wire rack before serving. The cookies will get crunchier as they cool.

Russian Borscht

Yield: 6 servings

5 raw beets, peeled and thinly sliced (they should look like matchsticks)
3 potatoes, peeled and thinly sliced
6 cups beef stock
2 tablespoons butter
3 onions, chopped
2 stalks celery, chopped
2 carrots, chopped
3 cups shredded cabbage
1 cup tomato puree
1 tablespoon honey
1 tablespoon apple cider vinegar
½ cup fresh dill
Dollop of sour cream, for garnish
Sprigs of dill, for garnish
Salt and pepper, to taste

Place the beets and potatoes in a stockpot and cover with the stock. Boil for 20 minutes. Remove the beets and potatoes from the stock so they don't continue to cook. In a large skillet, melt the butter, then add the onions and sauté until soft. Then add in the celery, carrots, and cabbage. Cover and cook until the vegetables are tender, about 10 minutes. Transfer the potatoes and beets back into the stockpot with the broth as well as the sautéed vegetables. Add in the tomato puree, honey, and apple cider vinegar and add salt and pepper to taste. Add the dill and simmer for about 45 minutes. If liquid seems to be evaporating, add a little more water. Serve with a dollop of sour cream and a couple sprigs of the fresh dill.

Note: *The borscht always tastes better the next day, after all the flavors meld together.*

Sure to Make You Feel Special Shirley Temple

Yield: 1 serving

3 ounces lemon-lime soda
3 ounces ginger ale
Ice
1 tablespoon grenadine syrup
Maraschino cherry, for garnish

Pour the lemon-lime soda and ginger ale into a glass with ice cubes. Then add the grenadine. Stir and top it off with a cherry.

3

A Night at Bubbe's

....

Bubbe's Sweet Brisket with Coca-Cola Marinade,
Mushroom Barley Soup, Cinnamon Raisin Rugelach,
Schmaltz and Grebenes

....

I never thought my paternal grandmother, Bubbe Mary, liked me very much, even though every time I saw her, two or three times a year, she would hold out her arms, saying, "Who loves you the most in the whole world? Who loves you the most in the whole world?" I always wanted to respond, "Not you!" But Beauty told me that in certain situations honesty is not the best policy: "You catch more flies with honey than vinegar." I didn't want to catch any flies, but I always let Bubbe hug me and squeeze my cheeks until they were bright red and stung with pain. "Bubbe loves me the most in the world," I would say, knowing I was not really being truthful. But our visits were so few and far between that I would force myself to smile instead of wince in pain.

My two grandmothers lived near each other on the North Side of Chicago, but the way they felt about me was worlds apart. Beauty could never get enough of me and insisted that I spend every weekend at her house, so I slept over most Fridays and Saturdays. I rarely saw Bubbe, and she only invited me to sleep at her house—once and only once—when Beauty and Papa had a fancy wedding to attend, and my parents were in Africa on safari.

Usually, Beauty would never pass up a night with me, but it was the wedding of one of Papa's most important customers. Papa delivered paper goods, aluminum foil, Saran Wrap, and olives to Jack's Restaurant on a weekly basis and wanted to secure his orders since Sidney Supply was not the only restaurant supplier on the North Side of Chicago. Beauty was nervous about leaving me, but she didn't want to upset Papa, so she made the necessary arrangements.

Beauty feared that my active baby sister, who was known for flipping out of her crib and screaming for hours on end, would give Bubbe a heart attack. So April would remain at home at our apartment on Hudson Avenue near Lake Shore Drive with our weekday babysitter, Sister Ann, who Beauty said didn't have any of the qualities a religious nun was supposed to have. But she maintained our weekday schedule when my parents were away—driving me to school and my Brownie meetings at the Hull House Recreation Center and feeding April a bottle of infant formula every three hours.

On the weekends when Beauty would pick me up, she would try to engage Sister Ann in conversation. "My Dawn is such a wonderful child, so thoughtful, and lovely to be with," she'd say, but Sister Ann would have her head buried in a Bible, looking up just long enough to ask Beauty for her weekly check. During the week, it was worse when April would cry. Sister Ann would close April's bedroom door while she sat in the kitchen eating her Hormel corned beef hash out of a can while praying on her knees with her rosary beads.

Most times I had to take matters into my own hands, climbing into the crib with April and making funny faces to soothe her. The minute I calmed April down, Sister Ann would rush in and yank me out of the crib. "You are a bad girl. I am going to tell your grandmother that you are always hurting your sister and making her cry. You are an evil child. Stop interfering with my job."

I never told my grandmother the hurtful words Sister Ann spoke to me, and I claimed that the scratches Beauty noticed on my arms were from my neighbor's cat. I once tried to tell my mom the truth about Sister Ann, but she didn't believe me. "She is there to change diapers and feed April, not to be interrogated by a nosey six-year-old with an overactive imagination or to coddle April every time she whimpers."

My grandmother didn't like Sister Ann, but she thought April would be fine. I was the one she worried about, since I was sensitive like her. She took extra care trying to build me up: "You are my little warrior; there is nothing that you can't handle," she'd often say, encouraging me to always hold my head up high.

On Saturday, we got all dolled up for the special night— Beauty for the wedding and me for the sleepover with Bubbe. Beauty had her hair set and teased once a week at the beauty parlor, and usually, when I went with her, I just had my hair untangled. But this time, Beauty insisted that I have my hair curled in fancy little Shirley Temple ringlets, which the lady sprayed several times with smelly hairspray that made my hair stiff. I even had a new ruffled dress with matching socks.

Beauty checked my nails before we left, using a sharp metal

pointy thing to get every bit of dirt out. "Bubbe Mary is a very lovely woman, but she can be very critical. Let's give her nothing to comment on."

Beauty was fond of Bubbe Mary even though she thought she was a little bit of a phony. And she knew Bubbe favored her other daughter-in-law, Cappy, and my cousins Elizabeth and Alyson. Whenever she and Beauty spoke on the phone, Bubbe would rave, "Cappy is the best daughter-in-law in the world. Every time she comes for a surprise visit with the kids, she brings me a little something. Just last week, she brought me this expensive box of Fannie May chocolate candy from the Water Tower Plaza, the kind with all the different fillings."

But Beauty forgave her little jabs. "If I held a grudge against every person who said something silly to me, I would be a very lonely woman. Your Bubbe had an extremely hard life, and she goes out of her way to host the Jewish holidays, never taking any shortcuts. She prepares kishke, gribenes, and Russian black bread, all from scratch. I don't know anyone who knows how to make that old world food like your Bubbe. I think it makes her feel closer to the traditions she left behind when she came to this country."

I guess Beauty was right, and I did like Bubbe's gribenes— the fried chicken skin with onions and apples was a treat. However, once I found out that kishke was beef intestines stuffed with flour and fat, I could never eat it again.

Before Beauty dropped me off for my sleepover, she sat me down with a cup of milky, sweet tea, telling me about Bubbe Mary.

"Bubbe did not grow up in Chicago like me. She grew up in Romania and traveled by boat for a long time to get to the United States. Her parents, having no money, had to leave some of her family members behind. When they settled in Chicago, her dad sent Bubbe to work to help support the family. She was just thirteen years old when she got a full-time job in the garment district. She worked as a fluffer."

"A fluffer?"

"Yes, I know it is a funny name, but it was a very hard job. She sewed the pleats on dresses and skirts to make them look fancy. All the money she made, working ten hours a day with only a fifteen-minute break, went to saving enough money for her older sisters to travel here. One of them died before the family saved up enough money to send for her. You can spend all night asking her questions about Romania, and she can show you pictures of your daddy when he was a little boy. Maybe she can even teach you a couple of stitches or a few Romanian words."

Arriving with a box of jellied fruit slices and my class picture, I tried to smile brightly as Bubbe hugged me. "*Shayna madela!* Beautiful girl! Who loves you the most in the world?"

I hugged her, and Beauty admired the table set with gefilte fish, chopped liver, and homemade challah, braided with six strands.

"Look at all the trouble Bubbe went through for you."

"No trouble. If I did not cook, what would Alex and I eat?"

Alex was Bubbe's second husband, whom she married after my dad's father died of lung cancer. He died way before I was born, when my dad was just a teenager. My father once told me the story of how he helped care for his dad, having to inject him with pain medicine while Bubbe was at work. His name was David, and I was named after him.

After instructing us to take off our shoes, Bubbe Mary gave me and Beauty each a warm piece of challah to snack on. Then both of my grandmothers disappeared into the avocado-green tiled kitchen and began speaking in Yiddish. I sat on the gold, fluffy couch with plastic covers that made a tearing sound every time I moved. I wished Beauty were staying at Bubbe Mary's with me. I felt shy around Bubbe. She felt more like a stranger than a family member. I had rehearsed with Beauty all the questions I could ask to make conversation, but I was forgetting everything we'd practiced.

When she returned to the living room, I could tell Beauty looked a little uncomfortable. Bubbe explained that she was very happy to have me visit and spend the night, but some of her friends from shul wanted to come over for a game of cards. After dinner, I would need to sit in the den, where I could have dessert and watch the Tom Jones variety special while she played a couple of rounds of gin rummy and canasta with her friends.

Bubbe raved how she loved Tom Jones, and I could stay up as long as I wanted and watch the show on her new color Trinitron TV and sit on her brand-new couch that my uncle Melvin had bought her. Beauty looked at me. I could tell she wanted to say something reassuring, but Papa, who hated to wait, was outside in the car, blowing the horn nonstop. "I will call you from the pay phone in the powder room to check on you. Enjoy all of Bubbe's food."

"We will be fine. Maybe we can even fatten her up a little."

My heart sank watching the door close behind Beauty.

"You are such a little thing," Bubbe kept saying to me as she winked at me, while serving me dish after dish. "I made all your daddy's favorites." I kept complimenting Bubbe on how yummy everything tasted, but I was not used to eating so much food at one time and my stomach was beginning to hurt. But the food kept coming. It was hard to distinguish one dish from the next, and I hardly had a chance to swallow one thing before my plate was filled again. "Just a little more," she kept saying. "Food is meant to be eaten, not wasted."

I remembered my dad saying he felt like a stuffed turkey every time he left Bubbe Mary's after a holiday meal. "Unfortunately, willpower and I are not closely acquainted," he would exclaim as he joyfully indulged without coming up for air.

But other than holidays, we did not visit Bubbe Mary much. My dad said that he felt more comfortable at Beauty's house. She always made a big deal over him, laughing at all his jokes, telling him how brilliant he was, and displaying all the articles about him from the trade publications. He was a rising star in the ad industry, but Bubbe was confused about what he did for a living and was disappointed that he did not have a regular job like his brother Melvin, who was an accountant. I didn't know what an accountant was, but I knew my dad's job was super fun as he got to work with Tony the Tiger and the Pillsbury Doughboy. Bubbe was not as impressed: "A Jewish boy should be a doctor or a lawyer."

Even when my dad was a child, he did things that she did not understand, like creating satirical comic books or questioning why they had two different sets of dishes or opening and closing the lights on Shabbat when she strictly forbade it. Not knowing how to relate to him, she fed him constantly. Bonding over roast tongue, pickled herring, and rolled cabbage made both of them feel closer to each other.

But then, when he was in the sixth grade, my dad got beat up by a bunch of bullies who jumped him from behind, hitting him with lead pipes until he was unconscious. "Fat mama's boy. Fat mama's boy," they taunted. The beating was so bad he spent a week in a coma and the doctors didn't know if he would live.

Helpless, Bubbe Mary cooked all day and all night, praying

for his recovery, hoping the smells of her mushroom barley soup, stuffed peppers, and sponge cake, which she schlepped to the hospital, would revive him. When he awoke, Bubbe was standing there with a banquet, fully believing in the healing powers of Jewish food. My Bubbe fed my father bite after bite while he was in the hospital—feeding him but never telling him she loved him.

My dad wanted to feel comforted by all the wonderful food she had worked so hard to prepare, but he felt angry. He wanted to be thin. He wanted to be popular. He wanted to have self-confidence. The very food that brought him such extreme pleasure caused him to be bigger than the other kids, leading to ridicule and, worse, landing him in the hospital. Even the doctors were alarmed by his weight. But my Bubbe said, "It's just baby fat. He'll grow out of it."

But as he got older, he got bigger, and his cravings for food— as well as his need to be thin and popular—intensified. When my dad dieted, he felt like he was betraying my grandmother and dissolving the one bond they shared. My dad felt that if they were not talking about food, the room was silent, so he made jokes—most of which Bubbe did not understand—to break the silence. Conversation seemed to flow so easily between his brother Melvin and their mother. My father wondered why it couldn't be like that for him and his mom.

Of course, at six years old, I didn't know any of this; I didn't understand the relationship between my father, my grandmother, and food. I just knew that Bubbe Mary stuffed me to the gills, and now I'd have to sit in the den and watch Tom Jones all by myself. I asked Bubbe if I could shuffle the cards for her and her friends, but she hurried me out of the room with a half loaf of sliced banana bread and a box of old photographs that she said I could look through.

The bread was delicious with big, sweet chunks of bananas. I ate the entire half loaf, not so much because I was hungry, but because I didn't want her to be mad at me. My dad had once told me he would get in trouble if he ever left crumbs, so I made sure I didn't leave a single crumb.

I tried to watch Tom Jones, but I was bored. I kept peeking my head out of the room. Hoping Bubbe would include me, I kept smiling at all her friends. Beauty said my smile was contagious, and she always wanted to show me off, but Bubbe seemed happier with me in the other room. "You do not want to miss Tom Jones singing his biggest hit, 'It Is Not Unusual,'" she said, sending me away with an ice cream parfait topped with rainbow jimmies, strawberry syrup, and a cherry. "This should entertain you for a while." But I was lonely, not hungry. I tried to finish the cool treat to please Bubbe, but my body said no, and before I could take one more bite, I was shivering. Before I knew what was happening, there was vomit all over Bubbe's new couch. I remembered what my dad had told me, how Bubbe worked so hard to put food on the table, and how Beauty had told me to be a good guest. Panicked, I crept toward the bathroom. If I could just clean everything up, no one would have to know, and no one would be disappointed in me. I remembered how Sister Ann cleaned April up after she burped too much. I just needed a warm cloth.

I quietly shut the door behind me, hearing Bubbe Mary call out, "I have rugelach."

Embarrassed and dirty, I splashed cold water on my face and put a little Ivory Soap in my mouth. I was looking everywhere for rags, but all Bubbe's towels had a floral pattern and looked so fancy. I grabbed the first thing I could think of. I put some warm water into the tissue box and snuck back into the den trying to wipe up my mess, but the tissues broke into little pieces and started sticking to the fabric. I took off my dress and started wiping furiously. I thought if I could just change into my nightgown and stuff my smelly dress into my suitcase, everything would be okay. Just as I was figuring everything out, Bubbe came into the room, announcing that Beauty was on the phone. She saw her couch. She saw the shredded tissues. She saw me in my underwear.

"*Oy vey iz mir! Oy vey iz mir!*" The Jewish words of doom made me panic even further. I was shaking while she rushed me into the bathroom, forcing me to drink an Alka-Seltzer out of the cup where she kept her dentures. "Drink up," she said, making me lie down on the cold bathroom floor. She put a hot water bottle on my tummy, telling me to stay in the bathroom so she could say goodbye to her friends. I was hoping she would stay in the bathroom with me and say, "Who loves you the most in the world?" but she did not.

After what felt like forever, the door opened. It was Beauty. "What happened to my little pussycat? You must be coming down with something," she cooed, pulling me into her chest and wrapping a towel around me. "You can wear my fur while I help Bubbe." Beauty didn't seem concerned that I might mess her brand-new coat. "I am going to help Bubbe clean up the mess."

They were both quiet, no chattering in Yiddish, as they scrubbed, armed with plastic gloves, buckets of water, and boxes of baking soda and a bottle of vinegar. Hanging the slipcovers to dry, they both said in unison, "The one couch without plastic!"

Bubbe was grateful for Beauty's help, insisting that she stay for a cup of coffee and some goodies. "I have enough rugelach for a small village. I usually make them with just a little jam, but I used my grandmother's recipe making them with raisins and nuts as well."

"I will try just one," Beauty said. She started moaning as she tasted them, "So light, so delicate! Is that cream cheese I taste in the crust?" she gushed.

Feeling better and relieved that both my grandmothers were kibitzing, I inched toward the table. Bubbe poured me a glass of ginger ale to soothe my stomach, and Beauty scooped me onto her lap. While Beauty was enjoying the rugelach and coffee, Bubbe was busy in the kitchen. She was making several doggy bags. She even had some frozen challahs and marble cake for my dad when he returned from his trip.

"Don't forget to feed these to your daddy. Nothing says love like a little something from Bubbe's oven."

Retrieving our shoes from outside the door, Bubbe blew kisses. "I will see you in a couple of months for Passover. I would give you a kiss, but I will just blow one in case Dawn is coming down with something."

We enjoyed Bubbe's care package the following evening. The brisket was so flavorful and tender, immersed in a thick gravy of onion soup, ketchup, and apricot preserves, and the rugelach just seemed to melt in our mouths. In Beauty's kitchen, I was able to enjoy every sweet and savory mouthful. I kept waiting for Beauty to offer some pearls of wisdom about Bubbe, or my dad, or eating slowly. But all she said was how thoughtful Bubbe was to make us a care package and what a marvelous cook she was.

I had a feeling it would be a long time before we would see Bubbe again.

Bubbe's Sweet Brisket with Coca-Cola Marinade

Yield: 8 servings

4–5 pound brisket, with fat trimmed
½ cup ketchup
¼ cup apricot jam
1 can of Coca-Cola
1 packet of dry onion soup mix, such as Lipton
1 cup water with 2 tablespoons ketchup for reheating

Preheat oven to 350 degrees.

Place the brisket fat side down in a 13 x 9-inch roasting pan and add water to the depth of the pan, about 1 inch. Spread the ketchup and jam evenly over the meat. Sprinkle the soup mix over the ketchup and smear in. Pour the Coca-Cola around the meat. Cover the pan tightly with aluminum foil. After about 2 hours open the foil and baste brisket. Continue to cook, covered, for another hour. Skim any excess fat.

When cooled, slice thinly and add back into pan with the juices. About a half hour before you're ready to serve, preheat oven to 350 degrees and reheat the brisket with the cup of water mixed with 2 tablespoons of ketchup. Then spoon gravy from the pan over the meat. Heat for 20 minutes.

Note: *Like many Jewish dishes, brisket should be prepared a day ahead. It is much more tender and flavorful on the second day, after the ingredients have mingled.*

Mushroom Barley Soup

FOR HOMEMADE BEEF STOCK (SEE NOTE):
 3 pounds beef bones
 1 pound chuck, cubed
 1 onion, quartered
 4 celery stalks, sliced in half
 4 carrots, sliced in half
 1 bay leaf
 Water, to cover

FOR THE SOUP:
 64 ounces beef stock
 Salt and pepper, to taste
 Beef from stock (see note)
 1 large onion, quartered
 8 celery stalks, diced
 2 parsnips, diced
 8 carrots, cut into rounds
 1 cup pearl barley
 1 pound fresh white button mushrooms, sliced
 2 tablespoons tomato paste
 2 large bay leaves
 1 bunch of parsley, finely chopped

In a very large soup pot, combine all the stock ingredients. Bring to a boil and then simmer for two hours. Strain the broth into another large pot. Save the meat, but discard the rest of the solids. If the stock in your new pot is greasy, let it cool for about 15 minutes and then place 6 ice cubes in the pot. The grease will immediately congeal and you can spoon out the ice cubes and grease in one fell swoop. Your homemade beef stock is ready.

Now it is time to make the soup. First, taste the stock and add salt and pepper to taste. Then add the onion, celery, parsnips, carrots, pearl barley, and sliced mushrooms. Bring to a boil and then add the tomato paste, bay leaves, and parsley. Simmer 30 minutes, until the barley is soft. Then add the saved beef and cook for another 45 minutes You might need to add a little water if too much liquid has evaporated.

Note: *If you do not want to make your own stock, you can use 64 ounces of beef broth from a carton or dissolve 4 large bouillon cubes (such as Knorr) or 8 small cubes (such as Wyler's) in 64 ounces of boiling water. If you did not make your own stock, brown 1 pound of cubed chuck in 1 tablespoon of oil and use that.*

Cinnamon Raisin Rugelach
("Little Twist" in Yiddish)

Yield: 12 cookies

Parchment paper or cooking spray to line the cooking sheet
2 ounces unsalted butter, room temperature, cubed
2 ounces cream cheese, room temperature
½ cup flour
⅓ cup sugar (plus a little extra for sprinkling)
¼ teaspoon salt
½ cup chopped nuts (optional)
½ cup chopped raisins
½ teaspoon cinnamon (plus a little extra for sprinkling)
Jam of your choice
1 egg, beaten
1 tablespoon cold water

Cream the butter and cream cheese with a hand mixer, then gently stir in the flour, 2 tablespoons of sugar, and the salt. Mix well, until dough is formed. Shape the dough into a ball. Wrap the dough in plastic wrap and chill for 2 hours. Right before the dough is removed from the fridge, combine the nuts, if using, raisins, cinnamon, and the rest of the sugar in a bowl and set aside.

Preheat oven to 350 degrees. Line a baking sheet with parchment paper or cooking spray. Remove the dough from the fridge. Now flour a work space and begin to roll out the dough into a round pizza shape about ¹⁄₁₆-inch thick, giving the dough quarter turns as you roll. Try to work quickly, because when the dough loses its chill, it is hard to work with. Spread the jam across the dough, and then sprinkle the raisin-nut, mixture over the dough and press it in with your fingertips.

Slice the dough into twelve wedges. Roll each wedge from wide end to narrow. Place the cookies on prepared baking sheet and chill for 20 minutes. While they are chilling, whisk the egg with the cold water, and then gently brush the egg wash over the cookies before putting them in the oven to bake. Sprinkle a little cinnamon and sugar on top. Bake for 20 minutes. Cool on a wire rack.

Schmaltz and Grebenes

Skin from a whole chicken, washed and sliced
¼ cup sliced onions
¼ cup sliced apples

Cook the chicken skin over low heat until the fat is almost melted. Add the onions and apples and cook until the onions brown. Remove from heat and allow to cool slightly. Pour the schmaltz—the rendered fat—through a fine-mesh strainer. Then transfer it to a mason jar, cover, and refrigerate. Schmaltz will keep for about a week in the fridge. You can eat the crackly skins—the grebenes—with the apples and onions alone or add the mixture to chopped liver, mashed potatoes, or kasha varnishkes.

4

Bye-Bye, Chicago

....

The Ultimate Chocolate Chip
Cookie with the Cream Cheese Dough,
Lo-Carb Chocolate Crepes

....

I remember boxes, lots of boxes—big boxes, small boxes, packed boxes, empty boxes, boxes marked "Fragile." I had flashes of hiding in the boxes when we first moved into the apartment on Hudson Street six years earlier. I had just turned three. The apartment looked so big and scary that I hid in one of the boxes all afternoon—scared if I ventured out of the box, I would get lost. I remember the sun spilling through the window of my room. I remember the room turning dark. I remember waiting for my dad to unpack me, as carefully as he unpacked his antique gumball machines, his diet books, his *Mad* magazines, and his vintage Coke bottles. I remember waiting, waiting, for the sea of boxes to dissipate, and this unfamiliar place to seem less scary and more welcoming.

I remember feeling nervous, small, lost—similar to how I felt on the first day of nursery school when I waited for my mom to pick me up after a long morning of finger painting, gluing macaroni on cigar boxes, and learning my right foot from my left foot, while dancing the Hokey Pokey. One by one, all the kids were picked up, nestled into their moms' warm embrace. I stood there with the teacher, Miss Newburger, waiting, waiting, till I was the only one left. As my jitters were becoming increasingly apparent, the soft-spoken teacher with her golden hair, her Benjamin Franklin glasses, and gentle open arms, offered me a cookie.

"There is nothing like a little snack to take the edge off." Her words put me at ease, as they sounded familiar. When my dad was tired or stressed from working, he would motion me to come sit with him. "Let's have a snack," he would say. "There is nothing like a little something sweet to help me relax." What my dad considered a good snack was always changing, depending on the diet he was on. One of my favorites was the Metrecal meal-replacement shakes, paired with Oreo cookies. The shakes tasted like maple syrup, and they came in chocolate and vanilla flavors. Sometimes, he would even blend the Oreos and the shake together in a blender for something a little more special, or mix the Metrecal powder with whipped egg whites to turn it into a paste, and fry it with a little Pam to make a low-calorie pancake.

Miss Newburger pulled the little circus boxes off the shelf and handed me two animal crackers, one shaped like a monkey, the other shaped like a lion, and a little container of milk. Folding back the cardboard opening and pouring the milk into a little three-ounce Dixie Cup, she proclaimed, "If you dunk the crackers, they not only become softer, but sweeter." I dunked just the way she showed me, watching the little pieces that broke off. Some crumbs floated to the top and others disappeared. I nervously stared into the cup, wondering if my mom would ever come for me or if I would remain in the classroom forever. After not successfully reaching either of my parents on the telephone, Miss Newburger was determined to cheer me up.

"Nothing like cookies and milk to turn a frown right around. When my children were young, we used to pretend the animals were drinking the milk. We would dunk their heads first before their bodies." Demonstrating how to dunk, her voice lifted as she made a slurping sound and began tossing her head from side to side. I started to forget that my mother was nowhere to be found.

I call animal crackers happy crackers; no child can have a long face when they are selecting their favorite animals. "Roar, Roar, Nay, Nay, Moo, Moo!" she bellowed, instructing me to reach into the box and pick five crackers. She proceeded to do the same. "Let's see how many matches we have."

"We both have a zebra," I said.

"Can you make a zebra sound?" I shrugged my shoulders.

"Of course you can."

"Nay," I said softly.

"Really let it out. The zebra communicates with high-pitched, loud noises. Let all the animals in the wild kingdom hear you." I struggled to make the best animal noise that I could conjure. I began contorting my face and turning up my nose, and out of nowhere came a loud snort.

"Bravo!"

I kept snorting so hard that I become light-headed, falling off the chair in a mixture of giggles that turned to uncontrollable tears. I was so faint that I could barely breathe.

"My, my. It looks as if you have just seen the Holy Ghost." Miss Newburger rubbed my back to calm me down, but I continued to laugh, breathless, with tears rushing down my face and milk squirting out of my nose.

"Why is my daughter hysterical? Did she fall? She is very fragile," my mother screamed, storming into the classroom. My teacher assured her I was fine and calmly explained that my mom was several hours late and that pickup was supposed to be at eleven not at three. Irritated, my mom responded, "All this money and only a half day?" She started inspecting me for cuts and bruises, whisking me out of the bright nursery, unapologetic and annoyed, oblivious to Miss Newburger's disapproving face.

Totally shaken up, I begged never to go back—even though I really liked my teacher and all the fun activities we did. But that fearful feeling of being left overwhelmed me. Each morning my mother dropped me in the classroom, I was filled with butterflies wondering if she would return. Each morning, she nonchalantly vanished into the morning air, never looking back, never aware of the terror and the sadness that consumed me during those first several years of school. Eventually, I started taking the school bus home, and that feeling of fear was replaced by chatting with friends, reading books, and the birth of my sister—and the ache was dull, not overwhelming or sharp.

But as all the boxes filled the halls of our apartment and my room was quickly being stripped of all the things that were familiar—all that brought me comfort—I had an old ache that ran through me like a current, causing me to feel nauseous, hot, and sweaty, like the time my mother forced me to eat McDonald's and I protested that the greasy, salty meat from the forty-nine-cent menu would make me sick. I had spent the whole evening doubled over in pain. But today, I had not eaten anything bad. I had not given in to one my mom's fits when she declared I was stuck up for not wanting to eat the contents of one of her surprise packages of aluminum-foil restaurant leftovers. I had not eaten the block of yellow Velveeta cheese that my mom had gotten on sale at the Jewel Market and that was now covered in green fuzz. I had not given in to the fried Oscar Mayer bologna with the funny smell. I had only eaten the delicious kosher food from school that was always fresh, always homemade—yet the nagging pain in my stomach continued to grow.

"Should we take it or toss it?" my mother said, holding up my favorite Raggedy Ann doll that my *bestest* friend, Jenny Isenstark, gave me for my ninth birthday.

"Take it, but I don't want to pack it! I want to carry it with me on the plane."

"You are not going on the plane for weeks. You will forget about it by then. I need to get everything ready for the movers, so they can put all our belongings in storage. I am leaving for New York with Daddy tomorrow. He needs to move into his new offices, and I have to find us a place to live. You and April will stay with Beauty while I'm getting us situated."

My mom never did anything the way other moms did; there were never any lists and there was never any discussion of plans, just a whirlwind of energy. She was frantically tossing my rumpled shirts, unpaired socks, and my drawings from school into the cartons. I tried to slow her down so I could organize them, but she was getting annoyed with me.

"Stop being so particular. You can fold and sort everything later."

"It's my stuff. Stop just throwing everything around."

My world was being spun upside down, and no one bothered to ask me how I felt. Instead of consulting with me, my mother tried to distract me by telling me the story about the first day we rented the apartment. When she began talking, I sat on the bed and listened to the story of how I chose my room, the room I was now saying goodbye to. Many nights I yearned for my mom to sit on the edge of my bed and pull the covers over me and tell me a story. While I sat, she talked and dumped the contents of my room into the brown moving boxes—my journals, my puzzles, my fuzzy orange rug that was shaped like a foot, and my lava lamp with the blue and silver bubbles that used to keep me mesmerized for hours.

"You were just three years old when we moved to this apartment," she said in her theatrical voice, imitating the sophisticated charm of Sophia Loren. "We had just moved into this big six-room apartment from our teeny, tiny, cramped apartment on Berwyn Avenue. I thought you would be so happy to have all this space to run around. I said you could choose any room you like to be your special bedroom. Walking around together, you pulled me into this room, which was going to be used as a closet for all your dad's hundreds of shirts." We both chuckled because nobody had more shirts than my dad. "But you insisted that this was the room you wanted. When I asked why you liked it so much, you said, 'I am a very little girl, so I only need a little room.' You gravitated to that hot little room and there was no convincing you otherwise. I used to always find you curled up in a ball on that window seat."

I felt lost in my mom's voice, remembering the day, remembering how cold I often was during the long Chicago winters; but somehow the insulation of the small space and the purr and the warmth of the radiator soothed me. I spent hours sitting on the burnt orange–colored cushion that separated the heat from my body, watching the neighborhood children playing hopscotch and riding bikes. I would often just sit there, hugging my knees, staring out the window. Eventually, my mom grew very concerned and dragged me outside to make friends with the kids in the neighborhood.

While my mother and I were having this special moment,

April came running in, leaping from box to box, jumping inside them, on top of them—flattening the ones I had so carefully built.

"Look at my talented Baby Boom Boom go! Jump, Baby Boom Boom, jump!"

Baby Boom Boom is what my mother called my sister because when she was in her belly, April would kick all day and all night. My mom was sure the baby would be a football star. But to her surprise, she was born a bouncing baby girl—full of spirit and spunk and void of all fear, which my mom admired. My mother was beaming, watching my sister jump and hop, wrinkling my crumpled clothes even further.

"Please do not destroy my stuff."

"She is practicing her gymnastics," my mom declared.

"She won't be practicing anymore if she bangs her head or cuts her toes on the corner of the boxes," I said, scolding.

My mother scoffed and reminded me that the only time my sister had ever been hurt was the time when I slammed her finger in the door. I had just come home from ice-skating with Jenny and her mother. It was my first time ice-skating, and I spent the whole afternoon on my bottom. When I arrived home, I was soaked and freezing, so I rushed into the bathroom to peel off my clothes and put a robe on. When I put my hand on the big, old, heavy door, it accidently slammed shut with April's finger caught in the hinge. She was only eighteen months. She wailed, her finger dangling and blood covering the floor. I remember my mother crying so hard she could barely speak or drive, so we had to ride in an ambulance. My sister now held up her pointer finger that was significantly shorter than the rest of her fingers, with a big purple scar running across it, as if to confirm my mother's story.

Suddenly, I felt sick again. Not necessarily because of the

memory of hurting April, although I will forever feel awful, but because we were leaving our home. All the chapters that had filled my life so far, both the good and the bad, had started or ended in this apartment.

I remembered the many afternoons spent with friends in my room; I remembered the time I accidentally cut my hand in the bathtub when I was carving a heart in the pink Dove soap bar with my dad's razor blade, and how I charged all my friends to see my blood. I remember how the red water looked like cherry Hawaiian Punch, and I remember filling my piggy bank with all the change I collected. I remember not allowing my mother to drain the tub for twenty-four hours so we could have a second and third showing.

I remembered begging my mother not to go out at night, and vomiting, screaming, and crying every time she left. Finally, Sister Ann would hold me down, and my mother would run out the door. If my father was home, he would slip me a candy bar from his secret hiding place before he followed her out. I remember how bad he felt, and how he would try to make it up to me by taking me with him to the swap meets he so loved on Sundays. We would spend hours together—just he and I— methodically digging through the piles of used stuff on the cluttered tables, rummaging, the way pirates would search for treasure, for some interesting items that would help inspire my dad to stay on a healthy eating plan. Each great find was the promise of a great new recipe: an ice pick for no-sugar Italian ices, a meat grinder for the leanest no-fat burgers, a hand-cranked dough mixer for the fluffiest low-calorie bread. Our kitchen counters were cluttered with possibility and hope.

I remembered my mom making friends at the playground before my sister was born. I remembered my mom in bed for weeks when she was pregnant. I remembered all the nights I slept next to April's crib, watching her sleep, listening to her breathe, pinching myself that G-d had heard my prayers. I remembered running up and down the hallways that connected our rooms as my sister learned to crawl, to walk. We played dress-up, made tea parties with miniature China tea sets—cups, saucers, sugar bowls, and dolls—and baked brownies in my Easy-Bake Oven. We spent hours in my room around my little old-fashioned tea table that used to be my grandmother Beauty's when she was a child—the table that my mom was now giving back to her because she didn't want us to take it to New York.

I had friends throughout the building. Danielle lived upstairs; her mother was French and cooked the most delicious leg of lamb and green beans with garlic sauce. Tracy lived downstairs; her mother was a ballet teacher, and every Friday afternoon ten girls came over for dance classes. Becky lived next door with many brothers and sisters and would frequently invite me over for tuna casserole with a potato chip crust, and Hamburger Helper, minus the hamburger.

I remembered Bubbe Mary and Beauty eating corned beef on rye with mustard and sauerkraut that they brought over from Ricky's delicatessen on April's first birthday, and talking about how they had both decided that they no longer were going to add sugar to their coffee since Bubbe Mary had recently been diagnosed with diabetes.

I remembered brushing my hair with my friend Tamar in my room while we modeled the clothes we were allowed to keep after the Marshall Field's fashion show that we were both selected for when a talent scout came to our school. We were each allowed to keep an outfit. I kept the red corduroy jumper with gold brass buckles that was paired with the rabbit fur coat and matching hat, and Tamar chose the patent leather knee-high boots, blue sailor dress, and tan pea coat. We both refused to take off our outfits for days, proudly modeling them in school even though it was the beginning of June and the temperatures were already well into the eighties. I remember how we practiced for weeks before the show—counting on our fingers who could balance the encyclopedia on her head the longest, each trying to outdo the other on poise and grace.

But my most vivid memory was of the giant chocolate chip cookies from Old Town, the fat, chewy cookies with the bittersweet chunks that my mom used to bring me back in lieu of saying sorry when she hurt my feelings or when she stayed out extra late. My mom was never good with certain words, like "I love you" and "I am sorry," but when she wanted to apologize, she would dash out in her red Mustang and appear shortly after with the massive chocolate chip cookie from Old Town. "The cookie that smelled and tasted like homemade," she always said.

My mom would hold the giant cookie up like a peace offering and say, "I can not believe how expensive they are." Something about my mother buying something she thought was overpriced, and the true emotion in her voice when she presented the offering, made the cookie taste almost as delicious as my grandmother Beauty's homemade ones, the ones that filled her house with sweetness when she baked them. My mother didn't bake, but I smelled the sweetness, the familiarity, and the comfort of the cookie the moment she flashed the white waxed bag.

One by one, the boxes were taped shut, and the memories were locked away as the movers loaded the boxes onto the moving van.

The Ultimate Chocolate Chip Cookie with the Cream Cheese Dough

Yield: 12–14 giant cookies

Parchment paper for lining the baking sheets
1½ sticks cold unsalted butter, cubed
¼ cup cream cheese
¾ cup granulated sugar
¾ cup packed light brown sugar
2 large eggs, beaten
1 teaspoon vanilla extract
2¼ cups all-purpose flour
1 teaspoon salt
1 teaspoon baking powder
1 teaspoon baking soda
2 cups semisweet chocolate chips

Preheat oven to 375 degrees. Line 2 large baking sheets with parchment paper.

In the bowl of an electric mixer, beat together the butter, cream cheese, granulated sugar, and brown sugar on medium-high speed until well combined. Then add the beaten eggs, vanilla, flour, salt, baking powder, and baking soda. Beat on low speed until well combined. Fold in the chocolate chips.

Refrigerate the dough for at least 2 hours. Remove from the refrigerator and form into balls. Place the dough balls on the prepared baking sheets, spaced far apart. Bake for 15 to 20 minutes, or until the cookies are slightly browned at the edges. Remove from the oven and cool.

Note: *Bake longer for crispier, chewier cookies; bake less for ooey, gooey cookies. Serve warm or at room temperature.*

Lo-Carb Chocolate Crepes

4 egg whites beaten
1½ scoops vanilla protein powder
½ teaspoon vanilla extract
1 level teaspoon of coco powder
Cooking spray for pan
½ cup sliced strawberries

Put all the ingredients in a blender and blend until smooth. Spray an 11-inch nonstick pan with cooking spray and pour the batter, covering the whole surface. When the crepe bubbles, flip and cook until edges are brown. Remove from the skillet and fill with fresh strawberries. Fold over and serve.

PART TWO

5

Taking a Bite from the Big Apple

....

Lamb Stew with Sweet Potatoes,
Beauty's Baby Shell Kugel with Golden
Raisins, Aranacini di Riso

....

M y best friend Jenny told me horror stories about New York City: murders, people living on the streets, and subways and buildings covered in graffiti. But far more horrible was leaving Beauty and all things familiar. In New York, there would be no more special weekends at my grandmother's house, no more car rides on Lake Shore Drive, and no special noshes by the stove. It would be a latchkey, total independence, and self-survival.

I was heartsick. My parents and sister were thrilled. April would be going to school for the first time, and I would be leaving the only school I knew.

My mom boasted that with her ingenuity and a little bit of coercing, she had not only managed to enroll April in a wonderful preschool around the corner from our new house in Murray Hill, she had landed me a spot at the famous progressive

West Village elementary school, the Little Red School House. She said they accepted me without even meeting me due to her brilliant power of persuasion. My mom believed she could talk anyone into anything, and since she never took no for an answer, she usually could.

Even though I had to take two subways to school and walk a couple of blocks, my mother said I was extremely fortunate. "You will be going to school alongside the kids of famous artists, musicians, and playwrights. This environment is different than what you are used to, but I know you will thrive. And you were terrible at Hebrew anyway. Your teachers always said you were much more creative than you were academic. You have the soul of an artist! You will be happier in New York."

How did my mom think I was going to be happier? I was leaving the school I loved. I was leaving all my friends, and I wouldn't be able to see my grandparents for months. Besides, Anshe Emet had the most delicious kosher lunches and Manischewitz Tam Tam crackers with grape juice every afternoon for a treat. Not only was I going to die of loneliness, I was probably going to starve to death, or get mugged, or fall onto the subway tracks.

In the days before I left, I pleaded with my grandmother to let me live with her. "We can visit my parents during the holidays. We can take our first plane ride together." Neither of us had ever been on a plane before. "Also, Mommy and my dad are always out, so I doubt they'll even notice that I hadn't moved with them!"

Beauty felt my pain. "I am going to miss you so much," she said. "But you need to go with your parents. Your daddy is going to be a big shot in advertising—he is going to be like Darrin in *Bewitched*."

I wanted to be like Samantha and be able to twitch my nose

and land wherever I imagined, not where I was forced. Beauty reminded me that if I stayed in Chicago with her, who would look after April?

"You are the best big sister I've ever seen. Every time you leave April even for just a few minutes, she starts weeping. You are the only one who could calm her down. I need you to be brave—both for April and me." Beauty even shared that she thought my mother was a little scared, even though she would never admit to it. Vulnerability equaled weakness in my mom's eyes.

The night before we left, Beauty and I stayed up all night talking and making a batch of her famous noodle kugel with golden raisins and little shell pastas. She even divulged her special ingredient—lemon juice—the one my aunt had been dying to know for years. After the kugel cooled, she sliced it up and placed the pieces into twelve individual foil packs so April and I would have enough for a couple of days. The kugel never made it to the plane. We devoured it instantly and begged for more—scared it would be a while before we ate something so delicious again.

Beauty assured me that every week she would send me a recipe card and a twenty-dollar bill so I would have a little something to look forward to. "If I am cooking chicken soup for Papa, you can cook chicken soup for April. If I am cooking pot roast with green peppers and sweet potatoes, you could prepare pot roast with green peppers and sweet potatoes. I will walk you through every step. Just remember what I taught you. Food should taste like food. Chicken schnitzel should taste like chicken. Blueberry pie should taste like blueberries. If it is too sweet or too greasy, then you are losing the natural flavors of the ingredients. And if you need anything, I am just a phone call away—312-555-0783," she chanted.

"312-555-0783," I repeated.

"You have no idea how strong you are."

Beauty always said I was the strongest girl she knew, although I never really understood why she thought that. Both my parents always made fun of me for being too sensitive. Beauty said it was something that she knew, even if others, or I, didn't see it in me yet. Beauty believed in me so completely that I wore her love and confidence on me like a shield—making me feel protected from anything bad that could possibly happen.

The day we arrived in New York, it was extremely hot and muggy, and the sounds and sights of the city were mesmerizing—delis, fruit stands, bakeries, coffee shops, yellow taxis, pay phones, dry cleaners, bus stops, and take-out Chinese food places were everywhere. It was loud, fast, and dirty—nothing like our quiet neighborhood by the lake in Chicago. As much as I wanted to hate it, something about it was intriguing and electrifying. I was excited, scared, and curious all at one time. But I made sure not to let my mother see since she was being more attentive and thoughtful than usual. I guess she was probably feeling guilty about taking me away from the things she knew I loved most.

"You need to look at this like an adventure," my mother said, all gung ho, planning the sights of the day.

"I love adventures," April said, bouncing up and down. I said nothing.

"You were mad when I left you for a month to go to Africa on safari. This is your time to explore and have new experiences."

"I was mad because you left me with that mean babysitter, Sister Ann, who tortured me, saying I was going to Hell because I had not been saved by Jesus; and every time I showed her my drawings, she said they were ugly and I was a terrible artist."

"You know you are a very good artist. Don't I buy beautiful frames for all your pictures?"

"And she hardly fed us because she said you did not leave her enough money for groceries."

"She was a very reliable babysitter; she was always on time. I couldn't have left you with Beauty because she was too frightened to get her driver's license, so she would never have been able to get you to school."

"And you never called. I was worried that something happened to you. April was only one year old. How could you have not been worried?"

"You are just like Beauty, scared of the world. Didn't you like the little hand-carved wooden elephants I brought back for you girls?"

My mother always misconstrued what I was trying to convey. She always thought I was accusing her of something, instead of hearing me, which made matters worse. I learned at an early age that there were very few safe places to express myself—even Beauty would get uncomfortable when I read her my dark poems about death. No one seemed to be able to tolerate my emotions when I was sad, so most of the time I just smiled no matter what I was really feeling. The feelings I did not know what to do with, I kept locked safe in my diary—sealed with a little gold key that looked like it came off a charm bracelet.

Buckling my new Stride Rite white sandals with the rubber soles that my grandmother bought me for walking around Manhattan, my mother tried to convince me how lucky I was to be in a city of great public transportation and creative expression. "In New York City, we can walk everywhere, and everything is open late. I would have killed to get out of suburban Chicago when I was your age. My childhood was so boring. Every day was the same. I got up, ate breakfast, went to school, and practiced the piano. Nothing exciting ever happened in West Rogers Park. We had the same neighbors for most of my life, the same type of Jewish food day after day. It was just so ordinary. Everyone looked the same. I just love how people express themselves here."

Most days, I would have liked my life to be a little more boring and my mom to be a little more ordinary—from her wild, untamed, long frizzy hair; to her faded denim two-toned Levi bell-bottom jeans, to her low-cut tunic shirts to her dangling silver earrings, to her powerful voice, which always seemed ten times the volume of other people's. In Chicago, people always used to give my mother dirty looks; but in Manhattan, she didn't seem to stand out so much. Here, she was just part of the canvas and blended in as effortlessly as the bottle caps were embedded into the pavement. No one even looked twice at my mom while she hollered hysterically at April and me for wanting to sit down and get something to drink when there was so much more to see.

The first month we lived in the city, my mom was the ultimate tour guide. Her friend Joanne from the theater department at Northwestern University had moved to Manhattan after graduating college, and she mapped out the most exciting neighborhoods to explore. Since my mom loved Indian food, small avant-garde theaters, golden oldie movies, and foreign films, we explored the East Village. Since my dad used to be a disc jockey for the radio station at Northwestern University and his first job was as a music reviewer for *Rogue* magazine, we explored all the music venues and record stores in the West Village. My mom heard that there was a neighborhood called Little Odessa that made food like my Bubbe Mary, and she knew if she wanted to get on my dad's good side, eating there would be a fabulous idea. As for me, my mother wanted me to be comfortable taking the buses and subways because school was starting in a couple of weeks, and I would be traveling on my own. My mom said the school would provide me with a subway pass so I would be able to travel anywhere I wanted in the city for free.

"The whole city is like one big amusement park," she said, gesturing April and me to run through the water shooting out of a fire hydrant. When April balked because we didn't have bathing suits on, my mom suggested we take off our clothes and run through the sprinklers in our underwear. April didn't have to be told twice; she was off and running. When I refused to get wet, my mom shook her head in disgust. "Dawn, you are such a stick-in-the-mud. I don't know how I gave birth to such a Jewish grandmother." Noticing my eyes starting to well up, she looked at April and my dad and complained, "Not again."

"Dawny's going to cry, Dawny's going to cry," April teased in a singsong voice.

"I am not going to cry. I just have something in my eye." My stomach often ached from holding my breath so hard to hold back the tears from flowing. But unlike Chicago—where everything felt quiet, and I could easily get crushed by my emotions—in New York City, I was distracted by the street musicians, the clothes, the street art, and the sounds of the different languages being shouted in the streets. I was never too upset for too long. I was a part of something bigger than myself. I had only heard English and Hebrew before. Now I was lost in the rhythms and the dialects of the many languages spoken: Spanish, Ukrainian, Italian, Russian, Polish, Hindi, Chinese—each neighborhood a new language, a new culture, a new food.

There was so much to take in, and my parents, both experienced travelers, were determined to walk every street. They were like kids in a candy shop, sampling something new on every block. Chicago was the town of deep-dish pizza and ribs, but New York City was a mecca of cultures and flavors. "The city of many great cuisines," my dad said.

For the first time ever, my dad made no reference to any special diet he was on—the diet seemed to be eat as much as you can, and he did. Even though he was way over three hundred pounds and was not getting any skinnier from all the walking we were doing, he ate his way through the city. We enjoyed pasta in Little Italy, dumplings in Chinatown, pirogues in Little Odessa, curry on East Sixth Street, and falafels on MacDougal Street. Not only was I experiencing the food from different ethnicities bringing my family together, each dish had a story—a life before it touched our lips, a history that I found intriguing. It was one of the few times with my parents that I felt full, and we felt like a family.

On Bleecker Street in the West Village near my new school, there was an Italian sandwich shop called Faicco's Pork Store, filled with a dizzying range of imported Italian-style salamis hanging in the windows and hams, meatballs, sun-dried tomatoes, sweet peppers, and cheeses in glass cases. They even made their own homemade mozzarella. I remember the enthusiastic wrinkled man behind the counter asking me if I wanted to try the smoked or the marinated one. Both were incredible. I had tasted only Kraft Velveeta cheese before, but this cheese was so smooth and flavorful. The man who worked there had a passion for what he was selling, which made all the food taste that much more delicious. He told us food was *la gioia di vivere*—"the joy of life"—insisting that we try their house specialty, Arancini di Riso, crispy fried balls of risotto, crunchy on the outside and divinely soft and cheesy on the inside. They surely tasted better than my mom's boxed Rice-A-Roni.

A little farther east from the West Village was Little Odessa, which was famous for its delicious authentic old world Eastern European food: borscht with sour cream, blintzes, stuffed cabbage, pirogues, and potato knishes. As my dad bit into the chicken kiev, filled with melted butter and parsley and mashed potatoes on the side, he said, "Moving to New York was without a doubt the best decision I have ever made."

As I watched how happy my parents were, my uneasiness about moving to Manhattan and starting a new school was slowly beginning to fade.

Everyone had a favorite neighborhood. My mother loved Sixth Street in the East Village. In Chicago, there were only a few Indian restaurants, and she could never get her food spicy enough, but a whole street full of Indian restaurants with inexpensive lunch specials, all competing for your business, was more than she could have imagined. They would even make her food extra spicy. As my mother begged for more spice and heat in her lamb, she would joke how I was like Beauty since I liked my food so mild. While I watched my mother turn bright red, her nose dripping from the spices, I didn't think she realized how big of a compliment she was giving me. And even though I didn't like the food as hot as my mom, I loved learning about the different spices: turmeric, cumin, coriander, and saffron. I marveled at how the different spices created color and flavors that I had never experienced before, how the strands of red saffron and the turmeric turned the rice bright yellow when cooked.

Walking up St. Mark's Place, which had more smells, food, music, and vendors than I had ever seen in one place, I was in awe. There was everything from rock-and-roll posters, to sunglasses, to leather sandals, to T-shirts, to funny pipes. While my parents were debating which was the best part of New York, I started talking to the patch man. He had a whole stand filled with hundreds of different patches that you could iron on your jacket, jeans, or knapsack: peace sign patches, "Nixon Sucks" patches, "McGovern for President" patches, "Flower Power" patches. As great as the patches were, Jovan, the man who owned the stand, was equally wonderful with his six-inch 'fro, muttonchop sideburns, silk pajamas, and a neck full of beads. He smelled of sweet cigarettes and patchouli oil.

As April and I looked through all the patches, trying to figure out which one to select, he gave us each a patch for free and said, "Welcome to New York." He insisted that my parents take April and me to Veniero's pastry shop a couple of blocks up, where I experienced the most mouthwatering chocolate éclair filled with ricotta cheese instead of the usual custard, and my dad and sister indulged in the Italian-style cheesecake and chocolate mousse pie. My mother was content grabbing a little corner off of each of our pastries.

Whether we went east, west, north, or south, there was something spectacular to see, someone wonderful to talk to, and something delicious to taste. I was exhilarated and felt alive in a way that I had not known was possible. More than adapting to my new surroundings, I was falling madly in love with my new city. I couldn't wait to tell Beauty all that I had learned, and all that I had experienced in just a few short weeks.

Once summer was over and school started, my parents were not around as much. My dad started his new job at the ad agency, my mom started substitute teaching, and my sister was in an extended day program. As for me, I began wandering on my own after school, taking culinary adventures, buying new ingredients with the money Beauty sent me, and experimenting in the kitchen with different spices. My grandmother's boiled meat became lamb curry with the addition of garam masala powder and coriander that was sold in the little spice shop in Curry Hill, a few blocks from my new home.

I still missed my grandmother terribly and longed for the comfort and love of my grandparents' home, but learning about new cultures, cooking, and re-creating Beauty's recipes with an ethnic flare gave me an incredible sense of pride and purpose. With each new recipe card came a new challenge, a new taste of the Big Apple.

Lamb Stew with Sweet Potatoes

Yield: 4 servings

1 tablespoon oil
1 medium-sized onion, sliced thin
4 medium garlic cloves, pressed
2 tablespoons minced fresh ginger
1 pound cubed lamb
1 teaspoon garam masala (see note)
1 cup chicken broth
3 cups peeled and cubed sweet potatoes
5 cups finely chopped spinach
1 teaspoon turmeric
Salt and pepper, to taste

Heat the oil in a large skillet. Then sauté the onion, garlic, ginger, and lamb over medium heat for about 5 minutes, stirring frequently. Add the garam masala powder, mixing well for about 30 seconds. Then add the broth and stir in the sweet potatoes, spinach, and turmeric. Stir and simmer with salt and pepper to taste. Simmer, covered, on medium-low heat for about 30 minutes, stirring occasionally, or until the lamb, potatoes, and spinach are tender.

Note: *Garam masala is a pre-blended spice mixture that you can find in Indian markets or specialty shops. It is widely used in Indian, Nepalese, and other Asian cuisines. It is made of cardamom, cloves, mace, cinnamon, cumin, fennel, black peppercorns, and fenugreek.*

Aranacini di Riso

2 tablespoons butter
½ white onion, finely chopped
2 celery stalks, finely chopped
1 cup Arborio rice
Salt and pepper, to taste
½ cup white wine
4 cups vegetable broth, heated
¾ cup finely grated Parmesan cheese
1 egg, separated
½ cup shredded mozzarella
2 tablespoons chopped parsley
2 eggs, beaten
1 cup all-purpose flour
1 cup bread crumbs
1½ cups oil

Melt the butter in a large pan over medium heat, then add the onion and celery and sauté until soft. Stir in the rice and season with salt and pepper. Continue to cook for 1 minute. Then add the wine and stir until almost all liquid is absorbed, about 1 minute. Add 1 cup of the hot broth and cook, stirring, until it has been absorbed. Continue adding the broth, a cup at a time, and stirring until each additional cup has been absorbed. This will take about 15 minutes. Stir in ½ cup of the Parmesan cheese. Allow to cool and then put in the refrigerator, covered, overnight.

The next day, separate 1 egg and put the yolk aside. In a large mixing bowl, combine the chilled risotto, the egg yolk, and the remaining ¼ cup of Parmesan. Then add the mozzarella and parsley. Stir until all the ingredients are mixed together.

Place the beaten eggs in a large bowl. Next put the flour on a large plate and then the bread crumbs on another large plate. Roll your risotto into balls. Dip each ball into the beaten eggs, then

My Fat Dad   87

into the flour, then into the bread crumbs. Next, heat up the oil in a large skillet. When the oil is hot, start frying the croquettes. Keep turning them so they are brown on all sides. Remove the risotto balls to paper towel–lined plates. Give a quick blot and then serve.

6

Swapping Moms

....

Grandma Ethel's New York Egg Cream,
Saucy Susan Chicken Thighs and Legs

....

E ntering the Little Red School House in fourth grade was
akin to entering a foreign land. All the girls had long strag-
gly hair past their butts, and the boys did not look that much
different. It was 1972, and McGovern was running against
Nixon for president. The kids in my new class all seemed to be
a walking billboard for the McGovern campaign—sporting
several buttons and stickers on their clothes and backpacks. As
my first day of school began, a girl with bright red hair and
freckles named Marley led me to the circle of students already
seated on the floor, and another girl named Robyn handed me
a friendship bracelet made from daisies that she'd picked at her
country house in Upstate New York. Ginger, the teacher, who
we were to call by her first name, instructed us to one by one
introduce ourselves. Ginger told us that as we said our name,
we should make a hand gesture that represented our inner

essence. I made mine with big open arms above my head, representing that I was full of sunshine. When I told the class where I previously lived, David, the boy sitting next to me, said that he was a Cubs fan and proceeded to massage my earlobe. I was paralyzed as this strange, chubby boy with rips in his jeans was touching me, and I was even more amazed that the teacher just kept smiling at him with admiration. In my old school, we were always told to keep our hands on our own body. But here the rules seemed to be different.

Suzanne and I were the only two kids that were new. Suzanne was not from another city like me: she was just transferring from a public school uptown in Washington Heights, which she said felt like a different city. To close the circle and begin our learning day, we all took three deep tummy breaths in unison, honoring the beginning of a new school year. Thoroughly centered, we shook out all the stress from our bodies, then slowly and peacefully walked to our seat of choice, while Ginger hummed the melody to "Kumbaya."

Ginger, exotic and beautiful, with shiny hair as dark as licorice, began to tell us about the wonderful trip we were going to be taking the next day to the Bronx Zoo. The study of animals and their habitats was going to be our area of concentration for the year. For the trip, we were advised to wear sun hats so we would not get burned, and for a special treat we would be allowed to pack sodas in our lunch boxes since it was supposed to be a really scorching day. I raised my hand and asked, "If we bring ice cream sodas, won't they spill and melt all over our lunch bags?" Everybody started laughing, and Ginger clarified her statement: "I am sorry. I'm talking about sodas, like Pepsi and 7UP." In Chicago, those drinks were not called soda, but pop. I felt my face get flushed from embarrassment.

Next we had to line up to go to shop. Shop was something

I did with my grandmother on the weekends but never with my class. Little did I know "shop" meant woodworking, which I discovered upon entering the crafts studio. Our shop teacher's name was Leo; he had long, thinning hair, which was braided, and the longest beard I had ever seen—also braided. Most of my peers had been at the school since they were five, and they were very comfortable in the workshop, sawing and carving away. Some kids were making cabinets, others chairs, and one boy, Jonathan, whom everybody called Hucky, was making a go-cart—that would actually be able to go. I decided I would make a lamp. When Leo asked me if I wanted to shape it like a tree, I said, "Sure. A redwood, maybe." I was not sure why I decided that, but moments later, I was going through *National Geographic*s looking for pictures to cut out and then trace on three pieces of wood that I would cut with a jigsaw, before carving and chiseling.

Leo not only guided us on our projects, but also talked about activism, speaking passionately about his choice for the next president. Most of the kids, well versed on this subject, had walked in anti–Vietnam War protests in Washington and had raised money for Greenpeace. Some of them had even made inspirational cards for the inmates at the Women's House of Detention on the corner of Tenth Street and Sixth Avenue, before Mayor Lindsay shut the jail down. Although some of the inmates were actual criminals, many of them were writers, activists, and Communists—including former Little Red student Angela Davis, who fought for racial and social equality.

Recess was next, which was not held at our school but at a vacant lot around the corner. There were no swings, or slides, or monkey bars—just a big open space with basketball hoops and hard, gray concrete, which my head hit within moments of entering, when David knocked me over while playing Poison

Ball. Everyone was running around wildly, and I kept getting bumped and hit in the face with the volleyball that was supposedly poisoned. "You're out, you're out," the boys kept shouting. No longer able to take the danger, I removed myself from the chaos. I sat alone, against the warm iron fence that encased the play space, until it was time to go inside for lunch.

Lunch was held in a dingy, hot basement with large exposed pipes and red peeling paint. Following the other kids, I picked up an orange plastic tray and stood on line. A lunch lady plopped hard, crusty, lukewarm macaroni and cheese and mushy green beans onto my plate. I noticed that most of the kids brought their own food in square metal lunch boxes that had their favorite music groups on them, like the Jackson Five, Sonny and Cher, or the Partridge Family.

Hesitantly sitting down at the table filled with giddy girls, Robyn looked at me and said, "You are not really going to eat that, are you?" I did not want to, but I was famished and disoriented. "Don't worry. I have plenty," she said, handing me a couple of Wasa crackers with lobster salad that her mother had prepared. They were sweet, creamy, and crunchy all at the same time. When I rolled my eyes in delight, Marley told me I could have some of her lunch too. She offered me a piece of honey-glazed turkey with lettuce, tomato, and Grey Poupon mustard on a French baguette. Both girls assured me that eating the cafeteria food was very risky.

Thanking them for sharing, I explained how much different my school in Chicago was. "We would never address our teachers by their first names. We always had assigned seats. In the morning, we would trace cursive letters in English, and in the afternoon, we practiced writing sentences in Hebrew—from right to left—instead of left to right. Before we ate our lunch, we always said a prayer, and the food was always kosher, always delicious, and always blessed by the rabbi." Marley and Robyn were both Jewish but never said a Hebrew prayer before eating and didn't know how to write the letters. I showed them how to make a blessing over the food and write the first three letters of the Hebrew alphabet.

Robyn informed me that her parents were divorced, and whenever she went to her dad's, they would go to an amazing restaurant called the Palm, where they would order giant two-and-a-half-pound lobsters. Whatever was leftover from dinner, Robyn would bring home to her mother, who would make it into a lobster salad for her lunch the next day by adding chopped dates, pears, and mayonnaise so she would have something mouthwatering and special. Marley confided that her mother was usually working and suffered from bad headaches so she often made her own lunch or bought a sandwich from Zabar's near where she lived on the Upper West Side.

Both Robyn and Marley were extremely friendly, and by the end of the first day they had made me feel like I was a part of their group. They even invited me into their secret clubhouse under Ginger's desk, where, during free time, they congregated to trade Wacky Pack stickers. Robyn gave me some of her duplicates so I could start my own collection. I couldn't wait to purchase the stickers and show them to my dad, since they parodied everyday consumer products—like the kind he wrote commercials for. Some of the funniest ones were Grave Train Dog Food, Hurts Tomato Paste, Tied Laundry Detergent, and Hawaiian Punks Juice. Robyn's collection was the most impressive in the class since she was allowed to buy a pack every day. If she was with her mom, she would be allowed to purchase one or two packs, but when she was with her dad, he always bought her five packs at a time—even allowing her to chew the stale gum that came with them.

Arriving home, I began rambling about everything that had occurred. I was so excited to share my day with my mother. "Slow down, slow down," she insisted. "I can't understand a word of what you are saying."

"I need to pack a lunch, and I need some money for stickers so I can be a part of the club that hangs out under the teacher's desk. Please, please, please, can we go to the Palm so we can make lobster salad for lunch?"

My mom quickly went from confused to aggravated to ballistic. "Are you out of your mind? The Palm? Lobster salad for lunch? Did you do any reading? What did you learn? And why were you under your teacher's desk?" My mom's tirade squashed my excitement.

"I learned a lot, I just need some money for stickers and lunch."

"I have already paid for school lunch."

"But it is disgusting. Nobody eats it!"

I told her what my friends brought for lunch, and she said, "They must be snobs. What kind of spoiled child brings lobster for lunch?" But it was not lobster, it was lobster salad, and they were not snobs—just the opposite; they were really generous and warm. Why couldn't my mother understand that?

When Beauty phoned to find out about my new school, I fibbed. I knew she was worried about me, so I told her that my new school was great . . . which was kind of true. But I also told her the school food was wonderful. "You would be happy; we always have a vegetable with our entrée." And I guess that was kind of true too—except the vegetables were just canned, salty, and inedible.

I eventually figured out how to pack my own lunch despite my mother's protests and lack of interest. I had the twenty-dollar bill my grandmother sent me along with her weekly recipe card. I could shop, cook, and bring the leftovers to school. It was a lesson in ingenuity, independence, and survival. I was also learning to budget, which coincided nicely with what I was learning in school. In math, instead of having worksheets with tons of multiplication problems to memorize, we were given a fake checkbook and taught how to balance it.

Everything at Little Red was different from my old school in Chicago. They did not care about periods and commas, as long as you were expressing yourself when you wrote—luckily I had a lot to express. For homework, there were no books to take home, nothing that required sitting and memorizing. We were assigned to walk around the neighborhood pretending we were reporters asking questions about businesses and the history of stores and landmarks. We learned writing, math, and current events by asking questions like who, what, why, where, and when—culminating in the creation of a class newspaper. "The city is part of our classroom," Ginger would say, and I loved it! While my mother did not understand me, she found me a school where they absolutely did.

But both my parents were pretty much uninvolved when it came to school. They were not like Robyn's parents, who would always volunteer to chaperone on class trips and would always be involved in classroom projects.

Unlike Marley's parents or mine, Robyn's parents were very attentive and were always around—devoted to every aspect of her life. Robyn was an only child, and her parents were recently separated, so her parents were worried that she was lonely. Both parents were always more than happy to entertain Robyn and her friends after school. Marley and I were always happy to oblige.

Robyn's dad was in advertising like my dad. He even was a fan of my dad's work, telling me my father was a genius creative director, quoting his famous tagline for Schlitz: "Go for the Gusto." But unlike my dad, scheduling time to hang out with Robyn and her friends seemed to be his top priority. As soon as she walked out of the classroom, he would hug her tightly and fling her onto his shoulders. Marley and I would shout to her, "Duck your head, duck your head," as we exited the building, because he was super-tall. Sometimes, after school, he would buy all the kids in the class ice cream from the Mister Softee truck. While Robyn was on his shoulders, her vanilla cone would drip onto his wavy locks, but he never seemed to mind. Everything she did, he smiled in delight. I occasionally wondered if my dad didn't come to school because he was self-conscious of his size or if he was just too busy. I never asked or complained—but I thought Robyn was lucky.

I loved spending time with Robyn's dad. I learned a lot about gourmet ingredients and cooking from him. He lived on Ninth Street and Sixth Avenue, above Balducci's market, which specialized in upscale foods from around the world. And when we went to his house after school to do homework, he always had a spread of exotic fruits, like pomegranates, kiwis, and ladyfinger apples for snacks. If I was allowed to stay for dinner— which I usually was, unless I had to pick up April from preschool—he would show off his culinary skills by making Spinach Fettuccini Alfredo with real cream and butter or Caesar Salad with Portuguese anchovies, homemade croutons, and coddled eggs, so the yolk becomes thick and warm. I never made the fettuccini for my dad, but the salad with the anchovy dressing I made often, adding extra anchovies and eliminating the croutons. My dad's diets changed constantly, but the elimination of bread seemed to be a universal theme in most of the diets he was on.

While I loved going to both Robyn's mom's and her dad's

house, she equally loved coming to my house—although I could not figure out why. She said it was so much fun playing with April, and it was hard being the center of attention and being fussed over all the time. After being best buddies for many months and sleeping at each other's houses constantly, we came up with the brilliant idea to switch lives for a week. I was in awe of all the restaurants she went to with her dad, and how her mother tucked her in bed with a story every night. She loved the fact that I was not an only child, and my mother did not ask me questions every minute or rely on me for friendship or her own happiness.

Telling our mothers our brilliant plan, we were shocked when they both agreed to the idea, thinking it would help us to appreciate how lucky we each were. Whenever I felt upset about something, my mother would scream at me, "You are so spoiled; if you really want something to feel sorry about, I will leave you in the gutter with the rats for a night, and then you will really have something to feel sorry for." Robyn's mother would constantly tell her how she retired from the soap opera *As the World Turns* to raise her because her own mother had to clean houses to support her when she was a child and so she was never around. She wanted to be present for Robyn and did not want to miss one second of her childhood. Everything Robyn did or said seemed to be a monumental event for her.

Since Robyn and I had become friends, our moms, although their parenting styles were different, found they had a lot in common and also became friends. They both loved theater, poetry, and astrology, and struggled to find themselves with men who were immersed in the fast life of advertising, where spouses were usually not included in their social lives. Brenda, Robyn's mom, was very political and convinced my mom to work alongside her on the McGovern campaign. My mom rallied Robyn's mom, who was devastated about her separation, to go to the theater and dinner with her at night when Robyn was with her dad. My mom always had a two-for-one coupon for everything, and now she had someone to use them with.

They seemed to admire and respect each other for their common interests and their differences. For a New Year's resolution, they both read the self-actualizing book *Fear of Flying* by Erica Jong, which I used to hear them debate about late at night.

After a lot of conversations, the plan to switch moms was actually coming to fruition, with some compromises. Robyn was going to spend four nights at my house, and I was going to spend four nights at her mom's apartment. Robyn would help with April, and I would help train Robyn's new pet rock, which she promised wouldn't bite me.

When I blurted out the plan to my grandmother, she thought my mother had gone more crazy than usual and couldn't believe her daughter would agree to such a cockamamie plan. But our parents did agree. While Robyn was having second thoughts, I couldn't wait to have a home-cooked meal and be kissed good night—something Robyn's mother always did.

On the first day, I felt very awkward sitting at the little half table next to the kitchen wall in her mom's living room, where I used to always sit with Robyn. Now her mom and I were sitting there talking about my day, sorting my stickers, caressing her pet rock, and looking at the book *Where Did I Come From?*—which had explicit illustrated pictures of body parts.

Robyn's parents were very free and comfortable with their bodies—they were both nudists, along with Robyn's Grandma Ethel. The entire family walked around the house nude, even in front of guests. I remember the first time Robyn's mom answered the door without any clothes on—my face went white. Robyn told me it was normal, and her dad would walk around naked all the time too, but fortunately he never did this when I was at his apartment. While I had never seen a grown-up's bare body before, I thought my mom would appreciate the fact that they saved a lot of money on buying clothes.

Brenda, Robyn's mom, explained how there was so much shame associated with our bodies and it was wonderful to feel liberated. She said if I was sweaty or just felt constrained by what I was wearing, I didn't need to keep my clothes on. I said I felt more at ease covered, and she respected that.

She felt that it was very important for girls to love their bodies no matter the size or shape. She told me she used to be extremely skinny, but after becoming a mother, she put on a little weight due to the fact that she was always cooking and baking for Robyn. Also, her ex-mother-in-law lived upstairs in the same apartment building and was always feeding her—probably because she was feeling guilty that her son left Brenda. But I bet the real reason she remained close to her daughter-in-law was because of Robyn. Robyn was the glue that kept them together. Robyn was very close to her grandma Ethel—the way I was with Beauty. Ethel was always around, and the two were only separated by a quick elevator ride or a couple flights of stairs between their apartments.

During my stay at Robyn's, her mom made me the most delicious dinners—while standing over the stove naked—grilled lamb chops with Saucy Susan, roast chicken with Saucy Susan, veal chops with Saucy Susan, and stuffed shells with ricotta, spinach, and garlic powder. Brenda was not a gourmet cook like Robyn's dad, but she said that with a couple of tricks like garlic powder and Saucy Susan, anything could taste impressive. She even taught me how to use a basting brush so the meat would brown perfectly. When dinner—which always lasted a full hour—ended, we would go upstairs to Grandma Ethel's for two episodes of *I Love Lucy* and chocolate egg creams, which Grandma Ethel showed me how to make. To my surprise, it had neither eggs nor cream—just syrup and seltzer. At eight on the dot, which was much earlier than my bedtime, Brenda tucked me in with a good-night kiss, while humming the words to "I Am Woman" by Helen Reddy—the song Robyn always sang before her gymnastics meets. Everything felt warm there— even though they finally convinced me to un-robe. "When you let your body breathe free, your spirit will soar." I had a renewed strength and appreciation for my body. I wanted to stay forever.

As for Robyn, after four days of TV dinners, entertaining April, school lunches, and no showers—because my mother hated when the bathroom would steam and possibly make the raised velvet wallpaper peel—I never heard her complain again about how her mom was too doting.

7

The Hampton Diet

....

Diet-Friendly Jell-O Chiffon Pie, Lo-Cal Gazpacho Soup, Date Nut Bread Infused with Taster's Choice

....

Our move to New York was prompted by my dad getting a job as a creative director at the McCann Erickson ad agency. They offered him the job based on the successful campaign he launched for Taster's Choice freeze-dried coffee, making it the number one brand in the United States. The campaign ("The Fooler") put the coffee on the map and sales skyrocketed.

My dad actually loved Taster's Choice coffee and used it in everything, including his date nut health bread, which consisted of chopped dates, walnuts, and, of course—Taster's Choice. One evening back in Chicago, just as he was about to put the bread in the oven to bake, the phone rang; it was his secretary Molly Warner with an urgent message. My dad jotted down the number and name on a piece of paper towel. He would have waited until the morning to return the call since it was an international number, but Molly said it sounded urgent and he could call collect.

My dad called the operator and gave her the number. "This is Al Lerman with a collect call to Bob Reynolds. . . . Yes, I can wait. . . . Hello. . . . Yes. Hi. . . . No, it's not too late. . . . Of course."

I watched my dad's face as he listened in disbelief to the caller on the other end of the receiver. After a couple minutes of intense listening, he repeated several times, "Are you sure you have the right person? I am not sure. . . . I live in Chicago. . . . Tomorrow? . . . Creative director of the world? I thought only God had that title," he said, beginning to chuckle. My dad paced around the kitchen, continuing to talk while stretching the cord from the phone, which was mounted in our kitchen next to the refrigerator. The cord extended from the kitchen to the dining room, all the way into the living room.

I desperately tried to figure out exactly what the person on the other end of the line was saying. I hadn't seen my dad this excited since the time he discovered how to make a chiffon pie he could eat while on Weight Watchers. Watching the conversation continue, I saw my dad jotting down all kinds of numbers. "Am I hearing you right—double? I can never say no to anything double. Yes, I will see you tomorrow afternoon."

"Creative director of the world!" my dad shouted to my mom. "We might be moving to New York and they are going to double my salary! I will no longer be Al the copywriter; I will be Al Lerman, the international creative director."

Within moments, my mom was methodically calling airlines to book an early morning flight, imagining how wonderful it would be to live close to Times Square and the Theater District, while my dad was nervously pulling clothes down from his bedroom closet, shouting, "Too conservative! Too casual! Definitely not flattering!" Entering the kitchen to remove the moist, chewy bread with a little bit of crunch from the oven, he asked my mother if she thought they would reconsider once they saw how heavy he was. "The ad industry—especially the Madison Avenue types—are not only known for their cutting-edge work, but their hip, attractive, and impeccably dressed executives." As he buttoned his snug silk shirt, he eyed my mom and me for reassurance, and explained, "So far, I have been able to bypass the unspoken requirements of looking svelte and dapper with my catchy slogans and funny jokes; but this is the real deal, this is the big time."

"I know you will wow them with your funny jokes, Daddy," I said.

"I thank you for your vote of approval, but it's the agency people in New York that I have to impress. Tomorrow, I'm meeting the creative team and Mr. Reynolds, who is head of the agency both in New York and abroad. He is flying in from Vevey, Switzerland, where he is working on an account, just to meet me."

Tapping his chin, smiling at my mom, my dad was no longer aware that I was in the room. "Mr. Reynolds said if I could do for Nescafé and McCann what I did for Taster's Choice and Leo Burnett, I will be a star and I'll be handsomely rewarded with many great perks—a membership to the Friars Club, where George Burns and Milton Berle and other famous celebrities give roasts, VIP guest passes for the exclusive Atrium Club with its heated indoor pool, saunas, and Jacuzzis, and an expense account to dine at all the top restaurants: Le Cirque, 21, and the Four Seasons. You know this is a dream, right?" He beamed, gliding my mom around the apartment.

My mom pinched him on the arm—reassuring him that this was real, reminding him of his extraordinary talents.

For his campaigns my dad had already been receiving a lot of recognition and press in *Advertising Age* so it only made sense that he would be recruited by one of the biggest agencies in Manhattan.

Upon returning from his trip, he announced the good news over a celebratory Italian dinner of two deep-dish pizzas with the works—Italian sausage, ground beef, ham, and pepperoni. Mr. Reynolds and the creative team on Nestlé—the account that they wanted him to take over—adored him. And just like that, we moved.

The job proved to be glamorous way beyond my dad's wildest dreams. His new position was filled with trips all over the world, martini lunches, and wild soirees that seemed to last for days. This was not a nine-to-five position, and family members needed to understand what the job entailed. But during the Christmas holidays, wives and children were invited to the annual holiday bash, which my sister and I anxiously looked forward to.

The office Christmas celebration had a special area with a huge six-foot Christmas tree for the kids, and a Santa who listened to our wishes, and waitresses dressed like elves, serving kid-friendly food—pigs in the blanket, toasted cheese triangles, and frosted Christmas cookies. During the party, the kids of the agency employees got to stay up late and run through the cubicles decorated with posters from all the company's recent campaigns—Exxon, Nestlé, GM, and my favorite one from Coca-Cola—"I'd Like to Teach the World to Sing." I loved exploring the offices with the other kids, while the parents, oblivious to their children's whereabouts, socialized—smoking and drinking fancy cocktails like Kir Royales and Pink Squirrels. It was at the agency, watching the adults interact and looking at the gold, silver, and bronze Clio Awards covering the walls, that I experienced a glimpse into the world of advertising, the world that had seduced my dad. The world I was not really a part of.

With the demands of the agency, along with the enticing "Me Culture" that was exploding in Manhattan during the 1970s, staying home in the evenings or having family meals was of little interest to either of my parents. Their social calendar was busy—especially my dad's—and neither of them was about to give it up to spend time with my sister and me. But then one wonderful morning, fate intervened, and just like that, the beautifully engraved linen envelope arrived. I watched my mom open the invitation. We were to be guests, April and I included, for the Reynolds' annual Fourth of July BBQ at their East Hampton home. Not only were we invited to the party, we were invited to stay for the whole glorious weekend.

Mr. Reynolds was the president and CEO of the agency, so getting an invitation to his house was more than a polite formality; it was an honor. The Reynolds lived on Park Avenue, summered in the Hamptons, and were considered very fancy and affluent, living by the Emily Post School of Etiquette. My family never summered anywhere, and we were definitely not classy or fancy. We did not dress for dinner, we did not have especially good table manners, we did not play golf or tennis, and my mother had never been to a country club or engaged in the sort of gossip that wives who lunched and drank gin and tonics did. I did not go to school uptown like the Reynolds' three boys; I did not study Latin, sail in the summer, or ski in the winter. I did not wear pink Izod collared shirts, or pleated lime-green skirts, or own a monogrammed book bag.

My family represented the creatives, the bohemians, the purse-carrying men—free-spirited and informal. Mr. Reynolds's family represented the executives—the suits, the power behind the scenes that made the deals. The executives often came from Ivy League schools and had lavish lifestyles. A weekend in the Hamptons was something we only saw in magazines.

While my whole family was excited about the invitation, the pressure that accompanied the invite was huge. My mom had no idea what to pack, and my dad was embarrassed by how he would look in a swimsuit. His weight had ballooned to almost four hundred pounds since landing the job, due to the stress of the job, the late night production meetings, and the constant three-course meals—consisting of fried appetizers, rich meat dishes, imported wines, and decadent desserts. In recent months, keeping to a diet had been nearly impossible. My dad loved fine dining, but unfortunately he was cursed with a slow metabolism. When they were growing up, his brother Melvin had eaten the same heavy food as he did and was always super-thin. In the office, people were focused on what my dad was presenting, but in the Hamptons, appearances were important, and there was no hiding behind his storyboards and well-thought-out presentations—he was presenting us and showing himself in a more relaxed setting.

The three weeks leading up to the weekend trip to the Hamptons were filled with anxiety. My mom, who never seemed to care one bit about fitting in, seemed particularly unnerved. She did not know fancy people like this and wanted to make a good impression for my dad so he would continue to move up in the ranks of the agency. My mom, who hated to shop and usually would not purchase anything that was not on sale, took us to B. Altman's for new white pleated culotte skirts and ruffled ankle socks and did not even look at the price. And my dad pursued a new diet that he invented. He was convinced that he had a unique concept that would revolutionize the dieting world.

He believed that if he didn't eat and only drank for three weeks, no matter what he was drinking, he would lose at least two pounds a day, which would add up to forty-two pounds total—making a significant difference in his appearance. My dad said that when he sipped through a straw, he would get full faster and would consume fewer calories. He would call this diet *The Twenty-One Day Hampton Diet*. He believed that this would outsell Weight Watchers diet books since there was less cooking, fewer rules, and quicker results.

While for the first couple of days he carried out his plan solo, guzzling bowls of gazpacho and egg drop soup and drinking gallons of Diet Coke, I suggested that on Saturday mornings I could spend time with him and be his trusted assistant. I knew I could help him elaborate and expand his menu, making it a little healthier, adding all kinds of fruit and vegetable shakes that we could freeze for him to take to work in an insulated lunch bag. The liquid meals would defrost throughout the morning, being the perfect consistency by lunchtime. He could even carry the creations to meetings for his colleagues to sample. If the diet worked, not only would he feel better about himself, but also he would have a captive group of people that could help him market the quick weight loss plan.

I knew there was a lot riding on the success of The Hampton Diet, so I made it my business to wake up before everyone on the weekend and run to the store. I was allowed to go by myself to the D'Agostino's market on the corner, where I loaded up on a variety of ingredients that I thought would work well in our liquid creations: vegetables, fruits, vanilla ice milk. Beauty, who did not agree with the diet, suggested that I use V8 as a base and then enhance it with carrots, garlic, cucumbers, and fresh green peppers. I bought as much fresh produce as I could carry, and when I returned from the store, I charged into action—putting on my favorite polka-dot apron that my grandmother had made for me when my parents broke the news we were moving. Being that my mother didn't like to cook and barely ever went into the kitchen, Beauty knew her apron would get a lot of use, and wearing it made me feel confident and closer to her.

With my apron tied and my sleeves rolled up, I was ready for battle. My grandmother said being organized led to success, so I set out to turn our fridge into a liquid dieter's paradise. First was detoxing the kitchen. I tossed out everything that would lead to temptation, like the leftover candy from Halloween, as well as everything that was expired and rotten. My dad used to joke, "If you want to really lose weight, just pull out one of your mom's moldy leftovers that have been in there for God knows how long, and for sure, you will get food poisoning, so no diet will be needed, just a lot of magazines and toilet paper."

The clean refrigerator would symbolize a fresh start—not only for my dad's new diet but also for my family's social life. If the Reynolds enjoyed having us, they would invite us more, and my family could actually spend time together. I began tossing the moldy Miracle Whip, scrunched-up foil packs with half-eaten tuna sandwiches, and all the mini packages of ketchup, mustard, salt, and pepper—the kind of stuff you could grab free at the Bagel Nosh on the corner that my mom loved to store in the fridge. I hoped that I could inspire my dad, and hoped he would value my input.

Scrubbing down the insides, I made my mother promise to keep the refrigerator tidy and begged her to support the effort I was making to help my dad. While my mom usually became enraged when I talked about food or compared the way she kept our house to the way my grandmother Beauty kept her house, she miraculously consented. The refrigerator was always a battleground between my mother and me. For her, it was a place just to store things; for me, it was a place where I wanted to find order. I remember how my grandmother's fridge was always stocked with all kinds of delicious homemade food: roasted chicken and vegetable soup, as well as fresh milk in glass bottles, platters of cut-up radishes and celery, and bowls of sliced grapes and strawberries. Everything was so tidy, fresh-looking, and organized. I remember wishing that my mother would be more like my grandmother; but since that was not going to happen, I needed to take charge.

Our kitchen, like most New York City kitchens, was long and narrow, so for both my dad and me to work side by side required a lot of organization. I laid out all the ingredients in a way that was easily accessible, without either of us moving around too much. This way we could both make decisions together on what we were going to create. I could not wait to get started; there were so many possibilities—sweet shakes, savory shakes, hot shakes, cold shakes. My dad and I were on a mission, and we were not afraid to use our creativity. We would blend everything you could think of—from celery, tomatoes, and tortilla chips, to mashed avocado and banana shakes, to the spinach and ice cream Monster Shake that we both tried so hard not to spit out. My dad was losing a great deal of weight rapidly, so he stuck to the Hampton diet for a full twenty-one days, losing a total of twenty-five pounds before purchasing a bathing suit and tennis shorts at the Mr. Big & Tall shop for our weekend.

On the day of the trip, we went to Hertz Rent-a-Car, where we rented a brand-new white Pontiac convertible that had that new car smell, and loaded up our worn duffel bags that my mom had sent to the Laundromat so that we would look as good as new. As we drove to the Hamptons in our beach clothes, my parents kept arguing because my mom, who was in charge of directions, kept navigating us the wrong way.

The wind was blowing hard through my hair as my mother kept rolling down the window, sticking her head out, and screaming to cars speeding past us for directions. I watched the map fly out of her hand, landing on the windshield of the delivery truck to the right of us. My father slammed on the brakes to avoid crashing into the swerving truck. He began spouting words at the top of his lungs that I would never dare repeat.

When we made it alive off the freeway, my parents became calmer, admiring the quaint churches, old houses, and windmills planted on village greens. Nearing the Reynolds' home, we passed farmlands and riding stables and saw horses running free—and noticed that the homes were no longer houses but estates. Beyond them, you could see the water stretched into the horizon as my dad pulled the top down. Inhaling the salted air pushed any remembrance of Manhattan and the unpleasant car ride into the distance.

Arriving disheveled after a long drive in traffic, we were greeted by Ruth, Bob's wife, who was wearing a neatly pressed Pucci cocktail dress adorned with a single stand of pearls. Tucking her perfectly coiffed hair behind her ears, she offered us iced tea with orange slices, which she poured from a tall glass pitcher and served on a silver tray. We drank on the deck, and her three sons, dressed in blue button-down Oxford shirts, not tucked in but hanging over their khaki shorts, asked my sister and me if we wanted to head to the beach to collect seashells while the adults were having their aperitif. My mom looked uncomfortable as all the grown-ups smoked cigarettes and drank shaken martinis—my mother never smoked or drank. My mother always said, "I am happy enough; I do not need anything to enhance my mood."

Looking us all up and down, Mrs. Reynolds suggested we freshen up for the barbeque and congregate precisely at six-forty-five for dinner and a small fireworks display. The big one would be in town the next night. Relieved that we would be having a backyard barbeque, we went to our room, where my sister and I put on our new hot pants and matching T-shirts, and my dad put on his favorite jeans that now required a belt to stay up. My mother put on her new favorite skintight patriotic flag shirt that made her look like a blow-up Betty Boop doll.

Coming to the table, we saw that it was like no backyard party we had ever been to. There were several beautifully set tables and many guests had arrived over the last hour. Waiters were passing around trays of huge shrimps, rumaki, chicken livers wrapped with chestnuts and bacon, and celery stuffed with blue cheese. On the tables were fragrant bouquets of fresh-cut flowers from Mrs. Reynolds's garden. There were plates stacked on top of plates and more silverware than I had ever seen on one table—silverware to the left of the plates, to the right of the plates, and above the plates. The napkins were folded like fans and rested in shiny sterling silver rings. There were crystal glasses filled with water, crystal glasses filled with wine, and crystal glasses filled with milk for the kids. For dinner, we each had our own one-and-a-half-pound lobster and as many helpings as we wanted of mussels and steamers caught that day, as well as white sweet corn from the local farm stand. The kids and the grown-ups were served the exact same food, but we were not seated at the same table. Parents and kids sitting together was a no-no, according to the Reynolds's son Billy, whom I was seated next to.

Billy, who was wearing a jacket and a tie, was only a year older than me but had the demeanor of a grown man. When I asked, "Aren't you hot in that stuffy outfit?"

He responded, "Reynolds men always wear a tie and a blazer at dinner each and every night. It is as important as arriving to the table on time, sitting up straight, and being ready to discuss whatever pressing political event the *New York Times* is writing about." He motioned me to unfold my napkin and put it on my lap before I ate and explained what all nine pieces of silverware were used for while matter-of-factly conveying the story of how he once was unmannerly. "My fork fell, so I wiggled under the table to fetch it. When I came back up, my mother shot daggers at me. She rang her bell and the nanny rushed to her assistance, banishing me from the table. I never made that indiscretion again."

I followed Billy's lead, trying to imitate the way he ate, spoke, and sat. Being removed from the table was the last thing I wanted. He showed me the proper way to pull the meat from a cracked lobster claw in one smooth piece—not the easiest task, but well worth the effort.

Hearing the roaring laughter, I peered over to see how my parents were managing. They looked captivated while Mr. Reynolds told his favorite agency stories and quoted his favorite author, Nelson Algren. "Never play cards with a man called Doc. Never eat at a place called Mom's. Never sleep with a woman whose troubles are worse than your own."

My dad appreciated Mr. Reynolds's dry sense of humor, always saying he was the best boss, taking care of each and every person who worked for him as if they were family members. He had even been known to take employees shopping at his favorite men's shop, J. Press on Madison Avenue, if he thought that the way they dressed was hindering them from advancing in their career. My dad and his fellow creatives called McCann "Camelot" since working there felt like a fantasy kingdom, with Mr. Reynolds as their benevolent leader. He was equally kind as he was conservative, with his *Episcopalian Reformed Jewish Rules for Life*—"One should always dress for dinner, never eat a salad with a dinner fork, and the cocktail hour is sacred."

Licking my fingers, about to explode from all the delicious food, I noticed Billy glaring at me. I kept going on about how wonderful all the food was, amazed that I was the only one talking about it. How could no one be discussing the sweetness of each lobster bite or how the steak melted in your mouth—easy to cut, not chewy, and so flavorful, no need for ketchup—which I noticed wasn't on the table, anyway. The other kids at the table seemed unfazed as they ate and talked with poise. They remained neat while my sister and I were covered with melted butter and lobster juice in spite of wearing lobster bibs.

Returning to my room, sticky, greasy, and very content, I tried to recall every ingredient in each plate of food we had—the wine and the shallots in the mussels, the parsley in the sweet melted butter for the lobster, and the burgundy mushroom sauce on the steak. Reliving every glorious bite, I fell asleep to the sounds of the melodious, crashing waves.

The next day was equally as pleasant, filled with tons of physical activity and more wonderful food: wild strawberries, cantaloupe slices, and Eggs Benedict for breakfast, and for lunch crab salad with skinned tomatoes and key lime pie for dessert. My dad seemed to be enjoying himself immensely during meals, not being shy about asking for seconds and thirds of pie as he forfeited the tomatoes. He stated, "I need to leave room for the good stuff." But it was during a couple of rounds of tennis that my dad seemed to get winded and needed to sit out. He was having a hard time keeping up with Mr. Reynolds and his friends, most of them more than fifteen years his senior.

On the last night of our stay, Mr. Reynolds put his arm

around my dad with the utmost concern and general compassion and suggested that perhaps my dad would benefit from the agency paying for a weight loss camp, where he not only would be on a structured eating plan but would learn to play golf and get to take daily jogs. Losing weight would not only help his health but would help secure his job and the agency image. My dad was touched by his boss's generosity and hurt by his bluntness. He had worked so hard over the past couple of weeks losing some quick weight, but his diet, The Hampton Diet, which he had thought would be a quick fix, was unsustainable. My dad said he would consider Mr. Reynolds's generous offer, but he had researched a couple of diets on his own that he would like to try before he made such an extreme commitment.

During the drive back, my parents were very quiet and I could tell my dad was hurt, and a part of his spirit had been broken. As much as I wanted to help him, I remained silent—hoping we would be invited back, and that my first lobster dinner would not be my last.

Diet-Friendly Jell-O Chiffon Pie

Yield: 8 servings

1 (3-ounce) box sugar-free Jell-O, strawberry flavor
¼ cup boiling water
12 ounces sugar-free, low-fat strawberry yogurt
1 container sugar-free Cool Whip
1 graham cracker crust
Fresh strawberries, sliced

Dissolve the Jell-O in the boiling water. Stir 2 minutes until the Jell-O is completely dissolved. When partially set, fold in the yogurt and then the Cool Whip and blend with a hand mixer. Pour into the graham cracker crust. Refrigerate overnight. Garnish with fresh strawberries before serving.

Lo-Cal Gazpacho Soup

16 ounces V8 vegetable juice
¾ cup peeled and chopped cucumber
⅛ cup chopped green pepper
⅛ cup chopped onion
½ tomato, seeded and chopped
½ tablespoon chopped garlic
½ teaspoon lemon juice
Salt and pepper to taste

Place all the ingredients in a blender and puree. Cover and chill for at least 1 hour.

Date Nut Bread Infused with Taster's Choice

Yield: 1 loaf

1 cup pitted and chopped dates
1 teaspoon baking soda
¾ cup freshly brewed Taster's Choice coffee
4 tablespoons unsalted butter, softened
½ cup sugar
1 egg, beaten
1 teaspoon vanilla extract
1 cup chopped walnuts
1½ cups flour
½ teaspoon salt
Butter or oil for greasing the loaf pan

Preheat oven to 350 degrees. Grease a 5 x 9-inch loaf pan. Place the dates in a small bowl and sprinkle the baking soda over them. Pour the hot coffee over the dates. Set aside and let the mixture cool. In a big bowl, mix the butter, sugar, and beaten egg until well blended. Stir in the vanilla and nuts. Pour in the flour and salt, then fold in the date mixture. Mix well and pour into the prepared loaf pan.

Bake for 50 minutes, or until a toothpick is inserted and comes out clean. Cool before removing from the pan.

Note: *Cream the butter and sugar. Not overmixing is the key to making this bread moist. The more air bubbles, the lighter the bread will be.*

8

My Month at the Fat Farm

....

Salmon and Leeks Baked in
Parchment Paper, Duke University
Weight-Loss Rice

....

M y dad was an expert at dieting and losing weight, but
unfortunately he could never keep it off for long and
often found himself caught in a vicious cycle of yo-yo diets. "I
think I tried every diet in the world," he would say. "I even
tried the champagne and disco diet, dancing and drinking for
forty-eight hours straight. I didn't lose weight, but I had a hell
of a time."

He consistently tried every diet that came along in search
of the magic bullet that would make him thin, keep him thin,
and satisfy his constant hunger. He restricted food, weighed
his food, counted calories, and tried eating with chopsticks. He
even attended EST meetings to help explore the root of his
obsession. While each and every plan worked in the short term,
after a couple of weeks, the calling of moist chocolate cake,
cheesy pizza, and bowls of saucy pasta got the best of him.

When his boss, Mr. Reynolds, initially suggested that perhaps he needed a little extra support and a little more monitoring, like a fat camp where he could live for a while, my dad resisted— determined to tackle the problem without leaving New York City.

Frustrated with his fluctuating weight, which was fluctuating mostly in the wrong direction, my dad sought out the assistance of the popular diet guru Dr. Atkins. His town house, where he saw patients, was close to my dad's office and around the corner from the famous Friars Club, where Frank Sinatra had recently sworn my dad in as an official member—making him feel like a celebrity himself. My dad would pop into the private club on East 55th Street with the famous clientele for a power lunch or dinner—some days both. Dr. Atkins would personally take the liberty of phoning the club to place my dad's order, giving the kitchen strict instructions on how everything should be prepared. My dad had done many favors for Dr. Atkins, such as helping him with great marketing strategies so Dr. Atkins made sure to return his kindness, giving him extra care.

As with all my dad's diets, the first couple weeks went miraculously well. He lost eight pounds in a single week on the Atkins plan, eating bun-less, juicy, rare cheeseburgers wrapped in bacon and oversized omelets topped with sour cream and chives. The Atkins Diet was high-fat, high-protein, and low-carbohydrate, which worked for a while since my dad loved bacon and heavy cream; but soon the lure of warm, yeasty baskets of fresh bread and rum-infused pecan pie was too hard to resist.

The agency could no longer ignore my dad's appearance. He was now a creative director on high-profile food accounts like Coke, Kentucky Fried Chicken, and Nestlé. They wanted the clients to be as comfortable with his looks as they were with his writing, so his boss took it upon himself to arrange, through the human resources department, a six-month paid medical leave for my dad to attend Duke University's "Fat Farm" in Durham, North Carolina, where he would be expected to drop a significant amount of weight.

My dad loved creating slogans almost as much as he loved eating. He begged to work while he was on leave—as writing came as naturally as breathing to him. But Mr. Reynolds told him to commit his efforts when he was away to exercising and going to all the wonderful classes that the Fat Farm offered: How to Control Cravings, Water Aerobics, How to Love Yourself.

"You will not be alone. I have researched this thoroughly. There will be a team of doctors, dieticians, psychologists, and exercise specialists to help you reach your goals."

My dad was touched by his boss's genuine interest. Mr. Reynolds was the dad my father never had, and his support and his belief in him was paramount to his success. My dad wanted to lose the weight as much for Mr. Reynolds as he did for himself. But my dad was not used to taking charity, and he could never remember a time that he was not working. He even used to sing and dance on the street before he was old enough to apply for a real job, so he would have pocket money to buy a Vienna hot dog with the works—mustard, celery salt, hot peppers, relish, tomatoes, and pickles on a steamed poppy seed bun. My dad talked about Chicago hot dogs with the passion of a born-again Christian talking about Jesus. "You never spoil those babies with ketchup," he would say, smacking his lips.

Convinced that he would obsess about everything he could not eat if he did not have another outlet, he eventually convinced his creative team to put him on the TaB account. The zero-calorie soda was something that wouldn't be off-limits on his diet plan. He could drink unlimited amounts while he was dreaming up brilliant copy and eating rice for breakfast, lunch, and dinner.

My dad was to do all the phases of the "Rice Diet Plan," from detox to maintenance, which meant he would be away from home for six months. My dad traveled a lot, though never for a half a year, but he was ready to battle his demons, and the structure and support of the boot camp seemed to be a needed step in his life, for both his health and his career. Duke was not a spa to help you lose a couple of pounds, but an intense, controlled environment designed to produce rapid weight loss. The Rice Diet at Duke had the reputation of being a second home to many celebrities and comedians. Elizabeth Taylor, Shelley Winters, Buddy Hackett, Dom DeLuise, and, allegedly, even Elvis, had spent a significant amount of time there. It was the perfect hideout for desperate dieters.

My dad would leave in the beginning of March and would stay until September. We would join him at Duke for the month of June, when my sister and I were on break from school. The days before my dad left, he must have packed on an extra fifty pounds—in fear that he would never eat again. All the hidden Ding Dongs, Twinkies, and Yodels were unwrapped. Boxes of Cap'n Crunch, Coco Pebbles, and Frosted Mini-Wheats were purchased and emptied. He even made sure to try all thirty-one flavors at Baskin-Robbins.

The Rice Diet was the opposite of the Atkins Diet. It was high in carbohydrates and low in protein—consisting mostly of white rice and small bits of canned fruit, broiled chicken, and fish. Anything with salt or fat was a no-no. Even one speck of vegetable oil or salt would diminish the miraculous effects. There were no adjustments on the diet, no seasoning of your own food, no little cheat day when you achieved a milestone.

The plan required a rigid preset menu with no choices. If you wanted results, you would not stray from what was provided, especially in the first couple of months.

The night before my dad left, I remember him finishing several orders of baby back ribs, sucking the bones in delight as he scraped off every last bit of meat, not even thinking to offer a single rib to anyone else. Watching him gnaw on the bones, I remembered Beauty's words: "Monkey see, monkey don't. We all have choices. You should make smart choices, and only emulate people that have beauty, grace, and class." Beauty wanted me to love and appreciate food, not inhale and mindlessly overindulge. My grandmother would tell me to pretend I was the queen of England when I ate—to eat slowly, taste the food, and put my fork down between bites. She loved showing me how to sip tea while daintily holding my pinkie out.

But my dad would never taste food or uncover each and every subtle flavor the way my grandmother taught me. When he ate, it was fast, furious, and determined. It was as if he were filling in a hole inside himself, one that was large, deep, and hollow. I realized that my dad's desire to devour everything in sight was a disease, one he could not control, one I knew I did not want to catch. "I can do it, I'm going to change," he'd say, looking at the remnants of his frenzy. "I am just always so hungry." My dad's voice swung like a pendulum between hope and defeat.

By the time my mom, my sister, and I arrived at the Fat Farm, we hadn't seen my dad for several months, and we were shocked and amazed to see he had lost more than one hundred pounds. "Twenty-three pounds the very first week!" he proudly declared. My dad said he thought about food all the time, and while the first couple of weeks were difficult, he now was getting used to the feeling of being starving all the time. He had gone from eight thousand calories a day to eight hundred calories. The thing that kept him motivated was dreaming that when he came back to New York he would have a real international Continental breakfast—Belgian waffles, Canadian bacon, French toast, and Swiss hot chocolate.

My dad was in surprisingly good spirits, which was a relief. Often when he was dieting, he was cranky and irritable, and he and my mom would be at odds, but this time he seemed quite upbeat and thoughtful.

"Hurry up," he said, giving us a walking tour of the campus and some surrounding areas. My dad, who usually took cabs to go around the block, was now hard to keep up with, showing us the pool where he swam several laps a day and the tennis courts at a local hotel where he arranged for my sister and me to have a private lesson with a real tennis pro.

It looked like he was thriving—swimming, learning the city, and visiting the local malls, where he walked miles in circles, speeding up as he passed the fried chicken, doughnut, and hush puppy stands. From the time my dad woke up until the time he went to sleep, he wore a pedometer and was expected to take ten thousand steps a day. He said he was learning a lot of tricks to losing weight, including making exercise part of his daily routine and going to support groups, where he learned diet axioms that were helpful like "HALT"—Hungry, Angry, Lonely, and Tired. "Whenever I want to eat something that I know will not make me feel good, either physically or emotionally, I say to myself, 'HALT!' Am I hungry, angry, lonely, or tired? If I'm angry, I deal with that anger honestly. If it's directed at someone, I speak to them; if it's directed at myself, I deal with the reasons why."

My dad really seemed like he was changing, not only physically but also emotionally. My mom commented, "It was like

EST all over again, but the catch phrases seemed to be more effective, even though the price tag was equally as steep." Usually self-help knew how to shrink my dad's wallet—but not his waistline. My mom had little tolerance for people paying money to complain about their problems. "If something is wrong, why surround yourself with others who will just indulge you?" She seemed happy that my dad was accomplishing his goals instead of making excuses or cozying up to people who would give him sympathy while simultaneously draining his finances.

I felt relieved that maybe this time my dad's weight loss would be real, and everyday activities like going on a bus would not be difficult or cause such distress. He normally took up two seats on an airplane or a bus. He definitely looked as if now he could fit on one seat.

At mealtime, we joined my dad in the dining hall with the fellow "Ricers" and ate what they were eating, even though the portions were almost invisible and none of us were overweight. There was no such thing as seconds. We ate the same meal, the same portions as the "inmates." I felt like I was in the cast of *Oliver!*; I desperately wanted more. Breakfast was a miniscule bowl of white rice with a piece of either canned peach or pineapple. At lunchtime came a bowl of white rice with three ounces of chicken that had mineral oil rubbed on it. Dinner consisted of—you guessed it—white rice and three ounces of fish with no seasoning.

During meals, the dieters shared stories of their successes as well as their setbacks and escapades. Some followed the routine as instructed, weighing in at 7:30 a.m., eating only at the Rice House, and exercising six hours a day. The naughty Ricers spent their time cheating, ordering in pizza, and pulling pranks like duct taping doors shut to see who could not make it through the night without a junk food run.

One famous comedian told me how he poured apple juice into the required urine specimen container left outside my dad's door at night—making it look like my dad was cheating when they tested his sugar and sodium levels. Dr. Kempner, the creator and head of the program, reprimanded my dad in front of all the other dieters. "You, and you alone, are accountable for your actions," he said, embarrassing him and demanding he step on the scale.

"Al is such a bad boy!" they all said in unison. My dad looked boyish and modest as his new friends poked fun at him about getting singled out by the feared doctor.

"You should be proud of your daddy, he is really dedicated. No one can even get him to sneak out and head to 'Sin City,'" said a rather large lady with a funny accent, big frosted hair, and a sparkly velour jogging suit. I just smiled, having no idea what she was talking about.

She must have seen my confusion, so she clarified what she meant. "Sin City is the strip, baby. Every beautiful, greasy, fast-food restaurant that you could think of is there for the taking, beckoning me, 'Rhonda, come here. I know you want me, sweetheart.'"

"Everyone wants you here, honey. Are you going for husband number three or four?" shouted the comedian, batting his eyes at her.

"Keep this G-rated, people. My daughters are underage. Rhonda, I will not be back next year or the year after, nor do I have any intentions of cheating or losing my job," my father proclaimed.

"Oh yeah, we forgot you're a big shot now. Your dad has his picture on the community board. 'Ricer of the month!'"

"One hundred pounds and I'm not done yet!"

I was so happy for my dad and wanted to be as supportive

as possible, smiling every time the rice was presented to me, but every time I ate the overcooked white rice, it gave me a stomachache. Not wanting to offend anyone, I would push it aside, wrap the sticky, bland rice into my napkin, and then pass it to my sister, who would amuse herself by making little snowmen and spitballs out of it. My dad even caught her firing a couple at some of the people with really large bellies. No one wanted to encourage her, but everyone cracked up watching the rice balls flying through the air.

I think I was the only one, but I liked the chicken—not overly seasoned, the way Beauty liked to prepare her meat. The Rice Diet was a low-sodium, low-fat diet, so nothing had salt, which made a huge difference in the way I felt. Whenever I ate something salty, I swelled up. "I'm dizzy and my toes are popping out of my shoes," I would tell my mom. My grandmother told her it was salt, but my mom was skeptical. "You're just being picky." Maybe she didn't want to change our meals at home, which mainly consisted of high-sodium prepackaged frozen foods—Stouffer's, Oscar Mayer, and Swanson were as much as my mother could handle.

I loved talking to the experts at the Fat Farm, especially the dietician who diagnosed my iodine sensitivity. She validated what I already knew, what I instinctually felt. Everybody always made fun of me when we went to a restaurant and I asked for no salt on whatever I ordered or refused to eat fast food. A "snob," my mom would say. Her words hurt my belly almost as much as the food.

The experts at Duke were very welcoming. I asked questions, I sat in classes, I went to the family support groups. "Why does the rice give me such an awful stomachache? How do you know everybody should eat the same thing? Why are there no Red Delicious apples allowed?"

I asked why some people craved salty food while others craved sweet food. My sister craved fish and chips, the greasier the better. I loved things plain and was happy munching on cucumbers, carrots, and unsalted shelled sunflower seeds all day. My mom had an adverse reaction to all fruits. My dad seemed to be fine with all foods, but maybe that was because he was used to not feeling particularly great. While everyone was amused with my interest, no one really answered my questions, and even at the Fat Farm my curiosity about food and diet could not be satisfied.

My mother and my sister were getting sick of eating—or not eating—at the Rice House, meal after meal. Once a week, Dr. Kempner allowed my dad to eat off-campus at a Duke University–preapproved restaurant. A lot of the establishments in the area had a special menu for the Ricers. The whole town seemed to be focused around them. When you entered the town of Durham, there was a sign that read, "Welcome to Fat City." But the weight experts at the Fat Farm made sure the dieters were always prepared, packing them emergency bags with special condiments—a plastic spray bottle of salad dressing, a tin of saccharin, and some packets of salt substitute—for when they were off campus.

My dad even had some kind of weird stick that he dipped in his diet soda before he drank it to make sure it was really diet. The stick would turn colors if there was sugar. My dad had finally conquered his cravings and knew just one taste of sugar, salt, or fat could have undone months of work. My dad ordered grilled mushrooms and white fish for the table, "Without salt, bones, oil, or flavor, please."

The waiter smiled, bringing my sister and me milk in plastic-covered cups and a word scramble of local sights to amuse us. "We have been serving Ricers and their families for years. We know how to spoil you on your big night out." My dad looked nervous, hoping the boisterous waiter, who was rather plump, had heard his request—knowing that after months of deprivation, he would probably eat whatever the waiter put in front of him.

The mushrooms were covered with onions and parsley, and the fish was moist, steamed with leeks and lemon slices. While it was not osso buco or caviar, the taste of real food was calming and almost euphoric. We all ate slowly, knowing what our fate would be tomorrow back at the Rice House. It was one of the best meals my family ever had together, and no one missed the rice. My sister and I pinky swore that this was the kind of meal we would eat every night when we were grown-ups. When my mother asked what kind of secrets were we telling, we said nothing, knowing that she would be mad thinking that cooking a big meal was what we expected of her.

Arriving home from the Fat Farm, my mother was horrified to learn she had gained ten pounds. She immediately went back to her usual pattern of eating one small meal a day of tuna fish with hot sauce, while standing and chatting on the phone. My dad stayed on a couple more months, determined to lose another fifty pounds. He lost seventy-five. One hundred and seventy-five in total.

When asked how he could tolerate rice for so long, he answered, "It keeps you light on your feet," as he performed a little shuffle. That line became the slogan for his new campaign—the TaB Dance, featuring Gene Kelly and Broadway star Tommy Tune.

"TaB. It keeps you light on your feet."

Salmon and Leeks Baked in Parchment Paper

Yield: 1 serving, but make as many packages as needed
and lay them all on a baking sheet

2 16-inch sheets of baking parchment paper (or tin foil)
for lining the baking sheet
2 rosemary sprigs, or basil or dill, or whatever fresh herbs
you have on hand
1 6-ounce salmon fillet, rinsed
Salt and pepper, to taste
¼ cup chopped zucchini or other squash
3 cherry tomatoes, halved
1 garlic clove, chopped
1 tablespoon dry white wine
Juice of half a small lemon or lime

Preheat oven to 375 degrees. Place a double layer of parchment paper on a baking sheet. Lay the herbs in the center of the paper and place the salmon on top of the sprigs. Season with salt and pepper. Spoon the zucchini or other squash, tomatoes, and garlic over the fish.

Pour the white wine over everything. Seal the packet closed by folding the long sides of the paper together. Fold all ends to make a package and flip over. Place the sealed square(s) on the baking sheet. Make sure each square is sealed tightly so no steam can escape.

Bake for 15 minutes. Before serving, slowly open the package and squeeze the lemon juice over the fish. Use a spatula to transfer to a plate.

Duke University Weight-Loss Rice

Yield: 4 small servings

2 cups water
1 cup white rice

Bring the water to a rolling boil. Add the rice and reduce heat. Cover the pot and cook for about 30 minutes, until all the liquid has been absorbed. Fluff and serve with an ounce of unsweetened canned peaches or pineapple.

The Big Reveal

Macrobiotic Apple Pie, Tomato Aspic,
Sweet-and-Sour Meatballs

After spending six months at Duke University's Fat Farm in Durham, North Carolina, eating mostly white rice and small bits of fruit and protein, my dad had lost half of his body weight. When he returned to New York, no one recognized him—not the little Portuguese man at the corner newspaper store, which my dad frequented for diet sodas and candy bars, not our neighbors downstairs to whom my dad paid our monthly rent checks for the brownstone we rented, and not even his bosses who'd sponsored his leave of absence in the hopes that his image would match the success of the advertising campaigns that he launched. Mr. Reynolds was proud that his star employee had succeeded. My dad's first day back at work, his boss turned to the client and said, "Looks like we just lost half of our creative team."

My dad went to the Fat Farm weighing 350 pounds and

returned home at 175 pounds. With his new weight came a new confidence, a new hairstyle, and a new wardrobe. My dad permed his hair, shortened his sideburns, and went shopping—plaid blazers, turtlenecks, and tight pants now hugged his lean frame. When he left, he looked like a bloated Elvis; when he came back, he looked like *The Six Million Dollar Man*. For the first time in his life, my dad was not heavy, and he could shop at a regular department store, buying clothes off the rack that were in style. When he walked down the street, he was able to move rapidly, and nobody looked twice or gasped when he passed. He now looked like everyone else and was ready to take a break from what he basically called an extended fast.

To celebrate my dad's homecoming and success, my mom was going to host one of her lively potluck dinners. She hoped that my dad's weight loss would not only help his career but would help revive their marriage and our family life. My dad was usually so consumed with his diets that there was no time for my sister, my mom, and me. Before my dad went to the Fat Farm, he was tired and had a hard time getting out of bed in the morning. When he awoke, there was a complex diet regimen to follow that involved weighing himself and taking handfuls of pills—appetite suppressants, water pills, blood pressure pills, energy pills, cholesterol pills, even pills for special occasions—weddings and Bar Mitzvahs.

Nights were consumed with trying to impress his employers. My dad always felt he needed to work twice as hard and be twice as funny as anyone else to distract people from the way he looked. My mom hoped with his new healthy weight that he would have a little more energy to focus his affections on her and her attributes. My dad used to boast that my mom threw the best parties. "Nobody knows how to do it quite like your mom. She is the only person in Manhattan that can entertain a house full of people on ten dollars without lifting a finger. She is a real Auntie Mame," he'd playfully say.

My mom was at her best when she was surrounded by admirers—complimenting her on her wonderful Native American jewelry, her intriguing artifacts from all over the world, and her bubbly, magnetic personality that turned a simple gathering into live theater. My parents' close circle of friends were extremely eccentric—numerologists, musicians, artists, photographers, writers, dancers, and dramatic performers who had moved to Manhattan from all over the globe to pursue their creative endeavors. My mom had the talent of keeping in touch with everyone she ever met, and no one was ever turned away from our home or celebrations.

My parents' diverse group of friends represented that they had *arrived*, that they were a part of something fabulous—exciting, groovy, and mod. It made them feel accomplished that they had escaped their Midwestern upbringings. Their friends were a symbol of their success and also of their partnership. They needed each other to achieve their dreams. My mom kept my dad motivated, making sure he arrived to work on time and that he saved more money than he spent. My dad liked to spend money as much as he liked to eat, so my mom controlled their finances, usually keeping the refrigerator empty and their bank account full.

People seemed to genuinely adore my parents—my dad for his quick wit and charm, and my mom for her intellect and high energy. My mother was always upbeat and honest, and never burdened anyone with her problems. When my mom said she was having a party to celebrate my dad losing weight, all their friends were anxious to attend one of her legendary gatherings. Plus, they wanted to get a look at my father. Nobody could imagine my dad being super-slim.

"Joanne, you will never recognize him. I keep passing him in the halls thinking there is a stranger in the house. You have to see him; he looks like a movie star."

In preparation for my dad's debut party, my mom spent hours on the phone inviting everyone she knew to her potluck. She encouraged all the guests to bring a healthy dish. My mom would not be cooking or providing food, but she was providing the venue, an interesting array of guests, and the man of the hour, and as always, she assured everyone it would be an unforgettable night of music, performance art, and lively conversation. She instructed everyone on what to prepare, so there would be a variety of ethnic and eclectic appetizers, main dishes, and desserts. "Persis, bring that wonderful extra-spicy curried chicken stew with the hard-boiled eggs. Felicia, everyone flips for your tomato aspic and sweet-and-sour meatballs. Michael, bring that extra-strong sangria with apple slices that brings out the best in everyone. Joanne, bring your Jell-O mold; it always makes such a bright, beautiful centerpiece. Nadejda, everyone looks forward to your Bulgarian Moussaka with potatoes. No party of mine would be complete without it. Tandy, you are always so good at picking the perfect dessert. Just make sure it is not too fattening."

My mom spent the day of the party getting ready: rolling her hair straight with empty orange juice cans and picking the perfect outfit that would accentuate her cleavage. She waited until everyone arrived to fix up the house. Each time the doorbell rang with a new guest, the jobs started to flow. "Arthur, you are so good with set design, you are in charge of hanging the lights on the terrace! Joyce, set up your numerology station where everyone can see you. Len, you are the tallest, you can grab the card table from the top of the closet and water my spider plants. Charles, please warm and arrange all the food.

David, roll up the Oriental rug so no one spills wine on it. Gordon, start playing your magic flute for the belly dancer. Dawn and April, start pouring the Tang and tonic into the plastic champagne glasses and start passing them around to anyone who does not want alcohol."

I was always shocked at how many people would come to my mom's parties and how none of them seemed to mind being put to work the minute they entered. My mother was the director, and each guest was happy to be a part of her show.

"Vera is here. She has her magic violin. Oh my God, Sheila brought the new play that she has been slaving over for months. She is going to give everyone a part to read. Everyone, look how great Mordechai looks as Marilyn, and he brought his Ouija board to help us to remember our ancestors and friends that have passed. Linda has brought her new boyfriend, Mulligan. And Mulligan has a special pie." Announcing all the guests, she broke into applause. Everyone followed her lead, clapping for each new cast member.

One by one, they inquired, "Where is the man of the hour?"

"He will make a grand entrance when everything is ready," my mom said, surveying the room.

I was looking at what everyone had brought to eat, while my sister was running up and down the stairs telling my mom that my father was getting bored and hungry and was ready to make his appearance.

"Tell him five minutes. I will call him when the stage is set."

With the food displayed and everyone lined up at the bottom of the staircase, my mom instructed Gordon to play the theme from *Miss America* and screamed for my dad to make his entrance.

"Okay, Al, we're all ready!"

Everyone applauded and started gasping as my dad walked

down the stairs in his new leisure suit, giving a little Rockette kick, while holding up his old pants, which could now fit three of him. He tossed them into the howling crowd.

"Wow!"

"I can't believe this!"

"I wouldn't recognize him!"

"Who knew you could look this great from eating white rice?"

"Where is Albert?"

My dad took a bow. "Yes, ladies and gentleman, this is what six months of starving, three packs of Camels unfiltered a day, and peeing in a cup will get you. Autographs are accepted, but please no rice this evening!"

Persis applauded. "I am so glad you lost the weight and not your humor."

"Thank you, sweetheart. Now, get me a glass of skimmed water and some fillet of bone."

Everyone was complimenting my dad on how wonderful he looked. He seemed overjoyed, joking with all the guests who were gathering around him, listening to him share his new weight-loss philosophies and beauty secrets. "Seeing is believing," he kept saying—relishing the attention from all the female guests. Persis Khambatta, the former Miss India, whom my dad became friends with when he was casting a commercial, was sitting closer than anyone else. She was millimeters away from being on top of him. "Your dad is so knowledgeable. I learn so much from him. I can listen to him talk about diets all day." I wondered why she was so interested in dieting; she already looked like a skeleton, but according to her no woman could ever be thin enough. I knew I didn't agree as I watched her, ribs protruding through her sari.

"I especially loved your dad's stories about the liquid diet, the cookie diet, and the 'tapeworm diet,' on which your dad lost fifty pounds before marrying your mom. He is so romantic." The diet, which she thought made him a romantic, consisted of popping a pill that contained a tapeworm egg. Once in the intestine, the creature would feed off you, helping to consume the digested food. I thought it sounded disgusting. But she remained captivated, listening to him share his ideas for his new diet book.

"Persis, your flawless beauty will make my new diet book that I am planning on writing a huge success. *Bland, Boring and Beautiful* will reach international acclaim with you as the spokesmodel. The diet is a four-week plan, and each week you pick one food that has no sugar, salt, or flavor. You can eat unlimited portions of the selected food but nothing else. Eventually, you dull your taste buds and your desire for food. But each week, you choose a different food so your body does not plateau." Persis thought the diet was brilliant and agreed to be on the cover of the book pictured sucking on a big cucumber and standing between two life-sized carrots.

My mom was pleased that my dad had a captive audience. She wanted to be equally supportive, but she did not understand how people could spend so much time talking about food and diet. My mother ate to live. She did not understand people like my dad, my grandmother, and me who thought about food all the time. It was not so much that I wanted to eat all the time as it was that I was interested in all the different types of foods. I was so curious to see what everyone brought. It was such a rare event that we had so much food in our house.

My mother saw me peering at the food spread on our table and scolded me: "Enough with the food! Ask Sahara to show you how to belly dance or ask Joyce to do a numerology reading for you."

"I already know my past, and if something bad is going to happen in the future, I don't want to know."

"Joyce can help guide you."

My mom always thought I was too serious, too shy, and too stuck in my ways. And I did not know how to stand up for myself. My mom's words stung; but she would forget what she'd said moments later, and I would cry for hours. "Words can't hurt you," she would always say, but hers did hurt me.

Joyce muttered softly, "I will not tell you anything negative, just the number of your destiny and the personal year you are in. It will help you focus and unlock your potential."

Joyce was always sweet to me, and with her assurance, I hesitantly agreed to the reading. She started wildly calculating my numbers, eyes wide as saucers. Then her eyes closed and her body collapsed. I thought she'd had a heart attack. I knew this reading was not a good idea. Then she quickly rose, grabbing both of my hands, looking deeply into my eyes.

"You are in a five personal year. Get ready for many changes. And your destiny is a three. People with three destinies are very imaginative and often become great writers, artists, or great communicators. I am a three myself."

My mom jumped up, exclaiming, "I knew it! I knew it! I am always right. Remember, when you wanted to stay in Chicago and I told you New York and the Little Red School House would help bring out your creative potential. Joyce! Dawn has to be pushed. If I do not make her try new things, she would hibernate in my mother's house in Chicago or obsess about feeding April."

My mother always had to prove her point of how she made wonderful decisions for me. While I knew in my head my mom loved me, she often made me feel boring, and I felt overpowered by her. I was frustrated and upset at my mother's inability to see who I was and what I desired. I was different from her and had different needs. When Joyce mentioned some traits of the three destiny, I thought she was making it up and was in cahoots with my mother, but she pulled me aside and showed me her sacred book so I could read about the personality of the number three for myself. The characteristics of the three described me exactly. There was even a similar line in the book that I had written in my journal so many times before, but had never shown anyone. It said the eyes of a three destiny were like a camera that could remember details and events with great accuracy and sensitivity.

Ever since I could spell, I had kept a journal. I would write what I could not tell, I would write what I really did not want to feel, and mostly I would write because it made me feel better.

When we were done with the reading, Joyce asked me if I had any questions, and she gave me the paper with her notes. She said that I could share as little or as much as I wanted with my mother, and that I should always remember our conversation.

"You are magnetic. You are intuitive. You are a leader. Do not let anyone belittle your ideas or point of view. You are going to be a trailblazer. Big success awaits you," she kept repeating. "Remember you have a story to tell." Joyce's words were so powerful that I began feeling woozy.

As I was heading to the food table, finally hoping to sit and eat, my mom grabbed me and said, "Talk to Linda and her new boyfriend." Linda was my favorite cousin. She was way older—in her twenties—and way cooler than me, and had just finished working on *The Tonight Show*, where she worked closely with Johnny Carson. Mulligan, her new boyfriend, was a Vietnam vet. They had met a couple weeks ago on the subway, and now they were a big item. Mulligan wore a tie-dye shirt, had a metal plate in his head, and was a hard-core macrobiotic devotee.

Linda had told him I was interested in cooking and healthy food, and I had just won the award for the best peanut butter cookies in the sixth grade.

"In honor of your award, Mulligan brought over this special pie just for you, from our favorite vegetarian restaurant on the Upper West Side, Peter, Peter, Pumpkin Eater."

Mulligan held out a forkful, encouraging me to take a bite. "Let each ingredient dance on your tongue. Do not swallow until you have really tasted it. I usually chew one hundred times before swallowing—both for digestion and to honor the food. Pretty tasty, huh?"

I had to agree. It was one of the best pies I had ever tasted. The apples were so fresh, not syrupy or sweet. And the crust was nutty and firm.

"It is macrobiotic. There is no sugar, eggs, or butter in it and it is really healthy," Linda said enthusiastically.

How could this be? The pie had none of the usual suspects that made desserts delicious, and yet it was even more yummy. From the very first bite of the dairy-free, sugar-free pie, the most amazing feeling of excitement and satisfaction overcame me.

So while everyone else at the party wanted to find out what my dad ate or did not eat for the last six months, or wanted to talk to Linda about what it was like to work with Johnny Carson, I was focused on Mulligan. I drilled him about the ingredients of the pie, the location of the bakery, other places in New York that made such yummy healthy desserts, and what it meant to be vegetarian.

"Being vegetarian is about respecting life." Mulligan was happy to indulge me and share his philosophies. "Make love not war, eat food that is kind not killed, and love our earth." He was a recent convert since coming back from Nam. Injured and disillusioned, he was trying to make sense of his life, the world, and his fate. In order to heal, he felt like he needed to respect his body and Mother Earth, and that started with the food he was eating. After he had seen life taken right in front of him, he was not about to do that to any other creature. He was in Viet Nam for almost a full year before he was wounded and sent home. He felt beaten by both the physical and mental scars of war. But being involved in the health food movement was a positive step toward healing both his body and his soul.

In addition to eating vegetables, brown rice, millet beans, and tofu, in lieu of meat and chicken, he meditated and studied Eastern religions. He also had a daily yoga practice to keep his body lean and flexible and open his chakras so he could attain enlightenment and spiritual fulfillment. Mulligan seemed so centered and peaceful. A feeling I desired.

It was not only about food. It was a movement—a way of representing love and peace. I was so excited and enamored by Mulligan. I begged my parents to come over and hear what he had to say. I thought he could inspire them as he had me.

"It is not just what you eat, but how you eat it," he shared. "Respect your body and it will respect you. The right food is medicine for the soul." I loved how he chanted his mantras.

After that night, I needed to learn how to make that pie and understand why Mulligan felt so passionately about the vegetarian lifestyle, which was so different from my dad's or even my grandmother's way of eating. Since I had a subway pass, I had the freedom to explore. While my friends were participating in afterschool activities or playing Capture the Flag in the Bleecker Street Playground, I began exploring different natural food venues.

From the very first time I walked into a health food store, it was love at first sight. It gave me a thrill that filled every fiber of my being. I began reading nutrition books, and cookbooks, and cooking and baking as if my life depended on it. My eyes were opened to new schools of thought surrounding food. I learned about vegetarianism and macrobiotics. I read books by Jack LaLanne, Frances Moore Lappé, and Adele Davis—the movers and shakers in the health movement. I learned to cook adzuki beans, to make cheesecake from tofu, and how to substitute carob for chocolate in shakes and cookies. I tossed sprouts in salads and added wheat germ to everything imaginable.

While that party was an unveiling of my dad's most recent success, it was also a new beginning for me. Joyce had encouraged me to let my imagination run wild, and Mulligan opened my eyes to an exciting new movement. I was not ready to become a vegetarian, but I was interested to learn why Mulligan was one, and to incorporate some of the principles and staples into my own diet.

Macrobiotic Apple Pie

FOR THE CRUST:

¼ teaspoon salt

1½ cups whole wheat pastry flour

¼ cup vegan butter substitute, like Earth Balance

1 tablespoon barley malt

FOR THE FILLING:

4 apples, peeled and cut in chunks

1⅓ cups apple juice

⅓ cup raisins

½ teaspoon cinnamon

½ teaspoon lemon juice

2 tablespoons kuzu (see note)

Prepare the crust first by mixing the salt into the fresh pastry flour, then adding the butter substitute. Sprinkle the barley malt over this mixture, slightly mix, and add enough water to make a thick ball of dough. Quickly roll out between two sheets of wax paper or on a board used for piecrusts.

Shape the dough into a 12-inch circle and place into a lightly greased glass pie pan. Pierce the bottom and sides of the piecrust lightly with a fork so the crust will not puff up and let the liquid from the pie filling go under it.

Preheat the oven to 350 degrees. Combine the apples, ⅓ cup of the apple juice, and the raisins and bring to a boil. Cover and simmer 15 minutes. Mix in the cinnamon and lemon juice.

Remove from heat and allow to cool. Combine the kuzu and the remaining 1 cup of apple juice, stir until dissolved, and bring to a boil. Simmer about 1 minute, or until transparent and thickened. Spoon the apples into the crust and pour the kuzu mixture over them. Bake for about 40 minutes.

Note: *Organic Kuzu Root Starch can be used to thicken soups, stews, sauces, gravies, and pie fillings.*

Tomato Aspic

4 cups tomato juice
1 tablespoon Worcestershire sauce
2 teaspoons salt
5 tablespoons apple cider vinegar
2½ cups diced green pepper
2½ cups diced celery
1 cup diced onion
4 packages Knox Unflavored Gelatine
⅔ cup water
Cooking spray, for the mold

Place the first 7 ingredients into a heavy saucepan. Heat to almost a boil. Remove from heat. Dissolve the gelatine in water in a separate bowl, then pour into the saucepan and stir into the contents. Pour into a bowl or a mold that has been sprayed with cooking spray. Refrigerate until set. Overnight is best.

Note: *This aspic is like a congealed Bloody Mary.*

Sweet-and-Sour Meatballs

Yield: 8–10 servings

1 (12-ounce) bottle chili sauce
2 teaspoons lemon juice
9 ounces grape jelly
1½ pounds ground beef
2 eggs, beaten
1 large onion, diced
½ cup Rice Krispies cereal or bread crumbs
Salt and pepper, to taste

Whisk together the chili sauce, lemon juice, and grape jelly. Pour into a large pot. Keep temperature on a medium heat. In a bowl, combine the ground beef, eggs, onion, Rice Krispies, salt, and pepper. Mix well and form into 1-inch balls. Add to the sauce and simmer for 1½ hours. Remove from heat and allow to slightly cool. You can serve with a toothpick inserted into each meatball as an appetizer.

10

My Holiday Wish

....

Pumpkin Pie, Egg Coffee, Sweet Potato
Hummus, Creamy Cashew Butternut Soup

....

I n my daydreams, which is where I spent a good part of
my childhood, Thanksgiving would be a perfect time that
would bring my extended family members—some of whom I
did not know very well—together. My aunts, uncles, cousins,
and grandparents would travel from near and far, and they
would bring their favorite dishes that would contribute to a
picturesque meal. As we ate, we would swap stories, jokes, and
recipes; and we would compliment one another on the beautiful casseroles, entrées, side dishes, and desserts. Then we would
all retire in front of a warm, dancing fire, listening to the crack-
ling flames as we watched the first snowfall, ate dessert, and
played games like charades and backgammon.

I could taste all the delicious foods that I imagined would
be at our gathering as I pasted the cut-out food pictures from
Better Homes and Gardens magazine onto the back of my

Me and my dad.

ABOVE: *Family portrait in Chicago: Dad, Papa, Beauty, Mom, and me.*

RIGHT: *I loved spending time with Beauty as much as she loved spending time with me.*

I was always happiest in the kitchen.

Me and Mom in April's bedroom in Chicago . . .
It still looks like my dad's office.

Me and April playing in the kitchen.

ABOVE: *Mom and Dad on a Greek cruise . . . Dad always liked to be the life of the party.*

LEFT: *Walking through Greenwich Village with Mom and Dad.*

April and Dad, pre-Duke.

This is me and Dad right before he went to Duke.

Dad with Bubbe Mary after he successfully lost weight at Duke.

Dad and me on my wedding day.

seventh-grade binder. There was a turkey stuffed with apples and sage that had a golden brown skin, a creamy butternut squash soup with cashews, and roasted Brussels sprouts with a pomegranate reduction. And for dessert, there would be a choice of a pumpkin pie with a graham cracker crust or a warm berry cobbler. I was salivating studying the possibilities.

Since we'd moved to Manhattan, Thanksgiving was always at a restaurant, and there were never any extended family members, just big crowds of strangers and an all-you-can-eat buffet. Everyone would rush for the food and not really take the time to notice how it was prepared or how it smelled. I would watch my dad dash for seconds and thirds without taking a breath. His favorite advertising slogan was Alka-Seltzer's "I can't believe I ate the whole thing," and eat the whole thing he did more than once—especially when he was on the Stone Age Diet, which allowed large amounts of protein and fat, and small amounts of carbohydrates, so he could eat as much turkey as he desired without guilt. "Men are supposed to eat like cavemen," he would say—devouring the gigantic turkey leg, wing, breast, and thigh. Sometimes April and I would hardly even eat since we were always getting elbowed out of the way in our attempts to get into the food line. It was all about my dad filling and refilling his plate.

At mealtime in the restaurant at Thanksgiving, we would never sit and have a conversation and talk about what we were grateful for. I would pretend I was Harriet the Spy and try to listen to what other families were talking about—the families that went up only once for food and seemed to genuinely enjoy one another's company as they ate their meal slowly. I always longed to be back in my grandmother Beauty's kitchen, where she asked me if I was enjoying my meal, and if I liked how she made the sweet potatoes with brown sugar, crushed pineapples, and tiny melted marshmallows, and she always pinned my overgrown bangs off my eyes while I ate, using one of her special rhinestone bobby pins.

Finally, after three long years of living in New York and much pleading, the phone call came. My grandmother was going to come to visit! She and Papa were going to take an overnight Amtrak train, the kind with a sleeping section like in the Orient Express. Beauty had never left Chicago and was scared to take a plane, but she knew how important it was to me to have her with me for the holidays, so she decided to brave the train trip. She was also dying to see what my dad looked like. He had put back on thirty pounds in the last three months but still was down over a hundred pounds since the last time she saw him.

In anticipation of our first real homemade Thanksgiving feast, I began to prepare the menu. Not only had I become good at following recipes, but I had become pretty proficient at recreating traditional recipes with a healthier twist. Beauty said I was a natural in the kitchen, but she was much faster and far much more efficient. She could peel potatoes and apples in one smooth coil without ever breaking the skin, and she knew how to make real dark, decadent brown gravy by boiling the turkey neck and the giblets. Her butter for the corn muffins was never from the store, but always homemade—shaken by hand. My grandmother was very petite, but she was extremely strong from working in the kitchen, doing housework, and carrying groceries, so she could shake the heavy whipping cream in the glass jar vigorously for a full ten minutes with ease.

Before my grandparents arrived, my sister and I did our best to help clean our house. Beauty liked everything spotless. She never had a dish in the sink or a crumb on the floor, which she would scrub on her hands and knees daily. I wanted to make sure everything was perfect for her visit. I even went to the Third Avenue Bazaar and bought a bunch of tiny vases so I could put flowers throughout the house—yellow tulips, baby's breath, and daisies. I wanted her to feel at ease and relaxed. Beauty was a creature of habit, and since buying her house over thirty years ago, she had never slept anywhere else. "Why would I want to go to a hotel when everything I desire is right here?" she'd ask, pointing out her full cabinets lined with mason jars of dried beans, grains, oatmeal, flour, and sugar. When Papa traveled for business, she never accompanied him. In all her years of marriage—forty years total—she had never taken a vacation. I wanted everything to be as perfect as possible for her first big trip and for her to feel as special and comfortable as she always made me feel when I came to her house when I was a small child.

After a seventeen-hour train ride, my grandparents arrived, and my mom and I were waiting at the station to greet them. Beauty seemed totally unfazed by the chaos that was always at Penn Station. Before I could even say a word, she had me open her suitcase, right there, in the middle of the station with the crowds rushing by. Reaching into her bag, I felt many round metal tins, just like the ones she always had on her counter and in her refrigerator. She had me peek into each one. There were soft oatmeal raisin cookies, crispy sweet potato pancakes, salmon patties with chunks of green pepper, kugel slices with a cornflake topping, and peanut brittle squares with chocolate shavings—all my favorites. Papa handed my mother a big package of lox, packed on dry ice, and a bag of onion bialys—one of the few Jewish delicacies she enjoyed.

I couldn't believe my eyes. I had told Beauty we would cook together when she arrived and all she needed to bring was herself. "It isn't your job to take care of me," she said, "but mine to take care of you. You are only twelve years old. I should have not waited so long to visit."

Later that day, as we sat around in the living room munching on all the mouthwatering treats, Beauty and Papa shared their adventures of riding the train. There was a sleeping car with beds that pulled down from the wall, a smoking car for my Papa, where he was able to get a 7 & 7 (Seagram's and 7UP) while he read what horses were running at Aqueduct Racetrack, which he planned to visit while my grandmother took my mom, my sister, and me shopping, and a fancy dining car my grandparents dressed up to eat in. My grandmother said she had the most delicious veal scallopini with artichokes, and my grandfather was very excited about the clam chowder and the New York strip steak with baked potato that he ordered. "You can judge how good a restaurant is by the size and texture of the accompanying baked potato. The baked potato on the dining car of the train did not disappoint," he announced, nudging my grandmother to agree with him.

"It really was a beautiful baked potato, Dawn."

"Most definitely Idaho," Papa said.

"I usually buy those to make twice-baked potatoes for April; the skin makes such a great shell," I added.

"Did you guys really travel all the way to New York to talk about potatoes?" my mom complained.

"No," my grandfather snapped. "We slept in a cramped compartment with a hard mattress, so we could spend time with our daughter and grandchildren. Sit and have a little bit of the Nova I brought you."

"We have to get moving; otherwise, we are going to miss everything."

"What's 'everything'?" Beauty interrupted. "Everything I came for is right here. I don't need to go anywhere to have a good time," she said, reaching her arms around me and kissing me on both sides of my face while April played the piano.

But my mother had a different idea of how we were going to spend our evening, hurrying us to get our boots and coats on while rushing us out the door. "We can still beat the crowds if we do not get stuck in traffic." Once outside, she hailed a taxi. "West 77th Street and Central Park," my mom instructed the cab driver.

"Mother, I am going to show you how real New Yorkers see the Macy's Thanksgiving Day Parade. Tourists go to the crowded parade in the morning. Real New Yorkers like us," she said, pointing to April and me, "view the floats the night before." We didn't have many family traditions or rituals, but viewing the humungous balloons come to life once a year was one of them—one that I cherished. I was glad my mom was bringing my grandmother.

Exiting the yellow-checkered cab a couple blocks from our destination, my mom loosened up a little. She locked arms with my sister, my grandmother, and me so no one would get separated. We began strolling around the crowded streets while munching on roasted chestnuts, peanuts dipped in honey, and large soft pretzels from the pushcarts. Beauty was in awe of all the people and how huge Minnie Mouse, Snoopy, and Woody Woodpecker were when the balloons were fully inflated. "I never realized how big they were. You just can't imagine when you see them on TV. Papa should have come. This really is an incredible sight," she said, marveling at Smokey the Bear soaring above her.

My mother was pleased that Beauty was experiencing the real flavor of the city. We showed her Central Park, the Museum of Natural History, the Dakota, where John Lennon lived, and the San Remo, where we once spotted Dustin Hoffman.

Walking with my mom, my grandmother, and my sister, I realized how comfortable I had become in New York. I was not a visitor, but a real New Yorker. I knew the subways, the buses, the museums, and the stores like the back of my hand. I was excited to take Beauty to all the neighborhoods where I shopped. Her recipe cards had been my lifeline when I first arrived to the city—they gave me a focus. They were a starting point on a very long journey, one that I was now deeply immersed in. Now I wanted to be Beauty's lifeline to Manhattan and different cuisines—taking her to my favorite vegetable, poultry, and fish stands in Chinatown and taking her to lunch at my favorite macrobiotic restaurant, Souen on the Upper West Side. I wanted to show her how to use bamboo shoots, bok choy, and Chinese eggplant in a stir-fry and how to use dandelion greens in fresh juice. Beauty was not shy about trying new foods and was always delighted by everything I showed her—reminding me she still had many secrets yet to reveal.

Returning home, we found my grandfather and my father bonding over bagel and lox sandwiches while debating about where our Thanksgiving dinner would be held. My dad wanted to go to our usual spot, the Friars Club, where there were unlimited amounts of appetizers and desserts, and each table got its own fourteen-pound turkey, or Luchow's, where in addition to turkey, they had roasted suckling pig, Wiener schnitzel, apple crepes, and huge steins of beer. But my grandfather had never had Thanksgiving in a restaurant, and after traveling all night, he was not about to start. My father backed down, but he was disappointed. My grandfather assured my dad that in all his years of marriage, he had never left the dinner table hungry. With less than twenty-four hours to prepare our holiday meal, Beauty and I began dividing the tasks. I showed her the recipes I had been saving—even showing her many interesting vegetarian dishes, like pureed yams with grated ginger and apple cider, string beans with pine nuts, and a sweet potato hummus. We were ecstatic preparing our shopping list for the next morning.

While my grandmother and I were busy cooking our first homemade Thanksgiving feast in our Manhattan kitchen, my sister busied herself watching the parade on TV, periodically begging me to take a break so we could take a walk to see the holiday windows. And my dad kept announcing he was available to be a taster and offering to go on grocery store runs.

"It wouldn't hurt to get a little cheese. I am sure we can always use some ice cream for the pies. Maybe a little sorbet to cleanse our palates in between courses? Let me taste that soup; I'm sure it needs a little dash more of pepper. If you want, it is not too late to get some bacon to sprinkle on the Brussels sprouts."

My mother and grandfather stayed clear of the kitchen, arguing about why my mother did not want to move back to Chicago and work in Papa's store as an accountant, why she did not have a coffeepot, and why my grandfather wanted dishes and real silverware rather than paper plates for the dinner. The loudest argument of all was about why my grandfather had set up work meetings when he was supposed to be visiting us, and why he was going to the track alone instead of going to Rockefeller Center for hot chocolate with us the next day.

In spite of the bickering that we heard between my grandfather and my mom, Beauty and I stayed focused. Beauty said she had hoped Papa would be able to take a real vacation while in New York, but he couldn't wait to make an appointment at Tad's Steaks, Big Nicks, and Gray's Papaya to try and sell them his new super-sized cups for their drinks. "I am the king of Chicago. Now that Beauty has found a new love of trains, I can be the king of New York," he proclaimed, explaining why these meetings were so important.

"When your mom was a little girl," Beauty told me, "your Papa had planned a special outing with her. He was going to take her to his favorite ice cream parlor in Winnetka; ice cream and fountain sodas were a passion they both shared. But on the way, he realized that he had to fill an order and left her in the car by herself the whole day. She was only seven. She came home crying. Your mom said, 'It was light when he went into the restaurant and dark when he came out.' Apologies don't come easy for either of them and neither of them will acknowledge how similar they are." I always appreciated Beauty's insights about my mother, helping me understand why she was the way she was.

"You really are my little beauty. You are so easy to be with. We always understand one another," Beauty said, giving me a squeeze. I don't remember being happier in the years since we'd moved to New York than at that moment.

Grabbing pots and pans and putting things in the oven and fridge created an excitement in the air. Rich aromas of spices, onions, and celery cooking in sizzling oil brought new life into our kitchen. The smell of sage and poultry seasoning magically drifted into every corner of our house. I impatiently waited for the turkey to make it from oven to table, as Beauty had me start plating various dishes. "A watched pot never boils," she reminded me, while I kept peeking in the oven.

When dinner was ready to be served, Beauty and I set everything out on a metal folding table in our hallway. The table overflowed with delicacies: olives with red pimiento, endive salad, and marinated lima beans with garlic were peppered among the side dishes. Mashed turnips, apple-cranberry stuffing, roasted red peppers, and sautéed yellow zucchini brought pops of color to the table. And at its center sat a tray of perfectly sliced moist turkey and a boat filled with beautiful gravy. Beauty served small tasting portions of each dish, and oohs, aahs, and "yums" were passed back and forth about the flavor of the food. My dad did not even seem to notice the lack of buttered mashed potatoes or sausage stuffing, filling his plate with more vegetables than I ever saw him eat. My sister, who had a small appetite, asked for seconds and thirds. Even my mom seemed to miraculously sit and eat.

For the grand finale, I served my pumpkin pie and Beauty poured her old-world-style coffee. My pie was not made with sugar, and Beauty made her coffee without a coffeepot. She simply used crushed eggs shells to hold the ground coffee on the bottom of the boiling saucepan. My pie was sweetened with only bananas and a touch of maple syrup.

Seeing my family happily dig into the pie and sip the coffee— and my grandmother toss the turkey carcass into a pot to make bone broth, which she would freeze in ice cube trays for later use—I smiled, knowing exactly what I was thankful for this year.

Pumpkin Pie

Yield: 8 servings

FOR THE CRUST:

1 cup honey graham cracker crumbs, finely processed to a powder (from 7 to 8 2½- x 4⅞-inch crackers)

¼ cup unsweetened coconut flakes

3 tablespoons brown sugar

⅛ teaspoon salt

5 tablespoons unsalted butter, melted

FOR THE FILLING:

¾ cup, plus 2 tablespoons nondairy milk of choice

¾ cup pumpkin puree

1 large ripe banana

¼ cup maple syrup

1 large egg, room temperature

½ teaspoon vanilla extract

½ teaspoon ground cinnamon

Lightly grease a 9-inch pie dish and set aside. Make the graham cracker crust: In a small mixing bowl, mix the graham cracker crumbs, coconut flakes, sugar, and salt until combined. Add the butter and mix until the crust begins to clump together and resembles wet sand. Spread the crust out evenly in the pie dish and press it into the bottom and the sides. Bake the crust for 4 minutes, or until slightly toasted. Transfer to a wire cooling rack while preparing the pumpkin filling.

Position the baking rack in the middle and preheat the oven to 350 degrees. Combine the milk, pumpkin puree, banana, maple syrup, egg, vanilla extract, and cinnamon in a blender and mix on high speed until smooth.

Pour the pie filling into the crust. Bake the pie for 1 hour, or until the pie looks soft but set, with a mostly firm center. Transfer the pie to a cooling rack and let cool for 2 hours. Serve immediately or refrigerate until needed. The pie filling will firm up as it cools.

Note: *The graham cracker crust should be the perfect consistency, but if it seems a little dry, add a touch more butter. If it feels a little wet, add a touch more graham cracker crumbs. Since there are no eggs in this crust, feel free to lick the fork.*

Egg Coffee

1 egg
1 cup boiling water
1½ tablespoons ground coffee
½ cup cold water

Break the egg in a cup and set aside, reserving the shell. Crumble the shell and place it in a separate cup with the ground coffee. Add the cold water and mix it all together until it looks like sand. Dump the eggshell mixture into the pot of boiling water, mix thoroughly, and boil for 5 minutes. After 5 minutes, strain the mixture and serve.

Sweet Potato Hummus

1 large sweet potato (about 9 ounces)
1 (15-ounce) can chickpeas, drained and rinsed
5 tablespoons olive oil (plus additional, as needed, for thinning)
2 tablespoons tahini
2 tablespoons fresh lemon juice
2 garlic cloves, peeled
1 teaspoon ground coriander
1 teaspoon ground cumin
¼ teaspoon salt
Pinch of nutmeg

Position the baking rack in the middle and heat oven to 425 degrees. Wrap the sweet potato in foil and bake in a shallow baking pan until it can be easily pierced with a knife, about 45 minutes. Transfer to a cooling rack and allow the potato to cool completely.

Peel the skin off the sweet potato and transfer to a food processor fitted with a blade. Add the chickpeas, olive oil, tahini, lemon juice, garlic, coriander, cumin, salt, and nutmeg, and process until smooth. If the hummus is too thick, add a little extra olive oil or water and process until the desired consistency is reached.

Creamy Cashew Butternut Soup

3 tablespoons olive oil or unsalted butter
1 large onion, peeled and finely chopped
1 cup raw cashews
1 garlic clove, finely chopped
1 large butternut squash (about 2 pounds), peeled and cut into
    ½-inch dice
5 cups vegetable or chicken stock (plus additional, as needed, for
    thinning)
2 tablespoons minced fresh ginger
2 teaspoons ground cumin
2 teaspoons ground coriander
1 teaspoon curry powder
1 teaspoon ground turmeric
Salt and pepper, to taste
1 cup coconut milk (plus additional, as needed, for thinning)
1 sprig fresh rosemary

In a large stockpot or Dutch oven set over medium-high heat, warm the olive oil until shimmering. Add the onions and cook, stirring, until they begin to soften, about 5 minutes. Add the cashews and cook, stirring, until the onions are translucent and the cashews have slightly browned, about 3 minutes. Stir in the garlic and cook for 30 seconds. Add the squash, stock, ginger, cumin, coriander, curry powder, and turmeric and stir to combine. Season to taste with salt and pepper, and bring the soup to a simmer. Reduce the heat to low, cover the pot, and cook the soup until the squash is easily pierced with a knife, 20 to 25 minutes. Uncover the soup and let it cool for 15 minutes.

Starting on slow speed and increasing to high, puree the soup in small batches in a blender until smooth. Place a towel over the top of the blender in case of any splatters. You can also use an immersion blender (let the soup remain in the pot), but it will take longer to puree until smooth.

If using a blender, return the soup to the pot, add the coconut milk and stir. Then add the rosemary sprig, and cook over low heat, covered, until slightly thickened, 15 to 20 minutes. Serve immediately or refrigerate until ready to serve. If serving the soup later, while reheating the soup, thin it out with more broth or coconut milk until it reaches the desired consistency.

11

My Mom Makes Dinner

....

Cheese Fondue, Princess
Pancakes, Beef and Bean Cholent,
April's Mock Pecan Pie

....

M y mom's idea of a good home-cooked dinner consisted of boxed au gratin potatoes, canned tuna fish, or maybe some Franco-American SpaghettiOs. For all her virtues, my mom hated to cook, and she relied on packaged and frozen meals to make dinner as speedy and painless as possible. She would constantly tell April and me, as we scraped the last pea and the little piece of peach cobbler out of our Hungry-Man TV dinner, that my grandmother Beauty wasted her whole life cooking old-fashioned food, which to my mom meant anything made with fresh ingredients, especially vegetables. My mom said modern food came in a can, a box, or a foam take-out container. She boasted that she could get dinner on the table in just a few minutes, and since everything was disposable, including our plates, cutlery, and cups, there was no cleanup, so no one would have to waste the night doing dishes—especially her.

My dad hated coming home to a house with no real food. When he was growing up, his mother worked a twelve-hour day in the garment district, but she always managed to have a feast on the table for him. Liver with fried onions, brisket with roasted potatoes, and boiled beef flanken with kasha varnishkes were a few of his favorites.

In an effort to avoid arguments and keep peace in the family, my dad would choose dinners at Smith & Wollensky, P.J. Clarke's, and the Oyster Bar with his advertising buddies instead of having dinner with us. When he did make an appearance, he would dive straight for the drawer of take-out menus and order pizza, moo shu pork, burgers, fries, or a chocolate milk shake from the coffee shop. What he ordered depended on the diet of the moment—low-fat, high-fat, no carb, good carb, no sugar, sugar-free. I did my best to keep track. Luckily, Tivoli, the local coffee shop, had a six-page menu.

On one rare occasion, my mom did decide to cook a family dinner. Perhaps my mother was inspired by my grandmother's visit, or maybe Beauty scared her by telling her that the way to a man's heart is through his stomach. "If you don't feed him," Beauty would say, "someone else will." Or maybe it was because my dad was traveling for a couple of weeks working on a new ad campaign. As I pondered all the different scenarios, my seven-year-old sister, always wise beyond her years, taunted me, saying she knew the real reason for Mommy's special dinner.

"Did you know Mommy has a new best friend?"

"Mommy always has a new best friend. I think she has more friends than anyone in the world," I said proudly.

"Not that kind of friend," April said. "She has a different kind of friend, a friend who is not a girl, a friend who she looks at herself in the mirror for. Think about it, Mommy has been out really, really, really late every night after her acting class, and she is always in such a good mood when she gets home. I mean a really, really, really good mood!"

"I don't want to hear about it," I insisted, but April could not stop herself.

"Just this afternoon Mommy was on the pay phone in the pizza parlor talking baby talk. She bought me a rainbow Icee. How often does that happen? And then when I asked her for a pack of bubble gum, she didn't say no. She just handed me a dollar and waved me off without asking for a receipt or anything. You know Mommy always asks for a receipt."

"Maybe she forgot," I said.

"Mommy never forgets. I haven't even told you the best part. When I came back to bring her the change, she was laughing louder than I ever heard her. Mommy said she was talking to my piano teacher, but I don't think that was the truth."

I reprimanded my sister for spinning tales, trying my best to quiet her. "If we are on our best behavior, maybe Daddy will come home for dinner more." But April couldn't stop.

"Kissy, kissy," April kept whispering in my ear. "Kissy, kissy."

"That's not funny," I said, but before I could silence her, my mom announced that dinner was ready.

"Fondue and quiche, everybody." My mom's voice was really excited, almost childlike. When we came down the stairs, we noticed that my mom's hair was tied back neatly, and she had on her best bell-bottom jumpsuit with suede fringe, silver eye shadow, and her favorite dress-up, five-inch patent-leather disco platform sandals. She looked happy and pretty swaying about to the lyrics of "I Feel the Earth Move" by Carole King, which was blasting from our new hi-fi stereo.

On the table, usually filled with mail, receipts, and scripts from my mom's acting classes, were real plates and a red fondue pot with long three-pronged forks—each fork in a different color. My dad had bought the fondue pot months ago when he was in Switzerland on business; he thought it would be fun for parties, but now it was on the table ready for my family to enjoy. There were mushrooms, zucchini, and crispy cut-up French bread for dipping. The bread was for my sister and me, and the mushrooms and zucchini were for my dad, who was supposedly back on the Atkins Diet since the Rice Diet was impossible to maintain away from the Fat Farm.

When everyone arrived at the table, my mom proceeded to demonstrate how the cheese sticks to the bread when you dunk it in the pot. She made sure all eyes were on her, creating the perfect bite. "You do not want to over-saturate the bread with the cheese sauce; otherwise, it might break apart and the poor little pieces of bread will sink to the bottom and drown." She looked at my dad all bright-eyed and smiley. "I heard the custom in Switzerland is if the bread falls into the cheese, the man sitting beside the woman has to kiss her."

My sister started giggling, kicking me under the table. "Mommy is talking in that creepy voice again," she said.

My mom continued to gaze at my dad, declaring that the whole meal was Atkins-approved except the bread—"Lots of fat, protein, and no carbs. You can dip as many mushrooms as you like without guilt, and the quiche that I am about to get out of the oven has no crust—just loads of cheese, heavy cream, eggs, and bacon."

Just as April and I were about to indulge in this bubbly, cheesy bit of nirvana, we saw that my dad looked less than pleased. He said he'd had a terrible day. The series of Minute Maid commercials the he had spent the last couple of months filming were being shortened in the broadcast. The slogan he wrote was "The Juice of Juices," but the way it was transmitted sounded like the tagline was "The Juice of Jews," and the campaign wasn't receiving the praise and positive attention he thought it deserved. When my mom had phoned and said she was going to make him a meal to brighten his day, he envisioned comfort food like his mother would have made—tenderloin steak with rice and peas, a creamy tuna casserole with thick egg noodles, or meatloaf with oven-baked parsley potatoes. While my dad's face lit up remembering the kinds of dinners his mother made, I saw the light drain from my mom's. Hoping he was just experiencing low blood sugar from possibly dieting all day, my mom quickly cut him a slice of her quiche, sticking her finger in the middle of the slice to pull out a chunk of egg shell that had gotten baked in.

"How am I supposed to eat this soggy, runny mess with these long pointy sticks?" my dad exclaimed. "I need real utensils! Where are the utensils? There are no real forks, knives, or spoons on this table." I ran to the kitchen to look for everything when I saw my mother's eyes tear up. I fumbled through the drawers, the cabinets, the shelves, and even the refrigerator, which my mom used for storage of paper goods and plastic cutlery, but I could not find any utensils or napkins. Even worse, we were out of diet soda.

My belly was in knots. My mom was crying; I had never seen her like this before. My mom was always stoic and strong, but in that moment, my mother looked sensitive and unguarded, and it scared me.

"You know I do not like to cook, but I went out of my way to try and make a meal that was dietetic. I even bought two kinds of imported cheese and dry white wine for the fondue," she wailed, her voice quivering with anger. "I missed my class tonight. I went out of my way to please you. You don't appreciate me. I have a master's degree, I have tripled our savings in the stock market, I am a wonderful English teacher, and people tell me I am a talented actress. You're not the only one who matters in this house. The planet does not just spin around you."

My dad looked shocked. My sister, no longer playful, cowered behind my back. I was always the peacemaker, but I did not know how to make this better. I just stood there, frozen. Seeing my mom so upset hurt me in a way that I had never hurt before. I had felt pain before, lots of it, but this was excruciating.

I never noticed before how young and beautiful my mom was or realized that she needed love in the same way I needed love. I had never really understood my mom and often compared her to my grandmother, but she was different. My grandmother Beauty used to say that when my mom was little, she would lock herself in her room for hours reading and doing homework, occasionally not even wanting to come out for dinner. Who would not want to come out for my grandmother's delicious dinners? I thought. But my mom was always too busy to sit and eat; she was busy as a child, and she was busy now. "No one ever really knew what she was busy doing," my grandmother would say, "but she was always industrious and talented. She could play *The Moonlight Sonata* or Beethoven's Fifth Symphony as well as any concert pianist, and she could itemize my Papa's sale sheets and taxes better than any accountant when she was just a small girl."

I didn't always like my mother, but I always loved her. I wondered if she knew how much I loved her—maybe even I didn't know until this moment. My mom always thought I preferred being with my grandmother. "I know you like Beauty more than me," she would always say. "She dotes on you excessively, and no matter what you do, she thinks it is great. You will see when you are grown up, there is more to life than cooking and cleaning. You will be glad that I dragged you to museums, and plays, and thrift shops. I am the one that has made you an interesting, cultured child." There was a part of me that knew what she was saying to be true. And in that moment, with the tears running down my mother's face, I wanted to grab her and hug her and tell her that I appreciated her, and when she hurt, I hurt. But we didn't have that kind of relationship. I wanted to move toward her, but I could not.

"Where are those knives?" my mom said. "I know there must be some at the bottom of my purse."

My dad kept slamming his fists on the table. "I am not even sure why I came home. I just wanted one normal meal."

As my parents' argument became more heated, my sister and I ran upstairs and hid under my canopy bed, covering our ears, trying to drown out the sounds of their screaming. We escaped into a game we had invented called Big Sister, Little Sister. Whenever my parents argued, my sister and I would dodge under the bed—pulling all the covers with us. We would each get a flashlight and together pick who was going to be the big sister and the little sister. We spent a great deal of time under that bed in our secret world.

On the nights my parents went out, which was a lot, the game would become more complex. Whoever chose to be the big sister would also be the lady-in-waiting and had to provide a snack and entertainment for the little sister, the princess. I guess I invented the game so I would not always have the pressure of being the caretaker and the responsible one. When I was ten, I convinced my mom that I was more responsible than most of the babysitters she was hiring and I should be the main caregiver for my sister and myself. My mom knew that I would never let anything happen to April so she agreed.

While my parents were out at night immersed in the seventies party scene and the emerging disco scene, my sister and I were immersed in our own wonderful world. With no babysitters, the house was ours. April and I took turns swapping roles and making each other snacks that we would eat on my parents' king-sized bed while reading aloud stories in dramatic voices. We weren't really allowed to eat on my parents' bed, but in our fantasy game, the bed was our castle, and we stacked all the pillows really high to create a secure fortress.

I usually played the big sister, which was okay because I loved creating healthy snacks, using some of my grandmother's recipes as inspiration. Sometimes, the snacks I made for her were simple, like peanut butter and jelly sandwiches, or homemade granola and yogurt parfaits, drizzled with maple syrup. Other times, it was as elaborate as Princess Pancakes that I made by combining oats, cottage cheese, eggs, and a dash of vanilla in the blender until it turned into a smooth batter for frying. I then warmed fresh strawberries, which I spooned between two of the pancakes—making the most royal, double-decker pancake sandwiches, which I served to her proudly. I watched with anticipation as she ate, waiting for her smile of approval. And as we snacked, I read aloud to her my favorite passage from A. A. Milne's *Winnie-the-Pooh*, "If you live to be a hundred, I want to live to be a hundred minus one day so I never have to live without you." I read the line aloud several times while she sat on my lap.

April depended on me. I picked her up from school, tucked her into bed, and created a world where we would always feel safe. In reality, our house felt far from safe. It was an old brownstone from the late 1800s with glass doors located across from the Cuban Embassy. The embassy was bombed twice while we were home alone, causing our windows and front door to shatter. Even when the embassy was not bombed, our house looked as if it had been hit with something. It was messy and dark, with lots of cobwebs, which my mom said was a good thing because if any burglars were to break in, they would be scared off. But we had the greatest spiral banisters to slide down, big closets to hide in, a few mice that my sister named, and a huge terrace that overlooked a plush green garden. It was perfect for playing pretend.

I never let April or my parents see that I was actually terrified of staying home alone, and that I needed the game to escape and feel safe as much as I wanted to shield my sister from the turbulence that often occupied our childhood.

When it was April's turn to be the big sister, she said in her deepest voice, "Do not come out of the castle; your royal snack is almost ready to be served. Please sit patiently, my princess." Since April wasn't old enough to really cook, when it was her turn as big sister to make our snacks, she put together clementines, deli turkey, and raisins on a plate, and arranged them in the shape of a smiley face. Sometimes, she would mush a pecan between two un-pitted dates and crumple Cheerios on top of it and call it pecan pie. Or maybe she would put ketchup, pepper, and water in a bowl and call it soup. "For you, my princess," she would say. "I made this all by myself, for you."

My sister loved taking charge, and it was fun to watch her become empowered in the role of the big sister. I hoped my sister would always remain confident, knowing how much I loved and believed in her. What I did not realize was how much I loved it when she took care of me.

In the walls of our castle, the world was perfect, and no matter what snacks we dreamed up, they always tasted delicious.

Hearing my mom yell that the fondue was getting cold, we turned off the flashlights and left our safe haven. "Good luck," we whispered to each other, making our way back to the table. We ate in silence, neither of my parents speaking to each other or us.

That night, when my grandmother Beauty phoned, I told her it would be a long time before I wished for my mom to make dinner again. A couple of days later, the envelope that Beauty sent me was a little thicker than usual. It included a recipe for a beef and bean cholent, sweet potato fries, and chocolate fudge, and a note saying, *You can't fix your parents, but you can always make a hearty pot of love for you and April. Once in a while a dish might break, but do not let anyone or anything break your spirit.*

Cheese Fondue

½ pound Swiss cheese, shredded
½ pound Gruyère cheese, shredded
1 cup dry white wine of choice
2 teaspoons flour
1 garlic clove, peeled
Salt and pepper, to taste
1 loaf French bread, cubed for dipping
Lightly steamed or raw vegetables of choice, for dipping
Raw apple, for dipping (optional)

Melt the cheeses at a low heat in a pot on the stovetop. Add in the wine, mixing slowly. Make sure the mixture is smooth, with no lumps, and then add the flour. Don't let the cheese boil. Before transferring the cheese from the stovetop pot to the fondue serving pot, rub the inside of the serving pot with the garlic clove. This will give a garlicky essence to your fondue, adding extra flavor and aroma. Serve the cheese fondue with a variety of dipping choices: cubed French bread and lightly steamed vegetables or, if desired, raw apple slices.

Princess Pancakes

Yield: 4 pancake sandwiches or 8 open-faced princess pancakes

4 eggs
1 cup cottage cheese
I cup old-fashioned rolled oats
1 tablespoon milk of choice
Oil or butter, for frying
⅓ cup strawberry fruit spread, or 1 cup heated strawberries sautéed
    with 1 tablespoon of butter and 1 teaspoon of sugar
Powdered sugar, for dusting (optional)

Put the eggs, cottage cheese, oats, and milk into a blender and puree into a smooth batter-like consistency.

Grease a frying pan. When the pan is hot, ladle the pancake batter into the hot skillet—cooking one pancake at a time. When each pancake begins to bubble, flip over. When lightly browned, remove from heat and put on a plate. When all eight pancakes are made, spread the jam or warmed strawberry mixture between each pair of two pancakes and make a sandwich. Serve with a light dusting of powdered sugar, if desired.

Beef and Bean Cholent

···

Yield: 4–6 servings

¾ cup dry white beans
¾ cup dry kidney beans
2 pounds boneless beef chunks, cut in cubes
4 medium-size potatoes, peeled and cubed
1 medium-size onion, peeled and cubed
Salt and pepper, to taste
1½ teaspoons paprika
1½ cups water (plus additional, as needed, for thinning)
2 cups chicken broth

Soak the white beans and kidney beans in water, covered, for 8 hours. Preheat oven to 350 degrees. Drain and rinse the beans. Combine the beans, meat, potatoes, onions, salt, pepper, and paprika in a Dutch oven. Add the water and broth. Cover the pot tightly. Put the pot in the oven for 30 minutes. Reduce heat to 200 degrees and bake overnight, for at least 10 hours. The longer you cook it, the thicker it will be. Do not stir. The next day if it is too thick, you can add a little water and stir.

April's Mock Pecan Pie

Yield: 2 servings

6 medjool dates
6 teaspoons nut butter (pecan or almond)
6 crushed pecans
12 chocolate chips
Crushed cereal of choice (Cheerios or cornflakes work best), optional

Make a vertical slit in the date and remove the pit. Fill the center with a teaspoon each of nut butter. Then top with chopped pecans, and chocolate chips. Sprinkle with crushed cereal.

12

Annie *and the Eight-Month Auditioning Process*

....

Peanut Butter Love—
The Best Flourless Blondies, Rice Krispie
Treats with a Chocolate Drizzle

....

I had always been a dreamer; but as much as I was a dreamer, I was a girl of action. After seeing the Broadway play *Annie*, I was in love. I cried, laughed, and was filled with an overwhelming feeling of joy. I wanted to be in that show as much as I ever wanted anything in my life, but I couldn't dance or sing, and I had stage fright. I always dreamed of being an actress—being in a world where I was loved and adored, where the applause was for me.

Once, when I was seven, my dad let me audition for a Frosted Flakes commercial he was working on. Usually I couldn't because they wouldn't let employees' family members audition, but this one time, the agency made an exception and my dad realized that no kid could get as excited about food as me.

It was my big chance, and my dad said if I wanted to be in the commercial, I would have to describe the ecstasy of the way the sugar coating melted in my mouth, and how crunchy the flakes were before they dissolved on my tongue. He demonstrated what he meant with a big bowl of cereal, crunching with joy.

I took one bite and told him the cereal was too sweet. He said, "If you want to be an actress, especially if you want to be a commercial actress, you have to look directly into the camera and convince everyone watching TV that you've just tasted the most delicious food on earth. Liking the product is not your job. Making every kid in America desire the sweet cereal with the plastic collectible toy is your goal. *Capice?*"

The first couple of times I recited the lines, I tried to impress my dad with how animated I could be.

"You're only smiling with your mouth. Smile with your whole being. I don't believe you. Tasting this cereal should be as exciting as Neil Armstrong walking on the moon," he directed, grabbing a couple more handfuls of the cereal. "If you can't convey how mind-blowing this cereal is, you can't audition."

The next spoonful I took, I imagined it was my grandmother's cinnamon oatmeal cookies—sweet but not too sweet, crunchy but not hard, with just the right amount of nutmeg and raisins. I was feeling exhilarated just thinking about the cookies.

"I don't know what you are fantasizing about, but keep that look of pure delight on your face when you say the line!"

"Frosted Flakes are greaaaaaaaaat!"

"Louder, with more emotion."

"Frosted Flakes are greaaaaaaaaat!"

"One more time. Are Frosted Flakes good?"

"NO, they're GREAAAAAAAAAT!"

"That's it. You nailed it!"

The next day, at the real audition, I looked into the camera and stated my name and age. With pure conviction I recited my line, "Frosted Flakes are GREAAAAAAAAT!" My love of Frosted Flakes was so convincing that I got the commercial.

I was over the moon, but the night before the shoot, my front tooth fell out. In desperation, I called my Papa and begged for advice. He had worn dentures since he was twenty-three due to a quack dentist telling him his headaches would go away if he pulled out all his teeth. My grandmother always said, "Such a smart man, yet he is way too trusting of people." I thought Papa would be an expert on this subject and would know exactly what to do. Papa's teeth would float around all night in a wooden salad bowl, but in the morning, he had a million-dollar smile. Papa said he used denture cream to keep his teeth in place, but no matter what I did—not a whole tube of denture cream that my Papa had left in our bathroom, or even a piece of bubblegum that I had saved from Halloween—my prickly tooth wouldn't stay in place.

"We can't use a girl without a front tooth in our commercial," my dad said. "It will make consumers feel like the cereal will rot their children's teeth. We will have to recast the part."

I was replaced before I even made it to the set. But I loved the adrenaline rush of auditioning, and talking about food came very naturally to me. After my brief brush with fame, and once my front tooth grew in perfectly straight, I convinced my dad, who knew every commercial agent and casting director in Chicago, to please help me get representation so I could audition for commercials every day after school, like my friend Tamar.

"Please, Dad, I really want to be an actress," I begged, showing him all the different faces I had been practicing in the mirror for weeks: happy face, sad face, scared face. When he said no, I made my best puppy dog eyes and he finally gave in, calling some of his contacts.

"Most kids usually just end up disappointed. Your picture will probably just land in the trash."

"If I don't try, I will never know what it feels like to be inside a TV."

My dad was amused. "It just looks like you are inside a TV. That is the illusion of film."

"Okay, but I want the illusion."

My dad just shook his head. "You know, you are just as persistent as your mother when she has her mind set on something."

I wasn't sure if that was a good or a bad thing to be like my mom, but the important thing was my dad agreed to help me, setting up an appointment at the Shirley Hamilton Talent Agency.

During the interview, Shirley had me memorize some sides—which is a show business term for a part of a script. I enthusiastically recited my lines. "I love M&M's. They melt in your mouth, not your hand. I want the yellow, the red, the orange. I want them all!" I said, smiling, picturing myself on top of a chocolate-covered mountain. Pleased with my sincerity, Shirley signed me to their commercial division. She even gave my mom the name of a theater company for kids and a photographer for real headshots.

The day of the photo shoot for my composite card, I had to bring three changes of clothes and wear three different hairstyles to achieve different looks—all-American girl, tomboy, bookworm. My career was taking off. I had headshots, an agent, and was a member of Tom Thumb Players, where I played Yentl in *Fiddler on the Roof*. My mother wanted me to push the director for a bigger part since my only line was "We are going on a train and a boat. We are going on a train and a boat." But I was happy with that one line and was glad to be part of an ensemble.

The anxiety of being on stage by myself made my stomach turn somersaults, which is why I fancied myself a film or TV actress. I never felt nervous when I spoke into the camera. I felt like I was sucked into a wonderful dreamland where the words just effortlessly flowed and my smile was real. I was a hundred percent happy and confident in front of the camera, which was not how I felt in everyday life or school. While acting was pretend, the smile and the emotions that I experienced were sincere—even if I was describing something like green Jell-O, which I would normally never eat.

After several auditions, I really got the hang of the acting thing, booking three jobs: one for a Keds campaign, one for a Sears catalogue, and one for a Burger King commercial where I had to bite into a leathery cold burger over sixty-five times. Eventually, they gave me a spit bag so I wouldn't have to keep swallowing the greasy burger. When I finally said the line right, and the whole crew began clapping, it was as incredible as I'd imagined it would be.

But then we moved to New York, and I did not have an agent, and my mom didn't have time to drag me around to auditions, and my dad's new ad agency had a strict rule of not using children of employees in campaigns. So my acting aspirations fell by the wayside even though my desires lingered.

As the years passed, I kind of repressed my acting dreams. I had my sister to take care of, I was in a new school, I always had a lot of homework, and my real passion was becoming clear—re-creating traditional recipes with a healthy twist. I learned how to make my own high-fiber flour by pulsing oats in a blender, I learned how to make my own sweetener for cookies by soaking raisins in water and then pureeing the mixture into a syrup. I even learned to make my Bubbe Mary's stuffed peppers a little more calorie-friendly by using brown rice, ghee, and tofu instead of white rice, schmaltz, and beef.

But after seeing the show *Annie* on Broadway and watching the final encore where all the girls came out on stage for their second curtain call, I was filled with emotion and a burning desire to be on that stage. Hearing the applause growing louder, and seeing the orphans curtseying, and receiving a third standing ovation, tears started rolling down my face. I didn't know what was happening to me. It was as if I had been asleep for a very long time and I had just awakened from a deep slumber. I knew I was not sad, but the tears kept flowing. I was so close— only three rows and an orchestra between me and a Broadway stage. I couldn't stop thinking about how great it would be to be part of a cast.

About a month after I saw the show, there it was in bold print in my mom's *Back Stage*, the three little lines that would change my destiny and family life forever.

Casting

GIRLS 6–12 years old for an open audition for the First National Tour of Annie

No professional experience necessary.

I thought I was going to die from excitement. I fit the bill— no real experience necessary. I was twelve, but I looked young for my age, and I often felt like I was adopted. But as I looked at the requirements, even though there was no real experience necessary, I realized that not being able to sing and dance would be a big problem. Every dance teacher I had ever studied with told me I had two left feet and I had a dreadful voice. So there was no other choice than to do everything in my power to help my sister become an orphan. If I couldn't land the part for myself, I knew I could coach April. My sister was charismatic, precocious, sassy, and was able to sing any song that she heard on the radio, hitting every high note.

There was going to be an open call in a couple of weeks, and anyone could audition even if you were not in the professional theater union, Actors Equity. You just had to stand in line outside the Alvin Theatre on Fifty-Second and Broadway with a headshot and résumé and be prepared to sing a solo without an instrumental accompaniment. I had my work cut out for me, but I knew exactly what to do.

The first step was a photo. April didn't have a professional photo, but I had a Minolta camera that my grandfather had given me for my twelfth birthday. Making her look like an orphan was easy since my sister's hair was always messy and knotty, and my photography teacher, Miss Burdett, said I was wonderful at capturing people's true essence. The next task at hand would be teaching April a song, something that would make her stand out from the hundreds of girls that would be auditioning. When I told April about my plan, she was not nearly as overjoyed as I was.

"If you want to be in it so badly, you audition."

"I would if I could, but you know I can't sing."

"That's for sure. You are an awful singer."

"That's not nice. The point is that I would be so grateful if I had a sister who loved me as much as I loved you and would help me with this chance." I tried to convince April how much fun it would be, how people would stand at the stage door every night and ask for her autograph, and she would go to opening night parties and be in the newspaper. When none of my pleading worked, I resorted to bribery. "I will make you a batch of my carob-frosted Rice Krispie treats."

"The ones with the peanut butter that you made for my birthday party?"

"Yep, those are the ones."

"No deal until you tell me exactly what I have to do."

"All you have to do is rehearse a couple of songs with me and go to the audition and show them how special you are. You know you are the most beautiful, talented girl in the world."

"Just because you think that does not mean everyone else thinks that."

"Of course they do. You are perfect."

"If I was perfect, those mean girls in the second grade would not tell me my hair looked like a rat's nest and my uniform looked like an accordion," April argued.

"It's so obvious they're just jealous of you."

"No, I think they really think that. Who would be jealous of wrinkly clothes anyway?"

"You know you have trouble waking up, so Mommy's plan of letting you sleep in your uniform is not a bad idea. Anyway, when you get cast as an orphan, all those mean girls will be asking for your autograph."

"You promise you will not be skimpy with the frosting? And maybe throw in a batch of chocolate chip blondies, or fry up some salmon patties?"

"Deal."

"Okay, I'm in, let's get to work."

And so we began. After weeks of preparation, the big day was finally here. I had taken a great headshot of April that I developed and blew up at the photography lab at school, and I had written in my best handwriting a résumé that included April's height, weight, and a list of plays that she had performed in at school. We rehearsed and rehearsed an original song called "The Witch Is Dead" from her second-grade talent show. While I would normally tell my sister to brush out the knots from her hair or change her slept-in school uniform, I said nothing. She looked exactly like an orphan. My mother even joined us, genuinely delighted about her youngest daughter's prospects.

When we arrived at 9 a.m. at the Alvin Theatre for the open call, the line was already four blocks long—twisting and turning around corners. After waiting for hours, we were finally ushered into the basement of the theater with the hundreds of other hopefuls for a quick chance to come on stage and sing for the casting agents.

The stage manager scanned through the mass of girls to see who looked the part. "You!" she said to April, shuffling her into the group that would get the opportunity to sing. They liked her. Now she would have to show her stage presence. When they called her name, she skipped onto the stage, where there was a rope that went across to make sure that if you were auditioning, you were below rope level. If you were even a centimeter taller, you wouldn't have the chance to sing; but April was well under the height requirement. She said her name loudly and began belting out the song. April must have been nervous because she forgot the words, but she kept singing anyway, at the top of her lungs, and performing a crazy dance step with a bright smile.

"How about trying another song? Do you know how to sing 'Happy Birthday'?"

"Yes," she said and began singing, hitting every note with

perfect pitch. Then Martha, the stage manager, asked my mom if April could return the next week and sing "Tomorrow" and meet with the choreographer to see if she could follow the dance combinations from the show.

"We'll be there!" my mom shouted.

The next week was like a whirlwind. My mother sent me to Colony Music in Times Square to buy sheet music for "Tomorrow" and a tape of the show. I worked with April every night, making sure she knew all the words.

To keep April inspired, I made her a new batch of my Rice Krispie treats every day. Some days I added carob chips, some days I mixed in a little peanut butter, and one day I even added coconut flakes and Grape-Nuts cereal. My dad said if April won the part, I should market the treats as a power snack. "The treats that give you so much energy, you can sing from today until tomorrow." My dad always had a slogan ready.

My mother, who was normally absent from home most nights, was now home every night, chatting on the phone with some of her actor friends, who recommended vocal coaches. After thorough research, my mom found one of the top vocal coaches in the city. His only appointment was at ten at night, two days before the audition. But my mom said she did not care what time it was as long as he could give April a lesson.

I was glad for some professional input. April was starting to get annoyed with my coaching as I kept repeating, "Sing louder, sing with emotion, sing from the diaphragm."

Ned Hogan lived on the Upper West Side, at 116th Street and Broadway. I had never been above Ninety-Sixth Street before and had never been on a subway above the ground. We accidently missed our stop and got off at 125th Street. Making our way to Ned's house, I noticed many homeless people sleeping in cardboard boxes for warmth and many women wearing almost nothing at all. My mom kept running ahead so we wouldn't be late. I couldn't help but wonder if the people we passed on the streets had big dreams at one time, and what tragedies occurred in their lives that allowed them to just give up on life.

When we arrived at Mr. Hogan's house, he didn't seem excited to see us, even though we had trucked down the dark, gritty streets so late at night for the appointment. He immediately started playing the *Annie* overture and signaled April to start singing. April belted out the song, remembering every tip I'd given her. Ned seemed to brighten a little. When she was done, he took one look at April and said, "If you want this, you have a good chance." Something about Ned's approval transformed April's desire for the part. As Ned was giving April tips, he told my mom and me to wait in the dimly lit hallway outside the apartment with the worn-out, dirty red rug. We both put an ear to the door trying to listen to what he was saying. After about thirty minutes, both April and Ned came out smiling. "No more rehearsing—April knows exactly what to do."

At the next audition, there were not as many girls, and the kids were immediately broken into groups. I couldn't believe the way all the mothers fussed over their daughters. Most of the girls had big shiny ponytails or braids, and their mothers fed them healthy snacks of cut-up fruit, finger sandwiches, and hot tea with ginger and honey to coat their throats. While I always made April snacks, in the anticipation and panic, I had not prepared anything. I was now scared she might be hungry and it would affect her performance.

April did not have any silk ribbons in her hair, nor did she wear anything special. My mother and I were in the audience listening to Martin Charnin give directions as April stood among the girls, adjusting her jumper and curling a strand of hair around her finger.

"Sing as loud as you possibly can," Martin directed. "Make sure they can hear you in the back row."

My legs were shaking, and I could barely stay in my seat while April had her turn. I didn't know if she knew how to make her voice project that loud. But she belted out "Tomorrow" as if she had been singing professionally her whole life. Not only could they hear her in the back row, they could hear her in the basement, the dressing rooms, and the balcony. When she was finished, everyone applauded—the other mothers, the kids, the casting directors, Mike Nichols, the producer, Thomas Meehan the writer, and Charles Strouse, who wrote the music. We left that day feeling confident. The stage manager said they would be calling soon. The next day her name appeared in the *New York Times*, where they called April the next Ethel Merman.

A whole week had passed and we had not heard anything, so my mom, convinced that she had missed the call, hired an answering service. My mother and I both had the number for Actor Phone to check for messages, but after three months, we had given up all hope. As quickly as *Annie* had come into our lives, the dream was gone. We all tried not to speak about it.

Then the call finally came. April made it to the final callback, where she would read a script for her prospective role. April read for the part of Tessie. Her famous line was *"Oh my goodness, oh my goodness!"*

A couple of weeks later, April was cast. I felt like all my dreams were coming true and I was floating on air. Then reality set in. My sister was going on the road with my mother for a year, and I was to stay home alone with my father. All through the craziness of the audition process, I had been so caught up in the moment that I forgot what April getting the part actually meant. My sister, the person I adored most in the whole world, would be gone. I would remain at home without her.

That night when I tucked her in bed, I told my sister how proud I was of her and how much fun she was going to have traveling to so many spectacular new cities.

She said she was really happy but that she was also nervous. "Who is going to cuddle with me and read me stories? What if Mommy forgets to feed me? What are you going to do with all your free time?"

"Daddy said we will really get to know each other and spend some great quality time together. Don't worry about me. I will be fine. And you know, I will be at every opening night, and I will send you the most amazing care packages with Rice Krispie treats and blondies so you won't starve."

Hugging good night, we recited what we always said to each other: "I love you to the moon and stars and back again, I love you to the moon and stars and back again"—knowing that tomorrow my sister would be gone.

Peanut Butter Love —
The Best Flourless Blondies

Yield: 12 squares

16 ounces natural, no-sugar-added peanut butter
½ cup pure maple syrup
½ cup original soy milk or nondairy milk of choice (I use ones that have about 7 grams of sugar per serving)
1 ripe banana, mashed
2 eggs, beaten
1 teaspoon vanilla
½ teaspoon salt
1 teaspoon baking soda
¾ cup dark, semisweet chocolate chips
Butter or oil, for greasing the pan

Preheat oven to 325 degrees. In a bowl, mix the peanut butter, maple syrup, milk, and mashed banana. Mush it all up and combine well. Then mix in the beaten eggs, vanilla, salt, and baking soda. Mix together until well blended and smooth. Stir in half the chocolate chips. Pour the batter into a well-greased 8-inch-square Pyrex dish. Scatter the remaining chips on top.

Bake for 55 minutes, checking after 15 minutes to make sure the edges do not get too brown. If the top looks very brown, cover with foil and bake for the remaining 40 minutes. Cool and serve.

Rice Krispie Treats
with a Chocolate Drizzle

Yield: 12 squares

¾ cup creamy natural peanut butter (the only ingredient should be
    peanuts), softened
1 cup maple syrup
1 teaspoon vanilla extract
3½ cups brown Rice Krispies cereal
1 cup chocolate chips or carob chips (½ cup melted for drizzle)
⅓ cup unsweetened coconut, for garnish
Oil, for greasing the pan

Mix the softened peanut butter with the maple syrup over low
heat in a saucepan. Remove from heat. Add in the vanilla and Rice
Krispies cereal and stir, then add in half the chocolate chips. Press
into a greased 8-inch-square baking pan and refrigerate for a half
hour. In the meantime, melt the remaining chips in the top of a
double boiler and drizzle on top. At this point, you can also sprinkle on the coconut. Return to refrigerator until the bars are solid.
Cut and serve.

PART THREE

13

Home with My Dad

Sunday Gravy with Meatballs,
Oatmeal Raisin Cookies

April was going to be a real *Annie* orphan—touring for a whole year in the First National Company of the Broadway hit. My mom would accompany her, and I would stay home with my dad. I had never spent a whole day, a whole week, let alone a whole year with him.

The morning they left, I hid my face as the limousine pulled away. I tried not to let either of them see how distraught I was. This was a once-in-a-lifetime opportunity for all of us. April was going to be a star, my mom loved exploring new cities, and my dad seemed like he was really interested in bonding with me. "This will be our special time," he assured me. I was going to miss my mother a lot and especially April, but I was also kind of excited to have my dad all to myself and make him proud of me.

I had cooked for my dad often, making it my business to be

up on all his latest diets—even praying beside him while he read *I Prayed Myself Slim*, and I ate seven to ten apples a day while he was on the "Israeli Army Diet." But I never made him homemade meals seven days a week, twice a day. "We will have breakfast and dinner together every day," he promised.

Sitting next to him on the blue silk couch, I watched him smoke one cigarette after another blowing smoke rings, thinking with my mom and sister gone how quiet the house would be. It would be my dad and me for an entire year. Making food with fresh ingredients using Beauty's recipe cards—and now many of my own creations—was how I learned to show my love, first to my sister and now to my dad. I decided, since I no longer had April to fuss over, I could focus all my energies on him. If I helped him lose weight once and for all, I was certain that he would be grateful and love me more.

My dad was no longer morbidly obese like he was before he went to Duke University, but he was still heavy and still looking for that magic diet where he could indulge in sweets, cocktails, and fatty foods, and still stay thin. While he had not gained back the full 175 pounds he had lost during his six-month stay at the Fat Farm a couple of years earlier, eighty pounds had managed to creep back on him.

I was determined to show him that he did not need a divine intervention, a special soap that promised to melt fat, or a handful of pills to suppress his appetite, just some practical advice and healthy home-cooked meals on a consistent basis. I had been studying macrobiotics and vegetarian cooking. I knew that brown rice had more fiber than white rice; beans, tempeh, and seitan were good substitutes for meat, with no saturated fat; and eating green vegetables was very important to detoxify your body. I was sure my dad would be transformed by my culinary expertise and reach a healthy weight with my encouragement and healthy recipes. I even had a bunch of dessert recipes that I thought would inspire him.

During the first few weeks that my mother and sister were on tour, my dad and I spent a lot of time together. We even went shopping at my favorite health food store, Brownies, near Union Square. Unlike my mom, who had a real aversion to grocery shopping and trying new foods, my dad loved both. I could throw anything in the basket—miso paste, udon noodles, Brazil nuts, seaweed—and he didn't make a face, or study the price.

"What is this awful stuff you are cooking?" my mom used to sigh, refusing to taste anything I ever made. But my dad tried everything I cooked: broiled tofu with ginger, vegetarian nut loaf with red peppers, and soybean tortillas with rice cheese and nutritional yeast. For dessert: aduki bean mousse, carrot cookies, and a strawberry kanten. We were eating more than healthy food, we were eating happiness.

Some nights my dad even suggested dressing up and dining out—letting me pick my favorite restaurant, Au Naturel. I could never get my mom to go there. She much preferred a hot dog on the run. I suggested the millet with steamed vegetables and the avocado and alfalfa sprout salad. My dad said he really enjoyed the meal—even noticing that he felt satisfied.

"Rabbit food is not as tasteless as I anticipated. I feel full but kind of energetic like a little Easter bunny," he said, jutting his teeth out like a rabbit and pretending to hop up and down. I began cracking up at how silly my dad could sometimes be.

But as the weeks went on, our dinners together became less frequent. My dad spent more and more time at work. Some nights he came home; more often, he didn't. Even so, I never stopped cooking and experimenting with recipes, always making sure there was a little something new for my dad to try. When he was around, he was always very complimentary, noticing how creative I was, but signing up to be home every night was more difficult than he'd anticipated. He had obligations in town, out of town—even out of the country. Feeling guilty about some of his prolonged absences, he would sometimes invite me to come to a production stage where he was filming, letting me watch the commercial through the director's monitor. He even finagled a couple guest passes to the Atrium Club, the luxurious social club and spa at Fifty-Seventh and Park Avenue, so I could swim and shower there after school—even though the members were mostly business executives, and I was probably the only person under the age of sixty. And one day, he even let me use his charge card to go to Bloomingdale's and buy a navy tweed wool blazer that I needed for school and some emerald stud earrings, since I'd recently had my ears pierced without my mother's consent. But most days I was alone, sickened with a gut-wrenching emptiness.

Walking partly dazed down Third Avenue on my way home from school one afternoon, I tripped and twisted my ankle on a stupid crack in the sidewalk. With blood rushing down my knee, I remembered April always saying, "Fall on a crack and you break your mama's back." Unable to move and totally embarrassed, I noticed a man sitting on the sidewalk a couple feet away from me. He kept staring at me, trying to make eye contact. When I finally looked up to acknowledge him, I smiled.

"Is that a happy smile?" he asked.

"I suppose," I responded.

"It's not. I can tell. I know you."

"You don't know me."

"Sure I do. You pass by here at three-fifteen every day. You go to private school. You don't have many friends."

"That's not true. I have tons of friends!"

"Suit yourself."

"I have to go. My mother worries if I'm late."

"Nobody worries about you!"

I felt my face turning red and my voice starting to get really high-pitched and stuttery. "Why would you say that?"

"I see what I see. Comes with the job."

What job? I thought to myself. But he continued to intrigue me with his insights.

"See that woman who just passed in the black pumps? She has a boyfriend now. For the past year, she was pretty miserable; but now she's found love. See the guy in the gray suit? He just lost his job, but he has not told his wife yet and is still pretending to go to work. Anyway, my little angel, you are very lonely. I see it in your eyes. As a matter of fact, you have some of the saddest eyes I have ever seen."

"I just fell. And my knee hurts," I protested, defending my position and flashing him my normal cheery grin.

"Okay," the man said as he kept studying me. "But I see through that smile."

The strange man was wearing a red-and-black-checkered lumber jacket and a New York Yankees baseball cap. He was seated next to a cart loaded with a few leather suitcases and several hardcover books. He looked like he was in his late sixties, with straight but yellow-stained teeth and big bushy eyebrows. His clothes were worn, but not particularly raggedy. He kept looking me up and down in a caring kind of way. Then he asked, "Why are your heels so worn down? And why were you walking so slowly, like you were lost, before you tripped?"

Who was this guy and why did he care? Just as I was about to walk away, he asked me to stay for a bit. Somewhat curious, I agreed. As he continued to question me, I noticed his language was particularly articulate and he was relatively handsome—even resembling my Papa a little bit. But clearly, he wasn't just sitting on the dirty sidewalk to take a coffee break. I thought it was impolite to ask, but he was obviously a hobo. I had met many when I went to school in the West Village, most of them Viet Nam vets missing a limb or suffering some kind of post-traumatic stress; but this guy was different. There was something really wise about him. We sat quietly for a few minutes. I wasn't sure if I should stay, but I knew I didn't want to leave. All around me, kids and grown-ups were rushing by. I wondered why this man had asked me to sit with him.

"With all these people, why did you ask to talk to me?"

"Because," he answered, smirking, "you were already on the ground, but mostly because you looked like you needed someone to ask you how your day was. My name is Jim. May I have the pleasure of knowing yours? Or if you don't want to tell me, I can just call you Gimpy. Ah, now that is a nice smile."

I wondered why this man didn't have a cup to collect coins and how he knew so many things about my life. "I bet you love poetry," he said, "and I would bet this whole stack of books that you are a straight-A student. And you know what, I bet, people probably think you are a very good listener."

Jim seemed to know things about me, deep things, dark things—things that I never shared with anyone. He was like a guardian angel in one of those Christmas stories—here on earth to save me. I tried to sway the conversation away from me, to him. I kept doing a double take to see if he was real or if I had just imagined this whole strange scenario. Maybe I hit my head when I fell. But there he was next to me, and the way the rough New York City ground had felt against my body, it was surely real.

"Are you homeless?" I finally blurted.

"Yes. I am," he replied without hesitation.

"But why? Don't you have any family?"

"It's a complicated story."

"Please tell me." I'm not quite sure why I was so interested, but in that moment I was desperate to know what had happened to this man to get him to where he was today.

"There is no easy explanation, and it is not a story I am proud of."

"Please," I begged.

"If you're really sure . . ."

"I'm sure," I said, sitting a little closer.

"I used to be a psychotherapist. For twenty years, I had my own practice on the Upper East Side. Life was great. I had a wife, a child, a nice apartment, an impressive address—I thought I had it all. Life was going according to plan until the day I received a phone call from the police.

"'There was a tragedy,' they said. 'Your wife . . .'

"In the time it took for that impersonal sentence to be spoken by that cop, my world just stopped—unraveled in front of me—and there was no coming back. I tried support groups, consulted with other doctors, even started going to church, but nothing worked."

Perhaps his story would have made me suspicious, since it was pretty unbelievable. How could someone who counseled people for a living not be able to help himself? But I saw truth in the way he relayed the story and the intense look of sadness that washed over his otherwise friendly face.

"After losing my wife, I could no longer think clearly. Every time I went to that window, the pain was unbearable. I couldn't concentrate; I began drinking excessively to try to drown the guilt. My son blamed me for his mother's suicide and completely cut me off, not even permitting me to see my first grandson. But even if I could get dressed and make it to my office sober, I no longer had any desire or belief in myself or my abilities.

How could I help my clients if I could not save my own wife? I had known she was in pain and I turned my back on her. Everything I lived for was now gone. I've been on the streets ever since, just studying people. I share with them my sketches, my poems, my thoughts, and maybe a cup of coffee. But I never ask for charity or pity."

"How do you eat?"

"That is not for you to worry about."

I offered him a roast beef and cheese sandwich or a slice of warm apple pie from the Horn & Hardart automat down the street, but he declined. What could I say to this increasingly puzzling man who made me think about things in a different way than I'd ever thought before? When it started getting dark, he ordered me to go home, thanking me for talking to him, but reprimanding me for being so trusting.

I made sure from then on to walk down this stretch of Third Avenue every day after school, just hoping to see Jim. We became friends, real friends, even best friends. We talked about everything. Some of our conversations touched on issues that I wouldn't normally discuss with my schoolmates, most of whom I had distanced myself from in recent months. They didn't understand me. When I was with kids at school, I felt like I had to pretend to care about the things they cared about— mostly boys and clothes. But my life wasn't that simple, and the things that concerned me were different. Kids my own age made me feel like there was something wrong with me, but around Jim, I felt normal, smart—maybe even a little bit special.

On one of our visits, I brought Jim a bag of my homemade banana oatmeal cookies. He would never let me buy him anything, and my dad had forgotten the bag on the counter, so I hoped Jim would enjoy them. After taking a bite, Jim looked at me and said my cookie had transformed his world, and my parents were so lucky to have a daughter who was such a good cook. It was one of the first times in my life that I ever cried in front of someone other than a family member.

Jim was incredibly kind and became something of a father figure to me since my own father was usually unavailable. He also adored my recipes, appreciating the addition of chopped apples in the potato pancakes that I brought him over the holidays.

Once, when my father was traveling and the temperatures were becoming frigid, I even let Jim stay at our house for a little while. It took a lot of persuading, but finally he agreed to accept my offer. I gave him some of my father's skinny clothes. My dad had the most unbelievable collection of shirts in different sizes. No matter how much weight he lost or gained, he always was prepared. The shirts lined the walls of our brownstone like artwork on other people's walls. I didn't think my dad would mind if a couple of shirts went missing.

In addition to giving him my dad's clothes, I made Jim nice dinners, and he showed me how to chop onions without getting tears in my eyes by chilling them in the freezer for fifteen minutes before cutting. He also insisted on making me his favorite meal—Sunday Gravy.

"Sunday sauce is as important to Italian families as chicken soup is to Jewish families. It requires the perfect combination of fresh tomatoes, basil, red pepper flakes, sugar, and garlic. You can add whatever meats you want. Every Sunday, my wife and I made this together when my son was little. He would sit beside us reading the comics, noticing how the air became humid and sweet no matter how cold life was outside. I thought we had achieved the American Dream and we could withstand whatever life threw our way. I have not made this gravy since my wife died. I thank you for allowing me to make it for you."

I wanted to throw my arms around Jim and tell him to adopt me; that way we could both fill the void that was such a big part of each of us. But then my dad called with a surprise that his business trip was being cut short and he was coming home early. "Guess what?" he said. "I won the Peugeot account for the new ad agency that I am launching—Lerman and Van Leeuwen. I am going to be in *Who's Who in America* and so are you." I wanted to be excited. He was even bringing home the thick hardcover book that would mention that he had two daughters.

I looked at Jim, feeling guilty turning him back onto the streets, telling him I would visit him on a regular basis. He mysteriously said, "You won't find me on the corner anymore." He thanked me for our time together, saying he would never forget me.

I begged him to make a plan with me, to have a once-a-week place to meet for hot cocoa. But Jim refused. "I have a lot to make right in my own life. And you are at the beginning of a wonderful journey. Remember there is no such thing as chance encounters. It is what you do with life's chances that determine your happiness. I will always keep you with me right here," he said, pointing to his heart.

For weeks, I tried to find Jim, but he was nowhere to be found. I became fascinated by the fact that if one person could hear your story with an open heart, the outcome of your story might change. I heard Jim's story and he heard mine. With compassion and a little encouragement, he was able to move on, and so was I.

However, the school was concerned and called me in for an emergency meeting after I had shared my story with Sarah, who told her mom, who told the principal, who told the therapist.

Sunday Gravy with Meatballs

FOR THE MEATBALLS:

- 4 tablespoons butter or extra virgin olive oil
- 1 small white onion, minced
- 2 garlic cloves, peeled and chopped
- ½ pound ground beef
- ½ pound ground veal
- ½ pound ground pork
- ½ cup bread crumbs
- ¼ cup grated Pecorino Romano cheese
- 6 sprigs Italian parsley, chopped fine
- Salt and pepper, to taste
- 2 eggs, beaten

FOR THE SUNDAY GRAVY:

- ⅓ cup olive oil or butter
- 4 garlic cloves, peeled and chopped
- 2 (6-ounce) cans tomato paste
- 3 cups water (plus additional, as needed, for thinning)
- ½ cup red wine
- 1 teaspoon sugar
- 2 (28-ounce) cans peeled tomatoes, smashed
- 5 sprigs fresh oregano
- Bay leaf
- 1 teaspoon salt
- 4 whole basil leaves, coarsely chopped
- ¼ cup parsley
- Pinch of crushed red pepper flakes
- 1 pound beef stew meat
- ¼ teaspoon baking soda

To make the meatballs: Place 2 tablespoons of the butter in a skillet over medium heat. Sauté the onion and garlic for 3 minutes, or until the onion is translucent. Set aside and allow to cool. In a large bowl, mix together the three meats with the bread crumbs, cheese, the cooled onion and garlic, the parsley, salt and pepper, and eggs. Shape the mixture into medium-sized ovals. You should end up with about 12 meatballs. Brown the meatballs in the remaining 2 tablespoons of butter and set a side. They only need to be about 80 percent cooked as they will cook later in the gravy.

To make the Sunday Gravy: Place 1 tablespoon of the olive oil in a very large, heavy-bottomed saucepan over medium heat. Sauté the garlic for about 1 minute or until slightly golden and then add the tomato paste and fry it with the garlic for 5 minutes, or until the paste is bubbling, constantly stirring so as not to burn it. Stir in the water, wine, and sugar and allow to simmer for 20 minutes, or until thick. Add the smashed tomatoes, the oregano, bay leaf, salt, basil, parsley, and red pepper flakes. Bring to a boil then lower the heat so that the sauce barely simmers.

Place a wooden spoon under the cover to keep the pot partially opened. While the sauce cooks, place the rest of the oil in a large skillet over medium-high heat and begin to brown the meat and add to the sauce, then add the meatballs. Make sure the meat is completely covered by the sauce and continue to cook for 45 minutes, stirring periodically, always careful not to break the meatballs. You might need to add a little more water if your gravy is too thick. Add the baking soda and simmer for 15 more minutes. When the sauce is ready, skim the excess oil from the top. Serve over pasta of choice.

Oatmeal Raisin Cookies

Yield: 26 medium cookies

Parchment paper for lining the baking sheets
2½ cups old-fashioned rolled oats
½ teaspoon salt
¼ teaspoon baking soda
½ teaspoon ground cinnamon or pumpkin spice
3 large very ripe bananas, mashed to creamy consistency (if they are
    small add another half banana)
6 ounces applesauce or pumpkin puree, fresh or unsweetened, canned
3 tablespoons melted butter or oil
1 teaspoon vanilla
⅓ cup maple syrup
⅓ cup raisins

Preheat oven to 350 degrees. Line two baking sheets with parchment paper. In a large bowl, whisk together the oats, salt, baking soda, and cinnamon. Set aside. In a medium bowl, mix together the mashed bananas, applesauce, and melted butter vanilla, and syrup until thoroughly combined. Pour the wet mixture into the bowl with the dry ingredients and combine until well blended. Dough will be firm. Stir in the raisins until evenly distributed throughout the dough.

Use a small ice cream scoop or tablespoon to measure the dough, and then roll it into balls with the palms of your hands and place them on the prepared baking sheets. Flatten the dough balls with your hands. Bake for 10 minutes, or until lightly browned. Do not let bottoms get too dark. Remove from oven. Allow to cool before removing from the baking sheets with spatula.

Note: *Feel free to personalize these cookies. Add cranberries or chocolate chips instead of raisins. The riper the banana, the sweeter and moister your cookies will be.*

14

Olga's Lunch Room

....

Beef Goulash, Olga's Creamy
Banana Pudding with Nilla Wafers

....

A year earlier, when it was time for middle school, my mom had transferred me from my downtown hippie school, the Little Red School House, to a preppy uniformed school, Lenox on the Upper East Side. My sister had already been there since kindergarten. My mom loved the fact that she did not have to worry about what we were going to wear in the morning. Everyone wore the same navy-blue jumpers, white shirts with Peter Pan collars, blue kneesocks, and penny loafers with real pennies wedged into the front for good luck.

My mother was initially worried that Lenox would be too academically challenging for me, but it was just too inconvenient having kids in different schools on opposite ends of the city. Having us in the same school provided for easier mornings and less rushed afternoons. April and I could travel together to and from school; it would help my mom a lot, and she knew

I would not mind, and even if I did, it was not really up for discussion.

Every morning, I would be in charge of dressing April and making breakfast for the two of us before we rushed to the bus to head uptown. I would normally prepare something hearty and warm, like eggs in a hole with star-shaped eyes, or Cream of Wheat, a little bit lumpy, with maple syrup and raisins. I would let my sister make a menu for the week, and I would do my best to wake up early enough to cook, knowing that breakfast was the most important meal of the day.

Our mornings, although hectic, became my favorite part of the day. April would have me review her homework as she spoke in pig Latin, filling me in on all the second-grade gossip, like who was best friends with who, who was reading chapter books, who picked their nose, and who could do a cartwheel with their legs straight. But when my sister was cast in the First National Tour of *Annie,* our routine, which I cherished, came to an end, and cooking breakfast for myself just made me feel miserable. I couldn't wait to escape and get to school. I was usually the first one to arrive and the last one to leave. Some days, I would arrive as early as seven o'clock, when school did not officially start until eight-fifteen.

Walking through the big red doors of the school, I felt at home as the classical music played and the smells of Olga's home-cooked food—especially her Parker House Rolls—wafted through the halls. After saying hi to the early bird teachers, my first official stop was always to the kitchen to visit Olga, the lunchroom lady. Olga would say in her welcoming thick, broken German accent, "You want a Yumbo?" I would just grin and Olga would assemble her famous breakfast sandwich—two scrambled eggs with grilled tomatoes and melted cheese on a homemade biscuit. While I ate, she would pour me some fresh orange juice and tell me this was our little secret. "You can't come every day for breakfast."

"I know," I always said. But each morning, I appeared, and each morning she fed me.

Since the school was so small, just twelve kids in a grade, it felt like being part of a big family. The teachers knew each and every student very well and were extremely involved in their social and emotional growth. Olga, with her stiff auburn hair that was hidden in a hair net and her crisp pressed polyester uniform, was no exception. Olga didn't place a lot of emphasis on the way she looked. Her husband had passed, her kids were grown, and she felt like she was past her dating prime. Olga completely and passionately devoted all her efforts to her job—noting that all the kids at the school were like her grandchildren, so she prepared everything with care and love. Many of her friends who worked at other schools would take shortcuts, but not Olga; she sliced, seasoned, and baked and ensured that everything that was served in our school cafeteria was made from scratch. In addition to cooking, she made it her business to know every child's name, what the child ate, and what the child did not eat. If you did not like the main entrée, which changed daily—Chicken Chow Mein, Salisbury Steak, Turkey Tetrazzini—there was always Olga's special egg salad with onions or macaroni salad with lots of mayonnaise. Her biggest pleasure in life was watching us enjoy her food. "You like?" she would say if we came for another helping. When we did not come to the lunchroom with an appetite, or we had too much of an appetite, she always knew something was wrong.

After school, all the kids loved to visit Olga. She always had Scooter Pies, Triscuit crackers, and crisp McIntosh apples without a single bruise. I loved watching her write up the lunch menu for the week, bragging in her thick accent about all the kids she'd fed over the years. "They always come back for a bowl of Olga's banana pudding." I would follow her from sink to stove, watching her make the custard and arrange the Nilla wafers. I was amazed at how many recipes she could prepare at one time. There were always lots of pots and pans, bowls, blenders, and spices set up in a perfect line on her stove and countertops. Olga's kitchen was a place of order with the bubbling pots of Bolognese, rice, and goulashes all simmering in unison. Olga had no trouble creating several entrées and desserts while handing out snacks and hearing everyone's saga. Many of the girls confided in her about crushes, diets, or how unfair their parents were, and the obvious lack of boys, since the school had been all girls until recently. Everyone seemed to love Olga; even the awkward boys seemed to flock around her.

I first became acquainted with Olga a couple weeks after transferring into the school. She saw me sneak into the cafeteria during April's lunch period. I was eyeing what April chose to put on her tray. If I wasn't there to remind April, she would often just choose grilled cheese or a jelly sandwich and forget to eat something healthy. If I noticed April didn't have any vegetables or fruit on her tray, I would run up in the line and grab a couple of carrots, a slice of melon, and a few pieces of broccoli, and add them to her tray. April usually looked bothered, and her friends teased her, saying she had a weird sister who spied on her. I told the girls, "It is very important to eat fruits and vegetables every day if you want to grow up smart and beautiful." Most of the time April would stick up for me, saying I was not weird, but just a big worrywart, which is what my mother always called me. One afternoon when Olga caught me fussing with April's plate, she warned me that I had to wait until my own lunch period to enter the cafeteria; otherwise, I would be reported to my homeroom teacher, Mrs. Grand, for sneaking out of math class.

"But April will get a headache and will be cranky if she doesn't eat enough, and if her vegetables are not cut really small, and if her orange is not peeled and sectioned for her, she will not eat it."

"Go back to your classroom. Nobody is going to starve or get malnourished in my lunchroom."

Seeing the look of fear on my face, she smiled, assuring me that she would fill April's plate personally. After that day, I noticed that she also seemed to add extra vegetables to my tray. I felt like we had an unspoken bond, one that did not require words.

Since the Jim incident and the discovery of an apparent lack of parental guidance at home, Mr. Frank, the principal, thought it would be beneficial for me to visit the school psychologist, Ms. Thurman, who was always waiting for me to confess something horrible and disturbing about my home life. She would sit there in her big chair, with her pleated, black pin-striped suit, and just glare at me. I never spoke. After several sessions where she tried to bond with me over a game of checkers, she told me she would not blame me if I had a deep resentment toward my mother and sister for abandoning me. "It's okay to express your rage here," she would say, setting out a little plastic robot that I could throw fake punches at.

"I love my sister. I'm the one who helped her get the role as an orphan. And I'm excited for her, not jealous or angry."

"I see," she always responded.

I hated how coldly she looked at me, thinking she knew how I felt. She clearly had no clue. I loved my sister and I worried about her constantly. I felt sorry for Ms. Thurman, thinking that maybe she had never loved somebody so much that she didn't understand sacrifice. Week after week, I sat there, feeling like a therapy failure. I knew she wanted me to scream, to cry, to have some kind of emotional outburst. But every time she said in her stoic voice, "How does that make you feel?" the only feeling I had was wanting to escape from her small, claustrophobic torture chamber that smelled like mothballs and diner coffee.

The sessions were supposed to offer me some kind of relief and support, but they did just the opposite. The more Ms. Thurman wanted me to reveal, the more I felt I needed to conceal. She wrote down everything I said or did not say, scribbling her observations on her yellow lined legal pad. The more she questioned me with her dark beady eyes, her canned questions, and her false sense of empathy, the more I froze. I did not tell her that my dad often did not come home, that I wished I had some kind of talent, that I thought my sister didn't need me anymore, and how this was killing me inside. I could not tell her that I was completely alone, and I just wanted someone to love me, to take care of me. I could not tell her that I was insecure and not popular. I could not tell her anything that would get my parents in trouble or compromise my sister's career or make me seem weak.

Olga never asked me direct questions about my family, but she engaged me in conversation by asking me what I thought of the lunch. Did I like the turkey as an open-faced sandwich with gravy or did I like it better served with mashed potatoes and cranberry sauce? Did I like the hamburger meat ground in a rich tomato sauce or did I prefer it as a burger? Olga never wanted me to yes her or gratuitously compliment her cooking. She seemed genuinely interested in my opinion and what I had to say—and I definitely had a lot to say when it came to preparing food. I even offered her some suggestions on ways to make her delicious recipes healthier without compromising the taste, like using fresh garlic and chicken broth in her mashed potatoes instead of butter and cream. She encouraged my input, and my words effortlessly flowed when I was with her.

Olga always seemed amused by my stories. We talked about my grandmother, my visits with April, and the lavish cast parties with the most incredible spreads of food—and my dad, who was forever dieting. Olga could relate to my dad's struggles and was impressed with my healthy diet tips. Like my dad, she was overweight and loved hearing about new diets—even though she had no time or real motivation to diet herself. When people looked at her, they could instantly see she loved food, and she didn't mind that. She also could never imagine cooking without sampling everything she made.

"When Olga makes something, you know it is delicious," she professed, having me taste the goulash with tender chunks of beef, onions, celery, and tons of real paprika. Never McCormick in Olga's recipes. "A goulash is only as good as the paprika," she'd say, writing down the address of where to buy the key ingredient. "Schaller and Weber has more than ten different varieties of paprika," she'd add in her quiet voice. I never heard Olga talk so softly, but I guess the secret to her goulash was not for all ears to hear. "Remember to purchase one sweet and one sharp paprika, and make sure to tell them Olga sent you."

Olga loved that I was inquisitive and valued the importance of her life's work. "Cooking food that children look forward to is hard work. I love watching the children gobbling down my food, cleaning their plates even if it is something they have never seen before like roulades—thin slices of beef rolled with sour pickles and mustard."

Olga told me that both her daughters grew up watching her

cook and enjoying her food, but neither of them ever showed any real interest in learning to do it themselves. They had bigger dreams. "Magda is now an accountant and Heike a corporate lawyer. With their big fancy jobs, they can barely boil an egg or water for themselves." I told her I spent every Sunday making care packages of baked goods for April. Olga would just pat my head, telling me she knew how much I loved and missed my sister.

I did love my sister, and the idea of being jealous, which the therapist suggested, never occurred to me. "How can you be jealous of someone you love?" I asked Olga.

"When you are different, people try to put you into a box or define you in a way they can understand. Ms. Thurman is a very nice woman, doing her job the best way she knows how. We all do what we know how."

Although she never said it, I felt that Olga's relationship with her own children was probably not as close as she would like. She had pictures of them next to her food supply list on the corkboard near the refrigerator, and she talked incessantly about how brilliant and successful they were, and how proud she was of them. But in all the years she worked at the school, they never visited, and when she spoke about them, I thought there was a longing or a sense of despair. Whenever Olga and I would have emotional moments, she would tell me she needed to get back to work and I should try to spend some time with friends my own age. "It is not healthy to spend so much time with an old woman."

Olga encouraged me to make more plans with the girls in my class after school. "Ask Sarah to bake with you. I used to see you girls sitting together all the time at lunch."

Sarah had been my best friend in seventh grade. But now, in eighth grade, she was more concerned with being popular.

When we first met, we bonded instantly as we were both new to the school, we were both shy, and we were both the shortest girls in the class; but now Sarah wore makeup, and she was all chummy with the popular girls.

"Just because she is friends with other girls does not mean she can't be friends with you."

Serving me a heaping bowl of the banana pudding, Olga said, "Sometimes you have to look outside of yourself. You have no idea what is going on in someone's life unless you ask. And you cannot expect people to know what is going on in your head unless you tell them."

"Everyone and everything is changing and I am not sure how I feel about anything."

"Why don't you help me roll the dough for the biscuits?" As we put them in the oven and watched them rise, she said, "Things are always changing. And change is not bad, but necessary.

"You are changing, your sister is changing, but that does not mean your relationship will not be as special. She is enjoying her life, and you need to enjoy yours. It will not make you love her any less. I will see you at lunch tomorrow, but not before or after!"

Olga packed some warm rolls in a round Tupperware container. "Use the container to send the cookies to April. It is airtight and will keep them fresh longer than tin foil and a shipping box."

For the next week, I did not visit Olga. I just went home after school and moped, until finally I gathered the courage to ask Sarah if I could go with her, Natalie, and Lauren to Mariella's for pizza. While they were all wearing blue eye shadow and had cut their long hair into Farrah Fawcett flips, they were still the same girls as last year, deciding who would host a weekend sleepover, who they thought would make the volleyball team, who loved Olga's banana pudding the best, and who was most likely to be the class president.

During my next therapy session with Dr. Thurman, I realized that one of Olga's greatest gifts was not just her cooking—delicious though it was—but rather her ability to make each and every child feel special and cared for without words or questions. Each girl believed she was Olga's favorite, and for once, I was not the exception.

Beef Goulash

3 tablespoons flour
3 teaspoons Hungarian fine sweet paprika, divided
2 pounds stew meat (chunks)
4 tablespoons butter
Fat from 4 ounces of bacon or 4 tablespoons oil
2 garlic cloves, minced
1 large onion, peeled and diced
2 celery stalks, chopped
½ cup red wine
3 teaspoons tomato paste
32 ounces beef broth
Salt and pepper, to taste
1 teaspoon hot paprika
2 bay leaves
Dollop of sour cream, for garnish

In a small bowl, mix together the flour and a generous teaspoon of the sweet paprika. Dust the beef stew chunks with the flour and paprika. Mix and toss it so that all the pieces are well coated. In a heavy-bottomed pot or Dutch oven, melt 2 tablespoons of the butter on medium heat. Add a generous tablespoon of the bacon fat to the butter, to keep it from burning. Fry the meat pieces in small batches on high heat and brown them on all sides.

Scoop out the beef and set it aside on a plate. Repeat until all the beef is browned. Add some more butter to the same pot. Toss in the garlic and onion and sauté for a few minutes, until it all turns soft and translucent. Add the celery and sauté for a few more minutes. Then pour in the wine. Add the tomato paste and beef broth to the pot. Add the hot paprika and bring the liquid to a boil.

Next, add the meat back to the pot, including the juices. Season the stew with salt and pepper and half the remaining sweet paprika. Add the bay leaves to the pot, cover, and let the stew simmer on medium-low heat for 1½ to 2 hours. The longer you cook the goulash the thicker it will become. Stir occasionally. While the stew simmers you'll notice a film of fat form on the top. Skim off the fat and add in the remainder of the paprika. Serve over egg noodles or spatzles (see note) and garnish with a spoonful of sour cream. If you like a thicker goulash you can stir in the sour cream before you spoon over noodles or spatzles.

Note: *Spatzle is a German dumpling made from flour, milk, and eggs.*

Olga's Creamy Banana Pudding with Nilla Wafers

Yield: 8 servings

¾ cup sugar, divided
⅓ cup all-purpose flour
Dash of salt
3 eggs, separated
2 cups milk
1 teaspoon vanilla extract
40 Nilla wafers
6 ripe bananas, sliced
Additional wafers and banana slices, for garnish

Mix ½ cup of the sugar, the flour, and salt in the top of a double boiler. Blend in the egg yolks and milk. Cook, uncovered, over boiling water, stirring constantly, for 10 minutes, or until thickened. Remove from heat and stir in the vanilla. Spread a small amount of the custard on the bottom of a 1½-quart casserole and cover with a layer of the wafers and a layer of sliced bananas. Pour about one-third of the custard over the bananas. Continue to layer wafers, bananas, and custard to make a total of 3 layers of each, ending with custard.

For topping, beat the egg whites until soft peaks form; gradually add the remaining ¼ cup sugar and beat until stiff but not dry. Spoon the mixture on top of the pudding, spreading evenly to cover the entire surface. Bake at 350 degrees for 20 minutes, or until browned. Cool and garnish with additional wafers and banana slices just before serving.

15

Dawn's Desserts and Sarah's Sweets

Carob Chip Cookies, Protein-Packed Linzer
Cookies, Easy Peanut Butter Cookies

I n high school, my friend Sarah saved my life a dozen times,
a dozen ways. She lived around the corner from school, on
Seventy-First and Lexington, making her house the perfect
hangout and retreat. It was always clean, always the perfect
temperature, and always loaded with glass bottles of Perrier and
several boxes of Entenmann's chocolate chip crumb cake and
powdered sugar doughnuts, which her mother laid out on their
marble kitchen counter before she left for a long day of work.

Sarah had a lot of freedom, like me, as her mother Elaine
and stepfather Arnie did not come home most nights until after
eight o'clock. But unlike me, there was a structure and order
to her life. Her mother made sure that she was always impeccably dressed, her grades were the best in the class, and their
kitchen was meticulously stocked with groceries and fancy
leftovers from the best New York City restaurants, where the

family would dine on the weekends. Chicken Kiev from the Russian Tea Room, Veal Paillard from Café des Artistes, and Steak Diane from Les Pleiades were a few of the gourmet dishes that were left for nibbling.

The first time I ate at Sarah's house, I felt like I was in an episode of Robin Leach's *Lifestyles of the Rich and Famous*. Sarah was well-off but acted a lot haughtier than the Upper East Side life that her mother, a public relations executive for Sotheby's, and her stepfather, a marketing consultant and jazz musician, provided for her. Sarah liked to speak in an affected French accent and knew how to make the ordinary extraordinary—serving sparkling water instead of tap, which she garnished with slices of lime, or serving sweet cakes on china instead of paper plates, which she would decorate with fresh berries and lots of confectioner's sugar.

Everything Sarah did was fabulous, from the way she accessorized her uniform with silk Chanel scarves to the way she tucked her shirt into her perfectly pleated navy skirt to the way she had her closet organized. She had tons of sweaters and shoes that were arranged like a department store. The shoes were in boxes and labeled "summer," "weekend," and "school," and the sweaters were folded in special bags with tissue paper so as not to get moths or wrinkles. Sarah was like a sophisticated society woman trapped in the body of a little girl.

In every school that I had ever attended, I was the shortest, but Sarah stood four foot six, to my four foot eight, and she was rail thin—although she had one of the heartiest appetites I had ever seen. She could battle my voracious appetite, bite for bite, when we would sit around her kitchen table devouring the contents of her refrigerator and cupboards. Sarah introduced me to Brie and apples, prime rib with horseradish, and smoked salmon with crème frâiche and capers.

The only difference in the way we ate was when it came to sugar and carbohydrates. Sarah had a wicked sweet tooth and could eat three pain au chocolats smothered in Nutella. The nutty chocolate spread was sent to her by her cousins who lived abroad. I had never had a filled croissant with a big chunk of chocolate in the center, let alone one that was swimming in a sea of frosting. "More for me," she said, as I passed on the second croissant, opting for more pâté. Sarah thought it was weird that I would eat spoonful after spoonful of duck liver—but always refused the crispy baguettes or Carr's Water Crackers that she tried to pair with it.

"The way you eat is not very French," she would tell me in a disapproving tone.

"Well, the way you eat would never be Atkins-approved."

"I do not know what that means. Can you please explain yourself?" Sometimes when Sarah spoke, I had to do a double take to check that it was really her, not some old schoolmarm that had invaded her little body.

I started reciting the rules of the Atkins Diet as well as telling Sarah everything I ate and did not eat. But then I remembered what my mother had told me—how I would have no friends if I scrutinized and put down the way other people ate. But diet rules had been such a major part of my life, and it was what I was best at talking about. I knew how important proper food choices were, and my best skill was transforming traditional recipes into nutritional powerhouses. Most grown-ups were impressed with my expertise. I could create a meal plan for any of my teachers or my friends' parents without a second thought. But I wasn't trying to convert Sarah; I was just trying to make a good friend.

Just as I was about to stop, as I could easily get carried away when I sang the glories of whole wheat flour, oat flour, and nut flours, Sarah said, "Tell me more. I think what you are saying is quite fascinating. Do you know what foods help prevent skin breakouts?"

"Of course I do," I said, my heart racing as I began reciting, "Nothing too sweet, nothing too salty, nothing too greasy, and especially no chocolate cake, no chocolate ice cream, no chocolate candy bars, and no chocolate spread!"

"How would I survive?" Sarah asked in despair, looking down at her chocolate-filled plate.

"I will introduce you to carob."

"Who is Carob?"

"Carob is not a person. It's a food that will change your life. It tastes just like chocolate, but it is healthy and has one-third the calories of chocolate and none of the evil side effects associated with chocolate. I can show you how to make carob brownies, carob chip cookies, carob ice pops, carob mousse cheesecake, and carob-coated popcorn."

Sarah wrote down everything I was saying, asking me question after question. While she was not concerned with her weight, she was obsessed with her skin and would do anything to get a flawless complexion like the girls on the cover of *Seventeen* magazine. I promised her my recipes would not only clear up her complexion, but taste delicious. Sarah was willing to give my recipes a try, as she considered herself very cutting-edge and open-minded. Up to now, Sarah had always been the one enlightening me. She knew more about makeup and music, and was the only girl in our class who got French manicures on a weekly basis. I admired all Sarah's pretty clothes and jewelry, wondering how she decided each day what necklace, what jacket, and what shoes would transform our dull uniforms into something so glamorous. Sarah had a bulletin board with all the style do's and don'ts for teenage girls. Now it was my turn to teach her.

We made a plan to bake every Tuesday and Thursday after school. Monday she had ballet, Wednesday piano, and weekends were complicated—alternating between her beach house with her mom and stepfather and her dad and stepmother's apartment on Sixty-Ninth and Madison. But Tuesdays and Thursdays, we made a standing appointment to cook after we watched *General Hospital*.

"I Think Luke and Laura are the most romantic couple on daytime TV," Sarah said as she made our appointment official, entering it into her leather Coach date book. She had a plan for everything and was the most organized person I had ever encountered. Not only did she have her days of the week planned, but she also had her whole life mapped out.

"You know I am going to live in Paris as soon as I graduate college. But I am debating if I should be a film actress, a fashion editor, or the CEO of a major makeup and skincare line."

While there were a few variables, Sarah pretty much had her future planned. She would study at an Ivy League university, spend her junior year at the Sorbonne, have a villa in the South of France, and be married to a handsome European with a private jet. She even had the china and silver patterns that she expected to receive as wedding gifts picked out.

Sarah had a twenty-year plan. I was always just planning how to get through the day, wondering how we would pay for all the ingredients in all the recipes we were going to bake, if my dad would come home for dinner, and if my mom and sister would call. I was consumed with constant worry more about my mom and my sister than about myself. Even though two weeks earlier, a strange, disoriented man had found his way into our house. I was standing in our bathroom naked, just about to jump into the shower, when I turned around and there he stood. I screamed, and he screamed louder.

"You are not my social worker!" he cried.

I quickly wrapped myself in a towel, grabbed a scissor, and escorted him down the stairs and out the glass front door, where anyone could see in and open the door with a big shove.

When my mom finally phoned that night, I hysterically re-layed the mishap about the crazy stranger. She replied, "You are okay, aren't you? We're sure lucky to live across from the Cuban Embassy, where there are round-the-clock security guards. That's better than Sarah's doorman building."

But I definitely preferred Sarah's doorman building to my desolate, exposed brownstone—usually trying to stay at her house as long as I could. But her mother made it clear that week-days were not for extended visits; Sarah had responsibilities, piano practice, and an early bedtime. I had none of those so I could linger until Sarah's mother would take her in the other room and start muttering under her breath. When she politely excused the two of them, I knew that was my cue to leave. Her mom always looked a little guilty about sending me home, but not guilty enough to ask me to stay. I knew Sarah tried her best.

One day, during English class, when Ms. Lippincott was writing the characters from *Romeo and Juliet* on the board, Sarah passed me a quick note. She wanted to know exactly what we were going to bake every Tuesday and Thursday during each month. She already made pumpkin bread every year for her building Halloween party, gingerbread cookies for the an-nual Christmas dinner that her family hosted even though they were Jewish, and Linzer cookies with a big dollop of strawberry jam for the school Valentine's Day bake sale. She wanted to know how I would remake and improve on her nearly perfect recipes that were passed down from her grandmother, who was a fabulous cook. And she wanted to learn everything about carob, wondering how it would alter her cookies in flavor, texture, and sweetness. Once I satisfied her questions, it was time to satisfy her sweet tooth.

I gave her a list of ingredients that her mother agreed to purchase. The first Tuesday I came over to bake, Sarah had all the ingredients displayed on her kitchen counter and had rewritten my recipe into a pretty notebook, which she had propped up onto a little easel. There were glass bowls, measuring spoons, an electric mixer, and baking sheets, all perfectly laid out.

"I thought it would be more time-efficient if everything was ready to go, so I arranged it all last night before I went to bed."

Sarah was running our afternoon like a professional operation, and her precision was making me nervous. We didn't even have our usual snack, which sometimes substituted for my dinner. As we were dividing up the ingredients, separating the wet from the dry, I made Sarah try a carob chip on its own before it was blended into the dough.

I watched her as she chewed, eating a couple before she decided to speak.

"Well?" I said.

"Kind of chalky and gritty. But I cannot give you a proper analysis until they are melted and baked into the cookies."

I loved the flavor of the carob, although the chips did not melt as well as chocolate. I chose not to tell Sarah that. As we snacked on a couple more chips, we worked efficiently, blending the whole wheat flour, the wheat germ, the brown rice syrup, and the applesauce together and shaping them into little golf-ball-sized balls that we flattened with the back of a fork after we laid them onto the parchment-lined baking sheet.

"Why do some of your cookies have six chips and some have four or five? It is important that every cookie looks and tastes the same," said Sarah.

"It is important that every cookie tastes good," I corrected, as I sampled the raw dough. "Oh my goodness, they are really good, you really can't wait until they are baked," I said, holding a finger full of the dough up to Sarah's mouth. She hesitantly took her spoon and took a bite from the bowl.

"They are scrumptious, really scrumptious!" I could tell she was surprised, taking another spoonful of the raw dough from the bowl. "I could imagine these with peanut butter or with walnut chunks."

"I have made tons of variations. Sometimes I add in oats, or bananas, or carob powder, or whatever I have in the house."

"Wouldn't that usually be nothing?" she said and cackled. It was true, but it hurt my feelings nonetheless.

"Let's try one batch with just chips and one batch with raisins and oats," suggested Sarah.

While the cookies were baking, we went into Sarah's room. Browsing through her record collection, I grabbed a bright pink album cover. "Remember this one?"

"That album used to be my favorite when I was young."

"You are still young," I said.

"I am not! I'll be fourteen in a couple of months."

"Please put it on," I said, begging on my hands and knees.

"Okay, but do not tell anyone we listened to this album."

It only took a couple of bars of melody and a few carob chips before Sarah began blurting out the words to "Free to Be You and Me." And there she was, the girl I remembered meeting the first day of seventh grade, with her waist-length blond hair, matching Raggedy Ann socks, and big smile. She was back, the best friend I missed from before her mother remarried, before my mom and sister left on tour, before the mean eighth-grade clique stole her from me. She was just Sarah, and I was just Dawn, happy and carefree. We spun around until we were dizzy and fell to the ground. We danced around her house the way my grandmother and I used to dance around her kitchen while we cooked. We were not high school girls, we were not burdened with expectations, we were not cool, we were just us—silly and youthful in our own little world—the way we were when we used to laugh for hours after we made prank calls to Tommy Goldsmith. He looked like Barry Manilow, and we would laugh uncontrollably, hanging up before we ever got the words out, asking him if he was in love with Lisa or Lauren.

We baked batches of cookies on that first cool fall afternoon, testing them while they were still soft and warm. With each new batch and new inspiration, we improvised with different ingredients—throwing in chopped cranberries and dates to cookies that were only supposed to be flavored with honey. I showed Sarah that it was okay to make each cookie a little different. "After all, they are just for us," I said.

"What if they were not just for us? What if we started a cookie business?"

"Yes, we could call it *Healthy Cookies*," I shouted out.

"No! That's a terrible name. No one would buy them if they thought they were healthy. I will figure out how to market them. After all, this is not my first business." Sarah boasted that she was the only girl on Fire Island who was able to make a significant amount of money by selling painted seashell earrings and bracelets when she spent a summer there with her longest best friend, Madeline. "You can come up with the recipes and hand out the flyers. I will come up with the pricing, the logo, and the wrapping. Presentation is everything," she stated as she handed me a cloth napkin soaked with seltzer to remove the carob stains from my blouse.

Over the next couple of weeks we made dozens of cookies. We brought them to school for our friends to try. I even brought a batch to Olga—who was very encouraging even though she did not actually say she liked them. "I just like my cookies a little sweeter, a little more buttery," said Olga.

Sarah wrote down every comment and made a graph of which varieties were the most popular. We even added sweet potato bread and blueberry bran muffins to our menu. All the girls seemed to love everything we handed out. Before Sarah let anyone take a bite, she made sure to mention all the benefits of our baked goods. "Our products will whittle your middle and make your skin glow. Look at how bright my eyes are," she announced, having the girls observe how her blue eyes really stood out now. "How great is that?" she would say as all the girls in the class gathered around her. Sarah was already known as the resident beauty expert, and everyone who ever ate with me knew about my obsession with eating healthy, as I would go through handfuls of napkins blotting off all the grease and adding spinach and broccoli when we went for pizza after school.

Within weeks, we were ready to launch. Sarah had drummed up a bunch of business. She came up with the company name. I came up with the company slogan: "Dawn's Desserts and Sarah's Sweets—A not too sweet cookie for a sweeter, more gorgeous you." Together we distributed flyers all over the neighborhood, handing out samples to all the doormen on Sarah's block. Within the first week, we received several orders, and when we realized we did not have any money for supplies, Sarah's mother lent us thirty dollars to pay for the initial cost, provided we would pay her back from our profits. We both agreed, signing an official contract. I was hoping to make enough money to buy my sister an eight-track tape player shaped like a robot that I'd seen at FAO Schwarz. Sarah was hoping to make enough money to buy a pair of new Frye boots.

We both agreed that our first bit of profit would go toward a celebration lunch. I suggested Forty Carrots for frozen yogurt with berries at Bloomingdale's. She suggested the Magic Pan on Fifty-Seventh Street for chicken crepes. We finally agreed on Tavern on the Green for brunch, where we feasted on baskets of raisin bread and split an order of Salmon Benedict. The waiter did not even seem to be annoyed that we did not have enough money for two entrées. And I let myself indulge in a brunch of carbohydrates—being that it was a celebration.

For months, we baked on those Tuesdays and Thursdays, blasting show tunes and singing at the top of our lungs on her fire escape, hoping that someone passing by would not only be delighted by the smells coming from her kitchen but be charmed by our charisma and our voices. I taught Sarah every *Annie* song-and-dance combination, and she taught me to have self-confidence and pride in the way I looked. She even came over to my house and folded all my clothes. With me, she was not so serious; with her, I was not such a mess.

But then Sarah auditioned and was cast in *Pippin* at the all-boys school, Collegiate, where her mother thought she would hobnob with the right kind of people, and she was no longer free on Tuesdays and Thursdays. And I became obsessed with a group of kids at school called the Parkies who hung out at the Bandshell in Central Park smoking pot, playing Frisbee, and pledging their allegiance to Jerry Garcia and the Grateful Dead.

Even though our business venture lasted only a couple of months, and Sarah and I branched out into different social circles, we vowed to honor each other's secrets as well as our recipes for a lifetime.

Carob Chip Cookies

Yield: 12–14 giant cookies

⅓ cup oil or Earth Balance butter substitute or butter (plus a little extra for greasing the pan if not using parchment paper)

¼ cup mashed banana or applesauce

½ cup brown rice syrup

¼ cup maple sugar

1½ teaspoons vanilla

1¼ cups unbleached white flour

½ cup whole wheat pastry flour

½ teaspoon baking powder

½ teaspoon sea salt

1 cup dairy-free carob chips

½ cup walnuts, crushed (optional)

½ teaspoon wheat germ (optional)

Preheat oven to 375 degrees. Grease or line 2 large baking sheets with parchment paper. In a bowl beat together the oil, banana, brown rice syrup, maple sugar, and vanilla, and blend well. In a separate bowl, mix together the flours, baking powder, and salt. Add the dry ingredients to the wet ingredients and mix well. Fold in the carob chips, nuts, and wheat germ, if using. Using a teaspoon, drop heaping spoonfuls of dough onto the prepared baking sheet, placing them 2 inches apart. Flatten them a little with your hand or the back of a fork. Bake for 15 to 20 minutes, or until the cookies are slightly browned at the edges. Do not overcook; otherwise they will get too hard. Let cool for 10 minutes.

Protein-Packed Linzer Cookies

Yield: 12 cookies

8 tablespoons coconut oil or softened butter (put a tablespoon aside
   for greasing the baking sheet if you are not using parchment paper)
1 egg, beaten
1 teaspoon vanilla extract
2 tablespoons nondairy milk
⅓ cup maple syrup
½ cup almond flour or oat flour (plus additional, as needed, for
   thickening)
1¼ cups oat flour (you can make your own oat flour by blending oats in
   a blender)
Pinch of salt
¼ teaspoon baking powder
¼ cup strawberry jam or preserves
Powdered sugar, for dusting (optional)

Preheat oven to 350 degrees. In a mixing bowl, combine the oil, egg, vanilla, milk, and maple syrup and mix well. In a separate bowl, mix together the flours, salt, and baking powder. Then combine the ingredients from both bowls and mix together with your hands until they form a sticky dough. If the dough feels a touch dry, you can add a splash of water to thin it. If it feels a bit wet, you can add a touch more almond or oat flour. Roll the dough into balls with your hands; I like mine to be 1½ to 2 inches across. Place them on a parchment paper–covered or lightly greased cookie sheet, flatten them slightly with your palm, and push a thumbprint into each ball. Add a dollop of jam into the thumbprint. Bake for 15 minutes, or until lightly browned on the bottom. Let cool and sprinkle with powdered sugar, if desired, before eating.

Easy Peanut Butter Cookies

....

Yield: 18 cookies

1 cup brown sugar or sugar of choice
1 cup crunchy peanut butter
1 egg, beaten

Preheat oven to 350 degrees. Line a baking sheet with parchment paper. Stir all the ingredients together until smooth. Roll into 1-inch balls with your hands. Press down with the back of a fork and then press again from the opposite direction, to form the crisscross pattern on top. Bake for 12 minutes. Remove cookies from the oven and let cool before removing to a wire rack to finish cooling.

16

Chocolate Love

....

Fat Dad's "Closet" Brownies,
The Fudge That Says "I Do"

....

I was not looking to fall in love or have a boyfriend. As a matter of fact, I did not even really like boys—especially boys my own age. I understood falling in love with someone on TV, having a crush on some of the brilliant art directors at my dad's advertising agency, and every time Mr. Diner, our profound and life-changing English teacher, read selected passages from *The Metamorphosis*, a part of my soul was transformed. But to be enthralled with a boy my own age seemed unthinkable until Hank Thomas strolled into Miss Seawall's ninth-grade algebra class on a rainy September morning.

He had long, messy brown hair, big green eyes, and wore a Jimi Hendrix T-shirt. The first time he smiled at me with his amazing grin, I started to cry and had to run to the bathroom, as I was completely unprepared for the avalanche of emotions that invaded every fiber of my being. Something about the way he looked at me made me feel like everything was going to be okay, even though I could barely speak when he asked me if I knew the value of one thousand to the twenty-fifth power.

"One-e plus seventy-five," I managed to blurt out, hoping he didn't notice that I was sweating and shaking. I tried my hardest to appear mature, composed, and intelligent, but every time our eyes met and he smiled, I started stuttering and tripping over my words. No one except my grandmother had ever looked at me like that. He looked at me as if he loved me, as if he thought I was beautiful. With every slight exchange, there was the possibility that my life would be different. I had the dress, the shoes, the "I do" speech, and our prewar classic six-room apartment on Central Park West picked out before we even had our first real conversation. I imagined waking him up in the morning with fresh muffins that were made from blueberries that we picked together, and him sipping the piping-hot cup of coffee that I made from the freshly ground beans that I'd purchased the night before at Zabar's.

"Did you warm the milk especially for me?" he would say, pulling me in for a kiss. My grandmother always said, "You can tell if a man loves you if he notices all the little extras you do for him."

Feasting on the muffins—relishing the moistness from the chunks of berries and the sweetness from the brown sugar—he would hold me tight, asking, "How did I ever exist before you?" And I would just smile, hoping he would never let go of me, hoping we would stay enmeshed forever. As much as I knew my fantasy was premature, I also knew there was something real and not made up in my head about the connection we shared.

Hank could have had his pick of any girl in New York City: the disco girls liked him, the Parkie girls liked him, the jockey girls liked him—even the preppy and punk rock girls had his name written all over their notebooks—so the possibility of him picking me to be his girlfriend was next to zero, as Sarah pointed out.

"Every girl in the school wants to be his girlfriend. I heard he even dated Betsy, who is a senior, for three weeks. If you want him to like you, you need to at least pretend you're cool and experienced," Sarah said, showing me how to pucker my lips as she applied her third coat of Bonne Bell bubble-gum lip gloss, adding a little extra on the bottom to make her lips appear fuller.

But somehow I knew, as much as it seemed impossible, and even though I wasn't the most experienced or confident girl, it was meant to be. And he would see in me what I saw in him, and that would override any malfunction in my wardrobe or my lack of a chic style for my hair, which I still wore in braids most days. Hank would realize the future we could share, and he would acknowledge that nobody could love him as deeply and completely as I could.

Hank was unlike other boys that were popular only for their looks or their athletic skills. He was smart, mature, and talented—playing piano, guitar, and composing the most beautiful classical and rock concertos that left both teachers and students in awe. He had the soul of someone older, someone wiser, and someone wounded. He had an intensity that I related to. But unlike Hank, "I was not my best self yet," as Sarah constantly pointed out—trying to help me with style tips, demonstrating how to zip the latest selection of Gloria Vanderbilt jeans by lying on the ground and sucking in her stomach. But I preferred to be comfortable and have Hank love me for who I was, not who I was not.

But with every month that passed, and every equation we

successfully solved, my love for Hank became more desperate. Sarah said that I talked about him nonstop and that if I would not take any of her beauty suggestions—which most girls would stand in line to hear—I should at least entertain the idea of following her new plan that was pretty much guaranteed to move my crush to the next level. I was curious but skeptical.

"You have to swear not to tell anyone, not even your sister or Beauty."

"I swear," I said, promising her that if her idea worked, she could be the maid of honor at my wedding. I would even let her pick out all the bridesmaids' dresses.

She grabbed me close. "It involves Buddhism and baking."

"Okay, I am listening, but what do you know about Buddhism, and how will that help me with Hank?"

"When I want something really bad, I chant for it," Sarah nonchalantly stated, as she reached into her pocket and pulled out a little white card that had the words *nam myoho renge kyo* printed on it in calligraphy. "Some monk gave me this card when I was in the airport coming back from Israel with my dad. He said if I really want something, I should chant these words. I thought it was kind of creepy, but I decided to give it a try, and it has worked every time. My mother has even been coming home from work earlier, and yesterday, I was able to jump over the vaulting horse in gym. That had never happened before. Just as my turn was coming up, I said the chant under my breath, and like magic I flew over the horse, landing with perfect form."

I was hopeful and excited that what Sarah had said could actually work. Both my mom and Beauty believed in controlling fate through unusual rituals. My grandmother Beauty would say *"Kena hora, kena hora, poo poo, poo!"* several times a day as she threw salt and spat over her shoulder. If someone paid my sister or me a compliment or said something in a tone that my grandmother found envious, an extra round of *kena hora*, throwing salt, and spitting over her shoulder was required. My grandmother used very little salt on her food, but she kept several little restaurant packets in her pocketbook to keep us safe from the evil eye.

If my family were going to take a plane or a long trip, my mom had to sit in the dark for a couple of minutes with a deck of tarot cards. One time, when we were going to Florida on a family vacation, she stopped my dad as he was bringing down the suitcases. "We're not going," she declared. My dad explained that the tickets were not refundable, and she told him to trust what she was saying. My dad thought she was crazy but finally relented. That evening we saw on the news that the very plane we were supposed to be on had crashed and there were several fatalities.

So ritual and magic weren't foreign to me. To chant some words to bring lasting love seemed totally logical. I copied the words onto a piece of notebook paper that I was to keep with me all the time, and Sarah showed me the proper way to chant. I repeated the words over and over, turning in three clockwise circles and then in three counterclockwise circles.

"Don't forget to spin each way," she reminded me.

The second part of her plan was that I should infuse a recipe with desire to attract true and everlasting love. Sarah helped guide me on picking the perfect recipe. We both knew it had to be something spectacular, and memorable, and not something carob.

"I think you should make classic chocolate brownies with regular white flour, butter, and sugar. Now wouldn't be the time to mess with his taste buds or try to convert him to your healthy ways. Do not, and I repeat, do not mention that you are trying to be a lacto-vegetarian."

Back in my kitchen, I was overwhelmed with promise. With every ingredient I added into the bowl, I stated my intention, hoping that the brownies would be not just tasty but magical. If the prayer didn't work, surely the brownies could stand on their own merit. Beauty always told me that the way to a man's heart was through his stomach, and I knew my dad would not disagree. He even nicknamed my grandmother's recipe "Closet" Brownies, as every time I would make them, he would dash into the closet with them and devour the whole batch before they were even cooled and sliced.

I debated for hours if I should fill the centers of the brownies with peanut butter, or caramel, or just keep them simple and plain. I had made brownies hundreds of times before, but this time felt different. I could feel my heart pounding hard, like it might suddenly break out of my chest, as I chanted and circled, mixing and stirring, melting and tasting. I felt like I was going to explode or have a heart attack. I was not just making Hank brownies. I was creating my future. I said one more last round of the Buddhist chant before I sealed and wrapped the warm, soft brownies that would secure my fate. To make double sure they had the right combination of moist and crispy, I made an extra batch for my dad to sample when he got home from work. I wanted to see his expression when he tasted them. I was hoping for a thumbs-up review.

"Indeed these are a ten," he would announce in his Bob Barker *The Price Is Right* voice when I made something really outstanding.

I was careful to leave out only two pieces and hide the rest in the freezer so as not to thoroughly sabotage his diet. But he was a guy, and I needed a male opinion on both love and my brownies.

"You know I shouldn't have these," he said, smelling the brownies and looking even more delighted than usual since he had been on the Pritikin Diet for the past six days and hadn't been eating the "stop" ingredients, like butter, sugar, salt, and fat.

"I would never make you break your diet if it was not a desperate emergency. Please just tell me how these brownies make you feel," I said, then blurted out, "I'm in love, I'm in love and I need help!"

"Well, since it is an emergency, I can take a little nibble." My dad took a bite and then another and said, "Any man who would not love you after these would be crazy."

"What about you? Do you love me, Daddy? Do you?" I asked as he finished every last crumb.

"How can you even ask that? You are my little health coach even though you had me break my diet." He grinned and grabbed one more brownie before rushing out to a dinner meeting.

I spent the rest of the evening alone.

The next day I placed the wrapped brownies with the purple bow in Hank's locker, with a note saying, "Call me." I couldn't wait to get the phone call. Would he say he loved the brownies? Would he say he loved me? Or would he just ask me to be his steady girlfriend—realizing that the way the other girls felt about him was like saccharin—fake—but the way I felt about him was real—like honey.

But the day passed, as well as the next seven, and Hank did not say a word. Sarah said he was a jerk, and if I didn't say something to him, she would. I decided to wait for him to come out after band practice. I had hoped Sarah would hang out with me so when he exited the basement, our bumping into each other would look coincidental instead of planned. But she said she had better things to do than wait around for Hank. She had already put far too much effort into my relationship. She now had to pursue her own desires—mainly David Edwards, head of the Young Republicans, debate club, and star of *Pippin*.

"There are much cuter guys at Collegiate. Forget about Hank and come to rehearsal with me. Why wait for one boy when we can hang out at an all-boys school with tons of guys?"

But as far as I was concerned, there were no other boys. Not now, not ever. Hank was the one. I would wait for him as long as it would take. I waited outside the school, watching for the door to swing open and Hank to emerge. I watched and waited, daydreaming about how, after I'd confronted him, the rest of the evening, the rest of our lives, would pan out. I must have fallen asleep on the stairs, because the next thing I knew, Hank was shaking me awake.

"Hey! Are you waiting for someone?"

"You. I was waiting for you."

"Me? Why?"

"I just wanted to know if you got the brownies and if you liked them."

"The brownies were from you? They were rad! Why didn't you write your name? My family ate them in like three seconds. My mom even wanted the recipe, but I couldn't figure out who they were from."

He couldn't figure out who they were from? Who else would they be from? It seemed so obvious. Why was he not able to figure it out? I was a little hurt—well, actually a lot hurt. Just as I was about to forget about Hank forever and bury a little piece of my heart, he asked, "Do you like parties?"

I told him about all the crazy black-tie *Annie* cast parties that I'd attended, in all the different cities, and he said that with my busy social calendar I probably wouldn't have time for just a high school party at his house. Thrilled inside, I tried to maintain my cool, assuring him that I could rearrange my schedule since he was my math partner, and that was something I took very seriously.

He looked confused, but handed me his address on the back of a crumpled old matchbook.

"See you Saturday. This is no *Annie* party. No party dress required, but it is BYOB, so you can bring brownies if you want."

"I will, I will!" I shouted. "I can bring fudge and cookies too."

I ran to the closest pay phone to call Sarah. It seemed like the phone must have rung a hundred times before she finally answered. "Guess where we are going on Saturday, just guess?" I shouted.

"I don't know where you are going, but I am going to Serendipity for frozen hot chocolate with my cast."

"Wrong answer. You are coming with me to Hank's party. Please, oh please," I begged, knowing I would need her to get through the night. She agreed to accompany me to the party if I agreed to let her do a complete makeover on me. She would need the whole day, as there was a lot to make over.

On the morning of the party, before heading to Sarah's, I made my grandmother Beauty's homemade fudge—the chocolate fudge she'd made for Papa the night before he proposed to her, the fudge I'd promised Hank I would bring to the party. Stirring the melted chocolate, evaporated milk, and butter together eased my nerves. I had never been to a high school party before, and I didn't know what to expect or what to wear.

Sarah was in charge of my transformation, spending hours washing, conditioning, and blow-drying my hair, and putting cucumbers on my eyes, and turmeric powder on my face to make my skin look naturally radiant, before she went to town on my eye makeup—using both the blue and the fuchsia sparkles on my lids. She even selected an outfit that would show my curves instead of hiding them.

"Your baggy clothes look sloppy. Try this V-neck velour sweater with my new Fiorucci jeans, and you definitely need boots." The jeans were tight, and the boots were high-heeled, making me look taller, leaner, and older. I barely recognized myself.

"You look exactly like Brooke Shields, minus, like, eight inches," Sarah declared, adding the final touches to my brows, applying little brushstrokes to make them look really full. "See how they frame your eyes? I always knew you were pretty; now Hank will know too."

I could not stop admiring myself. I had no idea who that girl in the mirror was, but I liked her in a way that I had not liked my reflection for the past couple of years. Sarah had me practice my kissing pose with my eyes shut and one leg in the air, as we dusted the final touches of Clinique blush on the apples of our cheeks and sprayed Lauren perfume in the air before running through the mist and heading to the party.

When we arrived, the room was dark and smoky, and Hank was nowhere to be found. The tune "Brown Sugar" was blasting in the background as everyone was bopping up and down and screaming. I felt totally out of place drinking water while everyone else was drinking beer, even though we were all underage. Just when I started thinking I had made a mistake in coming, and was getting ready to go home to watch *The Love Boat*, I felt a hand on my back. It was Hank's. He hugged me and told me how different I looked.

"If it weren't for your green eyes and smile, I would have

never recognized you. Where is my study partner? What did you do to her? Bring her back!"

"I guess you think I look silly."

"That is definitely not what I am thinking." He grabbed my hand, leading me onto the dance floor, where we spent the remainder of the night dancing to the Rolling Stones and the Grateful Dead. He even invited me to the after party, which was supposed to be for only his closest friends. His father, who was a music and film producer, had a copy of *One Flew Over the Cuckoo's Nest*, and it was a tradition to let a small group stay a little later after Hank had a big gathering to view a movie.

We watched the film in his father's den, which doubled as a screening room with a row of real movie seats. One by one, as Jack Nicholson spit pills, Henry, Kenny, Sarah, Cathy, and Malcolm left. I stayed sitting next to Hank, our hands tightly clasped. With each person that left, Hank held me closer, till finally he turned his face to mine. "One flew east, one flew west, one flew over the cuckoo's nest," and while McMurphy argued with Nurse Ratched, Hank kissed me. In that moment nothing else existed.

After that night, we were inseparable. I even showed Hank's mom how to make my "Closet" Brownies, and she showed me how to make Hank's favorite dinner—rotisserie chicken smothered in a can of Campbell's cream of mushroom soup. I'd finally landed my big break. I was madly, deeply, and truly in love.

Fat Dad's "Closet" Brownies

Yield: 16 brownies

8 ounces bittersweet chocolate, chopped, or semisweet chocolate chips
6 tablespoons unsalted butter, plus extra for greasing the pan
¾ cup brown sugar
2 eggs at room temperature, beaten
1 teaspoon vanilla extract
¼ cup flour
½ cup chopped walnuts (optional)
Fresh berries or powdered sugar, for garnish (optional)

Preheat oven to 350 degrees. Grease an 8-inch-square baking dish. In a double boiler, melt the chocolate. Then add the butter, melt, and stir to blend. Remove from heat and pour into a mixing bowl. Stir in the sugar, eggs, and vanilla and mix well.

Add the flour. Mix well, until very smooth. Add the chopped walnuts (if desired). Pour the batter into the greased baking pan. Bake for 35 minutes, or until set and barely firm in the middle. Allow to cool on a rack before removing from pan. Garnish with berries, or powdered sugar, or both, if desired.

Note: *These brownies are more like fudge than cake and contain a fraction of the flour found in traditional brownie recipes.*

The Fudge That Says "I Do"

Yield: 16 pieces

2 cups semisweet chocolate chips
1 cup butterscotch chips
1 (14-ounce) can sweetened condensed milk
1 teaspoon salt
2 tablespoons unsalted butter
1½ teaspoons vanilla
1 tablespoon marshmallow cream
¾ cup chopped walnuts
Parchment paper to line the baking dish

Line an 8-inch square Pyrex baking dish with parchment, making sure the paper covers the bottom and overhangs the sides. Melt the chips in a small saucepan on low heat with the milk, salt, and butter, stirring briskly. When the mixture has melted, remove from heat. Whip hard and fast, then add the vanilla and marshmallow cream and combine well before adding the nuts. Pour the mixture into the baking dish. Place in refrigerator for a couple of hours. When thoroughly chilled, cut into squares and enjoy.

17

Visiting My Sister on Tour

....

Banana Bread, Beauty's Savory
Meatloaf Cupcakes with Mashed Potato
Frosting, Carrot Muffins

....

April's contract was renewed, and she and my mom were going to spend the summer in Washinton, D.C. I was going to visit them for three weeks after spending a month at Hillcrest Camp for the Arts in Connecticut with my friend Marley.

Hillcrest was a performing arts camp where kids were allowed the freedom to arrange their own schedules. The activities ranged from glassblowing, to silk screening, to acting, to stained glass making, to, most important, free choice—which translated into hanging out with cute, artsy boys. Marley was my best friend from Little Red. We spoke daily, even though we'd both left the school after sixth grade. She taught me how to inhale a cigarette, how to line my eyes on the inside ring, and the art of applying black nail polish to look edgy. She had already been to the sleepaway camp for the past three summers and was instrumental in convincing my mom to allow me to go. She said the experience was life changing, and she'd really found her voice as an artist in the printmaking shop. My mom thought I was getting too serious with Hank after I told her I loved him, so she signed me up immediately, even though she found the cost to be outrageous.

My mom equated every experience, every meal, and every activity with cost. She talked about money incessantly, not in the normal way, like other parents did: "We need to save up, we can't afford it, let's wait till it goes on sale, maybe next year." It seemed to have nothing to do with if we could afford it, but everything to do with the fact she thought she was always being gypped, unless it was a super-sale. Any normal purchase—food, clothes, toiletries—seemed to bring her physical pain, and enraged her, causing her to lash out. I was usually on the receiving end of these outbursts, swallowing her rage and internalizing the message that I was not worthy of normal comforts.

If we went to a restaurant, no matter what I picked to order, she would say it was too expensive. And she would never order anything for herself, mostly opting for the free bread dipped in ketchup; or she would help herself to other people's food using her bare hands to grab piles of French fries or onion rings, or cut hunks of meat without even asking. She wanted to make sure there was no confusion when we were out with friends that the check would be split into equal parts.

"Your father spends all the money on himself, so whatever little allowance he gives me to run the house needs to be saved for a rainy day. You always live in the moment! You never think about what will happen tomorrow," was my mother's familiar chant.

My mother felt no shame about screaming or humiliating

me in public. Beauty once told me, "When your mom was three years old, she hit her head while crawling under the table to get a napkin. At the time, I thought it was tomato sauce; but maybe it was blood, and I did not treat it as an injury. Maybe, that's why your mother gets a little *meshugganah*. You shouldn't take it to heart; just do your best not to antagonize her."

I knew Beauty's advice was sound, but it was difficult not to antagonize my mom—even if I didn't do it intentionally. She constantly hounded me, particularly when she was on the road with April, about how much I was spending on groceries. And when she was home, she would go through my shopping bags or my purse to look for receipts. "Twenty-five cents for a pear? I can buy one down the street for a nickel. Why would you buy chicken breasts when you could buy a whole package of legs for half the price? Your expensive eating habits will land you in the poorhouse."

I never really did anything wrong, but somehow I could never do anything right, and my mother constantly used words and tones that were so harsh that I was in a constant state of turmoil. The fact that I preferred fresh seafood and vegetables to soggy SpaghettiOs for dinner somehow irked her, making her feel unappreciated and enraged. I was not your typical kid, and my parents were not your typical parents, and the combination of our unique quirks and habits was extremely toxic and unsettling. So the thought of going to sleepaway camp, where I wouldn't have to worry what diet my dad was on, or if I would have enough money for food for the week, or what I was going to cook each night for dinner, was a welcome relief.

Marley had been to other camps before that had terrible food, but she said I would be overjoyed when I saw the quality and amounts of food at Hillcrest. She knew that if I were still a little hesitant about leaving Hank and cutting my summer short with April, the way to sell me was getting me to crave the food.

"For dinners, they always have charcoal-broiled meats. You can smell the hamburgers and barbecued chicken all the way at the lake. And there is a salad bar almost as long as a New York City block with cucumbers, chopped eggs, bacon bits, sliced avocadoes, artichoke hearts, and garbanzo beans. Breakfast is the best. They have the Hillcrest Slammer, which is like one of those Lumber Jack Specials that we have at the coffee shop with your dad. Just imagine scrambled eggs, French toast, grilled sausage, and the biggest bowl of fruit you have ever seen every morning." I was convinced.

Arriving at camp, I was assigned to bunk number 11 with Naomi Weinstein and the two Jills, both with last names starting with S. Jill Simon cried every night because she missed her parents and the comforts of home. Jill Schaffer was from Long Island and had a thick island accent and over-plucked eyebrows. She spent hours perfecting her hair with a curling iron, which she plugged into the single outlet in our bunk's musty doorless bathroom—while the rest of us waited for our turn to use the shower. Naomi Weinstein was a quirky girl with more mosquito bites than I had ever seen, but the two of us became inseparable. She was super–boy crazy and super-chatty, keeping us up all night with every detail of her rotating daily crushes, determined this was the summer she was going to have a boyfriend with big muscles to get past first base with. She was not going to let a little calamine lotion, which she dotted all over her face to soothe the itching, get in her way.

Marley, who had convinced me to take a break from Hank

to spend the summer with her, was on a different side of the camp. Even though we were both fifteen, she was a CIT (counselor in training) instead of a camper because of her experience from years past in the crafts studios, so it was often hard to see her. Her days were overrun by her many responsibilities, or her new boyfriend Eric, who was not a camper, but had a real job at the camp, cleaning the mess hall and disposing of the garbage.

Naomi and I would sometimes sneak out in the middle of the night and go to Marley's cabin, where all the junior staff would congregate and drink coffee with Kahlúa in water canteens after lights-out. For one of the first times in my life, I had the luxury of not having to care for anyone, not even myself. I could drift through my day with ease and even rebel without guilt. Naomi, my new best friend, was right there with me as her mother had just gotten remarried and sent her to camp while she was on her honeymoon.

While there was a designated time for rising, sleeping, eating, swimming, and socializing, the camp believed in free choice; you could choose to attend or not attend whatever activities you wanted. The setting was very tranquil with kids strumming on their guitars, batik-making in tents, and many other crafting experiences to choose from. I spent most of my days either in the tie-dye tent, where I made multicolored purple tank tops to wear to the weekly dance, or in painting class, where I learned how to re-create the lush greenery of the camp by using dots instead of brushstrokes.

At night, my bunkmates and I would dress up to sit on our porch and make bracelets and headbands out of daisies and play jacks by moonlight. Each bunk contained four campers with two bunk beds and no live-in chaperone. The cabins were arranged boy girl, boy girl—the girls living in the odd-numbered cabins, and the boys living in the even-numbered ones. The cabins were all in a row, and there was one counselor for a block of ten cabins. Ethan Clark was next door in bunk number 10. He had a bad reputation from years prior, and Naomi had heard from Sally, who heard from Katie in bunk number 15, to stay away from him. But after everyone was asleep, he would throw rocks at my window trying to get me to come outside and sit behind the bunk with him. He laughed when I told him I was not interested, and that I had a very serious boyfriend that I would someday marry. It took him about a week and a batch of chocolate cupcakes made with imported chocolate to convince me to sneak down by the lake with him. I remember the sounds of the crickets and the eerie feeling sitting in the pitch-dark eating the cupcakes.

I was so impressed that Ethan had made them himself and transported them all the way to camp from Manhattan. He said he had been saving them for a special night, and he would not share his cupcakes—his own special recipe—with just anyone. I was so moved by his gesture. I did not know any boys who baked, and certainly no boy had ever baked for me. Perhaps Ethan was thinking of becoming a chef. I had so many questions for him. Did he have a girlfriend at home? Why did he choose this camp? Was he an aspiring artist? Where did he live in the city? How did he get his curls to hang so perfectly, framing his face while not covering his beautiful brown eyes with the little flecks of green? I began firing a list of questions at him, trying to remember as he stroked my cheek and ran his hands down my back, that I had a boyfriend—a serious boyfriend who loved me and had given me a thin silver-knot promise ring, which he had purchased at a street fair the night before I left, to remember him by.

But suddenly, I couldn't remember anything. Everything was fuzzy, I was slurring my words, and Ethan was making fun of me. "Wow, those treats really hit you," he laughed. I had no idea what he meant. I was shivering and sick to my stomach. I told him I thought the hamburger from dinner was undercooked and that I might have food poisoning. I felt strange and wanted to go to the infirmary to get my temperature checked. He just kept looking at me and laughing, telling me I would feel good in a minute, tilting my head back and pushing my body into the mushy, wet mud. I begged for him to let me up and take me back to my bunk. He kept shushing me. "If you stay quiet, this will be the best night of your life."

When the morning bugle sounded for breakfast, I found myself in my bed. Naomi was standing over me with a cold washcloth. Ethan was nowhere in sight. I didn't know how I'd gotten back to my bunk and had a hard time piecing together the events of the previous evening. I just remembered Ethan's curls and his firm embrace. Naomi explained that what Ethan had given me was no ordinary cupcake. She said he was dangerous, and she made me swear never to see him again. I promised, but I betrayed her and Hank and continued to sneak out with Ethan, night after night. Until one night, he didn't come to my window to pick me up. I made Naomi sneak out of bed to help me look for him. When we found him, he was with a younger camper. Naomi simply said, "I told you so," when we found him in the exact same spot he always took me. He looked unapologetic as Naomi shined the flashlight on him, then the girl.

"He's not worth it . . . none of them are," Naomi said.

I didn't know if she was talking about Ethan, the boys who

didn't notice her, her father who'd abandoned her, or her mom's new husband. I didn't ask, absorbed by my own embarrassment and despair. We clung to each other silently, trying to find the path back to our bunk. The night was damp, and a chilly feeling of disbelief and sickness washed over me, worse than when I ate Ethan's special cupcake. I tried not to obsess about what I had witnessed—knowing it was my own fault, knowing it was only a couple of weeks till I would be reunited with Hank.

The last weeks of camp I took advantage of all the different workshops and tried to tap into my creativity as a diversion from my emotions. I found it pretty easy not only to get lost in all the artistic endeavors but to bond with other boys at the camp as well as my bunkmates. The month had gone fast, and I was truly sorry that I hadn't committed to attend the second session like Marley. On the last day, both of the Jills' parents came to pick them up. Jill Schaffer's parents drove from Long Island in a nondescript faded blue station wagon; Jill Simon's parents drove from Manhattan in a beautiful, shiny white Mercedes with brown leather seats. No one came for Naomi or me.

Jill Simon's parents insisted that we drive back to Manhattan with their family instead of taking the camp bus. They even made reservations at the fabulous Maxwell's Plum for an end-of-summer celebratory supper, where no one talked about the cost of what we ordered. They thanked Naomi and me for encouraging Jill to make it through the four weeks—even though it was just as painful for them as for her to be separated. Jill was a change-of-life baby whose mother was so astounded by her good fortune that she kept Jill as close as possible most of the time. Nothing was too extravagant for Jill and her friends. They even encouraged me to order the most expensive items on the menu.

Even though my parents were not there, I heard their voices

echoing in my ear as I ordered. "Only a stupid person would waste all that money on a meal." "I wonder how many calories this meal will set me back." But my parents' voices faded as I feasted on escargot with herbs, Rock Cornish Hens a l'Orange, and chestnut cake with a side of strawberries. It was a fabulous dinner, and I was grateful both for the meal and to be included in their family dinner.

Outside the restaurant Naomi, Jill, and I exchanged numbers before we parted ways, swearing we would make sure to call one another every night. Jill's dad hailed taxis for me and Naomi and even paid the cab drivers in advance to cover our fares. I gave the driver Hank's address, anxious to see him.

"Good luck with lover boy," Naomi and Jill screamed out as my taxi pulled away.

I nervously rang Hank's doorbell. We hadn't seen each other in a full month, and guilt about what happened with Ethan weighed heavily on me. Hank seemed genuinely happy to see me, despite the big hickey on his neck that he tried to conceal with his puka bead necklace. Not knowing how to react, confused and guilt-ridden myself, I shouted, "I never want to see you again!"

I raced down his long hallway, dragging my camp duffel bag behind me. I hoped he would follow me and get down on his hands and knees and beg for my forgiveness, sobbing, "Dawn, Dawn, forgive me!" as passionately as Stanley Kowalski called for Stella in *A Streetcar Named Desire*. I imagined I would melt into his arms like soft butter and we would be inseparable forever. But he never came after me.

I exited his building into the hot summer night and plopped myself on my favorite stoop. I felt lost, hot, and dirty. I didn't want to go home; my dad wouldn't be there, and I couldn't bear the thought of sitting in that dark, oppressive brownstone all alone. The train I was scheduled to take to Washington did not leave till mid-morning, so I spent the night at the twenty-four-hour Hamburger Heaven on Sixty-Second Street. I passed the time drinking iced coffee with skim milk and smoking unfiltered cigarettes—a habit that I'd acquired at camp.

I was exhausted and disheveled by the time I arrived at the Sheridan Hotel in Washington with my army jacket and my long peacock-feather earring that I'd made in the camp jewelry workshop. The hotel was really nice, with a pool, a kids' game room, and a coffee shop where all the orphans and their moms would congregate for a buffet breakfast since it was included in the price of the room. April had told me awful stories about some of the hotels they had stayed in on the tour. She said the hotel in Detroit had bloodstains on the rug, and the one in Florida had giant water bugs. Some of the other families always stayed in luxury hotels, and the parents spent their children's salaries freely. Not my mom. My mother saved every cent my sister earned—and rather than letting April squander it on frivolous things like toys and new dresses—she invested it. But this time, she had bonus points from her credit card that would expire, so she was able to redeem her points for a two-room suite.

As soon as April opened the door, she inspected me, searching my pockets and bags for presents. "Where are you hiding my packages? I know you have banana bread somewhere in that bag of yours, maybe even those muffins that you think are so healthy with the carrot pieces. What about that new recipe you said Beauty just sent you for meatloaf cupcakes with mashed potato frosting? I have been dying to try those. Beauty was pretty convinced that you were going to bring me a dozen. Come on, where are they? I'm really, really hungry."

Totally immersed in my own drama, I had arrived empty-handed. I always had something for my sister, whether I was picking her up from school, a friend's house, or coming to an opening night. I had disappointed her and I felt terrible. I apologized, telling her I would make it up to her when I was less worn out.

"You never forget to bring me something. I hope you are not turning into Mommy. You are even starting to look like her. Your shoes look like her hooker platforms that we used to hide when Ugly George would follow her down the street trying to videotape her for his sleazy cable show."

She continued to antagonize me, stretching herself across her king-sized bed covered with Annie dolls and flashing her fourteen-karat gold *Annie* head necklace with the diamond eyes. "While you were at lame camp dances, I have been at wild cast parties. I know all about sex, homosexuality, and drugs that give you energy so you can dance all night. I even know how two men have sex, and two girls have sex, and how to turn a man on by sitting on his lap and calling him Daddy. I am not so innocent anymore. I probably know more than you," she said, shaking her ten-year-old hips from side to side. "I will tell you all the bad things that we do backstage if you tell me what happened at camp and why you're acting so weird."

As much as I wanted to share my woes about Ethan and how Hank and I broke up, and how I just wanted to curl up in a ball and hide for a little while, I listened to April as she purposely tried to hurt me for abandoning her for the first part of the summer. As April told me tale after tale, I was horrified at how both my sister and my life seemed to be coming apart.

"One night when all us orphans were bored from doing the same show night after night, we decided to do high kicks without our bloomers so the audience could see our underwear. And one night, I overheard some of the moms talking, saying that they felt sorry for me because Mommy was so neglectful, often leaving me in the room by myself while she sat in the lobby with the marionette man that she met when all the kids were invited to a special performance of a puppet show. And did I mention that I never get up before one p.m.?"

Before my sister could utter another word, my mother came bursting into the room. "You have ten minutes to get dressed. We are going to the White House for lunch. It is a good thing, April, that your sister is here. She can help fix you up."

"Who's going where?" I asked.

"Me and all the orphans are going to sing 'It's a Hard Knock Life' for Amy Carter," April boasted. "She's a fan of the show. She came backstage three times. After we sing, she is going to give us a private tour of the White House, and we are going to have a pizza party in their private bowling alley."

While it was an honor to go to the White House and meet Jimmy Carter, it paled in comparison to watching my sister perform. I never grew bored of seeing her on stage, or watching fans waiting outside the theater for the chance to get her autograph. Supporting my sister and being there for her was more important than any problem I had with any stupid boys. I was back on track, cooking in the hotel suite, talking to my grandmother on a daily basis, and helping my mom create album after album of all my sister's newspaper clippings. For the rest of the summer, I spent every minute with April, except when she was performing. We walked around downtown Washington, visited a house in Georgetown where the Wright Brothers once stayed, and went to a little convenience store every evening where they had frozen fruit bars made with real fruit.

On my last night in Washington before I had to return to New York to attend my sophomore year of high school, I gave my sister a little stuffed heart with big white angel wings for her dressing room. April smiled at me and handed the heart back to me. "I have my wings," she said. "Now it's time for you to find yours."

Banana Bread

Yield: 1 loaf

1 cup sugar
¼ cup unsalted butter, softened, plus extra for greasing the pan
2 eggs, beaten
3 ripe bananas, mashed
½ cup full-fat plain yogurt (not Greek yogurt)
1 teaspoon vanilla
1½ cups flour
1 teaspoon baking soda
½ teaspoon salt

Preheat oven to 350 degrees. Grease a 9 x 5 x 3-inch loaf pan. In a large bowl, beat together the sugar and butter. Add the eggs, bananas, yogurt, and vanilla; blend well. Add the flour, baking soda, and salt to the wet ingredients. Mix well. Pour into the greased loaf pan. Bake for 50 to 60 minutes, or until a toothpick inserted in the center comes out clean. Cool for 20 minutes and remove from the pan.

Note: *This recipe was given to my grandmother Beauty by my grandmother Bubbe Mary. Bubbe used twice the sugar and sour cream instead of yogurt.*

Beauty's Savory Meatloaf Cupcakes with Mashed Potato Frosting

....

Yield: 12 cupcakes

FOR THE CUPCAKES:
1 teaspoon olive oil
1 cup finely chopped onion
½ cup finely chopped carrot
3 garlic cloves, minced
1 teaspoon oregano
1½ pounds ground turkey or extra lean ground beef
½ cup ketchup (plus more for topping)
1 cup saltine crackers (about 20), finely crushed
2 tablespoons mustard
1½ teaspoons Worcestershire sauce
¼ teaspoon freshly ground black pepper
2 eggs
Cooking spray

FOR THE ICING:
2 potatoes, boiled, peeled, and cubed
2 tablespoons butter
2 tablespoons milk
Salt and pepper, to taste

Preheat oven to 350 degrees. Heat the olive oil in a large skillet over medium-high heat. Add the onion, carrot, garlic, and oregano to the skillet and sauté for 2 to 3 minutes. Set the veggies aside to cool. In a large bowl, combine the meat, ketchup, crackers, mustard, Worcestershire, and pepper. Add the cooled veggie mixture and the eggs, and mix it all together.

Coat a 12-cup muffin pan with cooking spray. Divide the meat mixture evenly among the cups. Top each muffin with a spoonful of ketchup that you spread over the top. Bake for 25 minutes. While the cupcakes are baking, mash the potatoes with the butter, milk, salt, and pepper. When the meatloaf cupcakes come out of the oven, serve with a scoop of mashed potatoes on top.

Carrot Muffins

¼ cup oats, divided
1 cup whole wheat flour
1 cup all-purpose flour
2 teaspoons baking soda
½ teaspoon cinnamon
½ teaspoon salt
1 cup light brown sugar
¾ cup oil or melted unsalted butter or butter substitute
1 cup full-fat yogurt (not Greek)
½ cup unsweetned applesauce
3 eggs, at room temperature
2 teaspoons vanilla
½ cup unsweetened coconut
2 cups finely shredded and dried carrots
½ cup raisins
½ cup walnuts

Preheat oven to 350 degrees. Line muffin pans with baking cups. Evenly divide half the oats among the liners and set aside. In a medium bowl, sift together the flours, baking soda, cinnamon, and salt and set aside. In a large bowl, with a handheld or stand mixer on medium speed, combine the brown sugar and oil. Beat in the yogurt and applesauce until thoroughly combined. In about 1 minute the mixture will be gritty and thin. Add the eggs one at a time and beat well. Mix in the vanilla, then stir the dry ingredients into the wet ingredients till well combined. Fold in the coconut, carrots, raisins, and walnuts. Pour into the prepared cupcake liners. Sprinkle the remaining oats on top. Bake for 20 minutes, or until a toothpick comes out clean.

18

Studio 54

....

Traditional French Onion Soup,
Pritikin-Approved Lentil Stew

....

The first time I went to Studio 54 was on a dare. My old friend Robyn from the Little Red School House called suggesting we get together. When I told her I would love to see her, she suggested meeting at Studio 54 on Saturday night. Hearing the hesitation in my voice, she questioned if I had ever been to the popular club before. I assured her that I had.

"So funny we have never seen each other."

"Yeah, so weird."

Panicked by my lie, I put Marley on the phone with Robyn to say hi.

"We go all the time," Marley said in a calm, convincing voice. "Don't worry. We'll have no problem getting in. Midnight it is. We will see you by the moon with the spoon."

As soon as Marley hung up the phone, she turned to me with

wide eyes. "Holy shit. I told her we would meet her inside Studio, by some moon."

"How are we going to get in?" The closest I had ever been to Studio 54 or any club was driving by in a taxi while going to the Alvin Theatre to pick up a contract for my sister.

"I don't t know how we'll get in, but we just have to. Otherwise, she'll think we are totally lame."

The night we were making the plan, my dad happened to be home and he overheard us talking. He chimed in saying he had been a few times, but he had no pull. He had always been on a guest list or been escorted by a model after a shoot. "My best advice is walk up like you own the place," he said, telling the story of how he had heard that Bianca Jagger rode up on a horse to enter the velvet ropes—and some other celebrity arrived in a helicopter that landed right on the roof of the building. "The club thrives on theatrics and variety. The owner likes the crowd to be like a 'tossed salad,' not too much of one particular type. So you girls need to look really different to stand out. And just in case you do get in, you should probably have an ID," my dad advised, handing Marley and me forty-five bucks to go to one of the souvenir shops on Forty-Second Street to purchase the fake identification cards—making us a few years older than our real age of fifteen.

"Whatever is left, you girls can use toward the entrance fee," my dad said, crossing his fingers as he wished us luck—even though he did not think the odds were in our favor.

Marley did not think we needed luck. She went to Music and Art High School and was an art major. She even took sewing classes on the weekends, so costuming was second nature for her. "I will make us harlequin outfits, mine will be black on the left and gold on the right; yours will be the opposite."

"We could also wear my *Annie* satin baseball jackets," I said.

"I hear all the girls from the Broadway cast get in all the time. We can go around eleven o'clock and kind of merge with the crowd."

Marley was nervous the whole week, calling everyone she knew for tips. "If we get in, this will totally change our status to super-cool. I have read about all the high-profile parties and celebrity sightings. It seems amazing."

I really just wanted to see Robyn, but somehow, I got swept into this elaborate plan of reading Page Six to find out what celebrities went there and running around to thrift shops and the garment district to pick out interesting materials to create our outfits, while fighting over which one of us would get to make out with Mick Jagger. We also had to decide if we would keep our real names for our IDs or if we would use the last name of a celebrity—Redford, Taylor, Newman—to make it seem like we were related to someone famous.

"Mr. Bouncer, Mr. Bouncer, my father is Robert Redford. My name is Shauna, did you not see me in the society papers the other day?"

"Beauty always says I look like Elizabeth Taylor when she was younger. I can pretend I am her daughter."

"Does she even have a daughter our age?" Marley questioned.

"I'm not sure. Maybe we should just stick to our own names since we both have some famous connections, my sister being an *Annie* orphan and your dad being a kind of famous coat designer. His winter tweed jacket even made it to the cover of *Vogue* magazine five years ago. I know your dad can definitely help us. Maybe he could even call Halston on our behalf. He is a regular at Studio. That would definitely get us in."

Marley said that her dad was not cool like my dad, and there was no way he would help us. "Besides, my parents would kill me if they knew we were going to a club. I told them we were staying home at your house, cooking all night. I even mentioned what we were making: your famous chili, homemade corn bread with the honey butter glaze, and the legendary China Town Fruit Salad with the lychee fruit. It was hard enough to convince my mom not to call your dad. Luckily, she trusts you. We just need to take the phone off the hook at your house so if she decides to check in, she will keep getting a busy signal."

"We can also make a lentil chili so you can bring her a big hefty portion—that way she will never question it."

"Who has time to think about chili?" Marley protested.

"I was just trying to help. Besides, I have the best new recipe. My dad has been on this new diet called the Pritikin Plan, and all the recipes are so easy to make and really low in calories and fat. We can eat a big bowl of chili before we go out, and make extra for my dad and your mom and still fit nicely into our outfits. It is a win-win situation."

"These outfits are definitely not forgiving, so anything that won't make us look bloated would probably be a good dinner choice."

"And when you walk in the door Sunday morning with the chili adorned with onions, carrots, and celery, your mom will think we were home slaving over a hot stove all night."

"Whatever you think we need to do so my mom won't get suspicious. You know how my mom gets. Lately, she has even been smelling my hair to see if it smells like smoke. I told her it was from the smoking lounge in school where I go to do homework, but I'm not sure if she believed me. Every day she gives me the same boring speech. 'Marley, if you smoke, you are not only hurting yourself, but our whole family. Marley, all you care about is fun. Life is about setting goals, and hard work.' I don't think either of my parents understands what it is like to be a teenager. This is our time," she said, falling onto my bed reciting the lyrics to the hottest new disco song, "Born to Be Alive."

Marley's dad was a Holocaust survivor and her mother was a workaholic, helping her husband make a success of his business, so the idea of frivolous, carefree fun was not in either of their vocabularies. Marley was the opposite; she loved having fun and was usually pretty good at orchestrating elaborate plans. And tonight's plan was pretty elaborate. I started on the chili while Marley got all our stuff ready.

The lentil chili needed to simmer an hour, so we had plenty of time to get dressed. With makeup strewn all over my bed, Marley got to work transforming us into disco divas—spandex outfits, teased hair, and makeup that glittered and shined. We dove into the eye shadow, lipstick, and rouge, smearing pink frosted lipstick on our cheeks, eyelids, and lips. As Marley blasted the disco single that she'd purchased at Tower Records, I began to feel in the spirit. She finished off our theatrical outfits with high-heeled red cowboy boots, before we ventured into the night.

To make sure we had enough money for an entrance fee, we opted not to take a taxi and instead walked in our six-inch heels from the East Side to the West Side. We definitely were noticeable, with our skintight clothes and clumps of wet silver sparkles on our faces and in our hair, and more than one guy approached us thinking we were working girls. I just kept my head down and walked as fast as I could, which wasn't fast at all with those boots. Just when I thought my throbbing feet couldn't take another step, we turned up Fifty-Fourth Street and there it was—Studio 54.

There were even more people and cars than we had imagined. The street was backed up with tons of long limousines lining it, and there was a sea of people—hundreds, maybe even thousands—all dressed in the most outrageous outfits. Some people were half-naked, wrapped in Saran Wrap, others in evening gowns, others dressed as Egyptian pharaohs, and still others dressed like the Village People—the cowboy, the biker, and the construction worker complete with a hard hat. I saw one woman completely painted gold from head to toe and wearing roller skates, and many men were dressed as women, with bright wigs that stood several inches high. It was a show in itself.

"Marley, there is no way we are going to get in. It's a mob scene! We can't even get close to the entrance. No one can even see us back here."

"No is not an option. Just follow me." Determined, Marley began pushing her way through the crowd, holding up two fingers.

Everyone was screaming out at the bouncers as they stood on fire hydrants to see above the masses, surveying the crowds to determine who would gain entrance.

"Steve, over here."

"Marc, please, I'm on the guest list."

"Steve, I am your cousin. We used to spend our summers together."

"Marc, I was just here last night. I'll just die if you don't let me in this evening. I will do anything," one woman promised, flashing her multicolored nipple lights. Everyone was trying to get Marc's and Steve's attention, and I had no idea how we would stand out amid all this chaos. But before I knew it, Marley had locked arms with Andy Warhol, and somehow we became part of his entourage sweeping past the velvet ropes. Going through the massive crowds, I was sure I was going to be squished to death. My heart was racing, pounding with both exhilaration and fear as we bypassed body after body.

"Can you believe it?" Marley exclaimed, jumping up and down once we were through the club doors. "Was that not the greatest moment of your entire existence? I will remember this day for the rest of my life!" Marley turned around trying to rejoin Andy's crowd, but he had already been swept away by another entourage, and we were shoved into the line to pay our fifteen-dollar entrance fee where nobody even asked for our IDs—or cared that we weren't eighteen, the legal drinking age in New York.

"The younger the better," one man commented as he admired our outfits.

"Told you we could do it," Marley said, dancing down the mirrored hallway.

"Let's see if Robyn is here yet."

"Forget Robyn. Look at this place."

"I thought the whole point of getting in was coming to see her," I said.

"We'll meet up with her. It's only eleven-thirty; we have a half hour to explore. Anyway, it is good to be fashionably late."

We made our way across the first floor, then took a flight of stairs halfway up to the next level. From the balcony, we could see the whole club. Studio 54 was originally a theater used to tape *The Ed Sullivan Show*. The owners kept the original structure of the theater, with a stage, backdrops, and pulleys that raised and lowered the blinking lights that were syncopated to the music. There was a row of bleachers, where I witnessed many naked bodies pressed up against each other—no one seemed to care about privacy as they frolicked freely. It was like nothing I had ever seen or experienced before, but I was immediately sucked in, as I peered over the railing to watch. Dry ice machines created billows of smoke that rose from the dance floor. An eccentric and eclectic crowd snorted various substances up their noses at the surrounding tables, and it looked like another party was happening in the unisex bathrooms on either side of the balcony.

All the patrons were fabulous, chosen at the front door for their distinct looks, beauty, and fame. Celebrities were everywhere; Jerry Hall, the supermodel, was right next to me in the bathroom. We even ate breath mints from the same candy bowl, and I could have used the same brush as her, if I had given the bathroom attendant one dollar to indulge in the spread of beauty products she had laid out for the evening.

While I was obsessed with all the celebrities huddling in the bathroom—trying to overhear their conversations and hoping they were talking about something newsworthy—Marley couldn't stop talking about the bartenders.

"I have never seen so many gorgeous guys in one place. Each one is hotter than the next. I love those cute little gold gym shorts and how they're all bare-chested. You know how I feel about well-defined, strong arms."

Marley wasn't the only one enamored of the bartenders. There were as many people surrounding them as there were people on the dance floor. They were an attraction all on their own—pouring both cheap mixed drinks at the bar and serving expensive bottles of champagne in chilled buckets to the VIP tables. Marley kept smiling at different men sitting in the booths, hoping that one of them would invite us to join him for a glass of Moët & Chandon or Dom Pérignon. I felt like we had been transported into a dream, as the beat of the disco music pulsated, matching the rhythm of my heart.

Heading back downstairs, we saw the lit-up man in the moon with the spoon where we were to meet Robyn. The spoon kept swinging back and forth over the dance floor to the nose of the moon and then back the other way. Right at midnight, we spotted Robyn. It had only been a couple of years since we had seen her, but she looked completely different and way older. She probably could have passed for twenty-five with her false eyelashes, crimped bleached hair, and revealing sequin halter jumpsuit. She looked like a real disco queen.

"I can't believe you made it," Robyn said.

"We told you we were coming," I said and beamed.

"Who did you come with?" Marley asked Robyn.

Without answering, she motioned us to the bar, where she had free drink tickets, which she made sure we saw, and began kissing a guy holding a tray of empty glasses.

"We're kind of an item. Have you guys ever dated one of the busboys or waiters?"

"A few," Marley said.

"Most of them are bisexual or gay. You know that, right?"

Marley just rolled her eyes, pretending everything Robyn said was common knowledge while passing me secret looks.

"If you date a busboy, he can usually sneak you through the back of the club, so you can avoid all that front door hassle. That is how I always get in. But if you date a waiter, you can get a VIP card, and you are invited to all kinds of important dinner parties, and get to take limos when the club closes, to Brasserie for brie and ham omelets with French fries, or to the Empire Diner for meatloaf and warm brownies with ice cream. They usually have so much cash on them that they do not mind picking up the tab."

"I so need to date a bartender," I declared.

"You and everyone else in New York City!"

Delivering that important bit of information, Robyn disappeared onto the dance floor with her busboy, and then moments later, she was not only with him but sandwiched between two other guys with even less clothes than the busboys. Marley followed, gyrating between them. At first, I thought it was a little creepy dancing with men who never asked my name, who were practically naked and probably didn't even like girls. But within minutes of hitting the dance floor, we were in the middle of this dance circle surrounded by Liza Minnelli, Mariel Hemingway, and Mason Reese, the redheaded kid from the Underwood Deviled Ham commercials who was shorter than me but apparently pretty popular, because people were taking his picture. He was not a busboy or waiter, but he liked girls and was fun to dance with as he broke out in all kinds of kooky dance moves—oblivious to how silly he looked. "We all look beautiful here!" he shouted, pointing to the lights shining on us.

The club was a frenzy of energy, music, and sweat. No matter where you turned, people were touching one another, dancing in pairs, dancing in groups—just dancing with total freedom as feathers, balloons, and confetti exploded from the ceiling. Filled with adrenaline, I could not stop moving, pinching myself that this was all real. I was in the center of something amazing, something unexplainable—something that just felt right.

That night came and went in an instant, but the lure of the club became an addiction. After that evening, I became a regular. I babysat, I worked in clothing stores, at a Fotomat—any odd job I could find to be able to buy fabulous outfits and have money for the entrance fee. Each and every time I made it past the velvet ropes, I felt like I'd won an Academy Award. And each and every time, my confidence and my belief in myself grew.

In the beginning, I was going only on the weekends with Marley or Sarah, sometimes even Robyn. But they could not get out of the house during the week, so I started going on my own—eventually realizing that I could just bring my school bag and an extra set of clothes and change in the bathroom of

Brasserie, where I went several mornings for a bite after the club had closed.

My routine was school, homework, and making a pot of soup for my dad and myself, followed by a disco nap before heading out of the house at midnight for an evening of dancing and then a breakfast of quiche lorraine and French onion soup at Brasserie before heading to school.

With my mom and my sister on the road for a couple more months and my dad wrapped up in his own life, I discovered the joys of being fifteen in New York City without a curfew. In the darkness of the clubs, I found my own fame. I no longer took a backseat in my life. The nightlife was my life. I spent every night—and I mean every night—dancing at Studio 54, Xenon, or the Mud Club. I was a VIP, never doubting my entrance as hundreds stood outside. I danced on speakers, met celebrities, and gained much attention for my underage status and youthful looks. I even got that kiss with Mick Jagger.

Many people I befriended fell victim to drugs and alcohol as an escape. For me, the escape was the music, the colorful people, and the before and after meals at Trader Vic's, Brasserie, and the Empire Diner that made my world euphoric—allowing me to realize my own dreams and fantasies.

Traditional French Onion Soup

Yield: 4–6 servings

3 tablespoons butter
5 Spanish onions, chopped fine
1½ tablespoons flour
2 garlic cloves, mashed
8 cups beef stock, boxed or homemade (page 53)
½ cup dry white wine
¼ teaspoon dry thyme
Salt and pepper, to taste
6 slices French baguette
1½ cups shredded imported Gruyère cheese

In a large pot over low heat, melt the butter and add the onions. Sauté the onions very slowly, until they are soft and golden, but not too brown. Add the flour and cook the onions a minute longer. Add the garlic and sauté for another 2 minutes. Add the stock, wine, and thyme and let simmer for about 30 minutes. Add the salt and pepper to taste.

Preheat oven to 200 degrees. Place the bread slices in the oven and let them toast. Portion the soup into ovenproof bowls, float the bread on top, cover with cheese, and broil until the cheese is melted and nicely browned. Serve immediately and enjoy.

Pritikin-Approved Lentil Stew

Yield: 4–6 servings

2 tablespoons extra virgin olive oil
2 carrots, washed, peeled, and diced
2 celery stalks, washed and diced
1 small, yellow onion, diced
4 garlic cloves, diced
6 cups low-sodium vegetable stock
1 sweet potato, diced
1 tomato, washed, peeled, and diced
1 cup brown lentils
1 bay leaf
2 teaspoons kosher or coarse sea salt

Pour the olive oil into a large pot and heat over medium-high heat. Add the carrots, celery, onion, and garlic, and sauté the veggies for about 5 minutes, or until softened, stirring frequently. Add the stock, sweet potato, tomato, lentils, bay leaf, and salt. Bring to a boil over high heat and stir. Let boil for a couple of minutes, and then reduce heat to low, partially cover, and simmer for about 1 hour. Stir the stew occasionally, until the lentils are very tender.

19

My Parents' Divorce

....

Violetta's Vitello Tonnato, Real Italian
Tiramisu, African Chai Tea

....

When my mom and sister returned from touring with *Annie*, my parents staying together was no longer an option, even though neither of them wanted to leave our three-story rent-controlled brownstone.

My dad had met a woman while working in Italy. Violetta was an Italian from the Bronx who re-created herself while living in Milan. She was as passionate about food as my dad, and after a couple of weeks of eating their way through Italy, my dad invited Violetta to move to New York with him. Of course, he was still married and living with my mom, but within a few weeks of meeting Violetta, he found a swanky, modern high-rise apartment a couple blocks down from our house.

The evening my dad moved out, I was on the phone with Sarah talking about a guy I'd met the night before at Danceteria. I was sitting on the patchwork, Moroccan-tiled kitchen floor,

278

and just like that, my dad started to walk out with his suitcases. When I asked him where he was going, thinking it was one of his usual exotic trips, he casually stated he was moving out. I stared at him for just a moment before I went right back to my conversation with Sarah. I may have mentioned to her that I thought my parents might be getting divorced, but then I continued to grill her, wanting to know if she thought the guy with the purple spiked hair, nose ring, and the Sid Vicious shirt liked me.

Sarah interrupted me. "Hey, are you okay?"

"Why wouldn't I be?"

Sarah was shocked at my response since I was usually so emotional. The truth is I was relieved, as most of the time I was walking on eggshells, hoping neither of my parents would provoke the other.

Since it was rare that either of them were home at the same time, the weeks between my dad leaving and my first visit to his new apartment felt fairly normal. Most of my friends already had divorced parents, and they were pretty okay with it. There was even a restaurant on the Upper West Side called Marvin Gardens where all the divorced dads took their kids on Wednesday nights. Sarah said they had the best cheeseburgers, and Marvin used to come out personally to talk to all the kids. If he heard that your parents had recently split, he would even bring you an extra scoop of ice cream with Hershey's chocolate syrup for dessert.

I asked April if she felt upset about the separation; after all, our family was finally back together.

"I think it's great. We'll get to have two houses. And when you have divorced parents, they usually feel really guilty, and each parent is trying to be the favorite so they act nicer and buy you more stuff."

"I am not sure if Mommy thinks that way," I said.

"You just don't know how to handle her the way I do. You need to make her work for your love a little harder. Give her the silent treatment when she screams at you. It works like a charm every time."

My dad wanted April and me to meet Violetta, so we were meeting up at his new apartment for an authentic Northern Italian meal prepared by Violetta. April kept pulling me along, urging me to walk faster. "Hurry up, I am starving. Why are you walking so slowly? Didn't you hear there was going to be homemade food?"

We were only going from Lexington to Second Avenue, but those two blocks felt endless, and I was having a hard time making my feet move in a forward direction. Walking into the modern apartment, with floor-to-ceiling windows, stark white walls, and an ivory-colored leather sofa, I was shocked at how clean, organized, and utilitarian it was—the opposite of our family brownstone, which was always in total chaos.

"Violetta loves Danish modern," my dad said. "She discovered this type of furniture while living abroad; all the stuff is so sleek and functional, the way we envision our little abode to be."

Looking at the Scandinavian-furnished apartment, I remembered all the weekends my dad dragged me from antique shows to flea markets in search of old gramophones, rolltop desks, and rocking chairs. He told me he dreamed of retiring from advertising in order to open his own antiques store, specializing in mission furniture and antique toys from the 1800s. One time, I even almost lost my foot when he got a hot lead on an old vending machine that dispensed signed original Beatles trading cards. He had me sit in the front of the shop with the German shepherd watchdog as he went with the owner into the back room, where he would appraise the cards signed by Ringo Starr and John Lennon. I swung my feet back and forth as I waited, and the dog became aggressive and began chewing on my rubber flip-flops, biting a huge hole in my foot. Before rushing me to the hospital, where I got sixteen stitches, my dad made sure the antique machine was carefully wrapped with two layers of bubble wrap.

April was wandering freely through the apartment and called out, "No second bedroom," as my dad fed me a piece of warm bread with a homemade bean dip topped with sprigs of fresh rosemary and pine nuts. Inhaling the intoxicating smells from the kitchen—roasted garlic with braised meat—I could not help but let out a big, fat "YUM," even as I realized that no second bedroom meant my dad had no intention of ever inviting April or me to stay for a night.

Violetta emerged from the kitchen. She was totally different from what I had expected—big oversized glasses, cropped hair, and a tailored suit. My dad kept looking for my approval, tickling me as he winked all googly-eyed at Violetta.

"Did you know that there are more than twenty different types of Italian cuisines?" my dad informed me. "Each region has its own specialty. Southern Italy is known for seafood, Northern Italy is known for their risotto, and Central Italy is known for their cheeses. Violetta taught me that while we toured Milan, Tuscany, and Positano. We not only went to the most amazing restaurants and vineyards, but I learned to eat like a 'real Italian'—small portions of pasta, a little meat, and a big salad after the meal—never before—to help with digestion. 'Real Italian food' is nothing like the greasy stuff from the New York San Gennaro Festival in Little Italy—sausages with green peppers, meatball heroes with gloppy tomato sauce, and fried zeppoli with powdered sugar heavily soaked in cheap oil."

"That is not real Italian food!" Violetta and my dad both said in unison.

I used to love going down to Mulberry Street for the festival. While I never thought the food was great, it was something we did almost every year as a family, and I looked forward to it. My dad used to say he loved it too.

While Violetta was busy preparing the meal of Vitello Tonnato—cold veal with a thick, creamy sauce flavored with tuna and garnished with anchovies and capers—and tiramisu for dessert in which she used real Italian espresso to dip the ladyfingers, April seemed to be joyfully bonding with her. She was amused by Violetta's story of how they brought Cheecho the cat all the way from Italy. And she nodded approvingly as she tasted Violetta's gnocchi exploding with gorgonzola cheese—the rich, fragrant sauce sliding down the side of her face.

"Dad, I can see why you like living with Violetta. These dumplings are heavenly, Violetta. My mom never cooks like this."

"It's not complicated, just put some cream, wine, and stock over medium-high heat in a cast iron sauté pan and cook it until it starts to bubble."

"We don't have a cast iron sauté pan."

"You're joking."

"V, there were never any proper pans and very few utensils in April's mom's place. I was always so frustrated. The first time you cooked for me, giving me a knife, fork, and a spoon, I fell instantly and madly in love with you. You didn't even need to cook me a thing."

"Oh, Al," Violetta said, gleaming at my dad.

Looking up, I saw April cozying up to Violetta, complimenting her on her silk blouse with shoulder pads, the chic apartment, even complimenting her on her musical taste and highlighted hair. I never felt any ill will toward April, but at that moment, I remember thinking both her and my dad were traitors. With all her flaws and wacky behaviors, our mom was still our mom, and she would die for us. She had given up the last two and a half years of her life touring with my sister. How could April forget that so easily and befriend Violetta, who my dad had left my mom for a mere month ago? Besides, Violetta wasn't even that pretty, with her short, sassy hair, her boyish figure, and her fake accent insulting everything that wasn't Italian. "Americans do not know how to eat. Americans are so behind on style. I just had to order the Italian newspaper so I can find out what is really going on in the world. Americans are so ignorant about politics."

Italian this, Italian that; the funny thing was she hadn't even grown up in Italy. She was an American transplant who lived in Italy for a few years because she worked for the Italian airline Alitalia, and now she seemed to have some kind of superiority complex. While she might have had a lot of knowledge about all things Italian, she certainly didn't know anything about kids, pouring my eleven-year-old sister a glass of wine and declaring, "It's Italian to drink with dinner."

Even though I didn't think having a glass of wine was a big deal, I turned her down when she offered me a glass. My dad just shook his head. "It would be polite just to have a sip for a toast." My dad seemed to agree with everything Violetta said. He didn't even mind being her sous-chef, taking orders on how to roll the basil to slice it into perfect strips for the bruschetta, or cleaning the kitty litter box, although he had always declared he was allergic when I begged for a pet.

Watching them hug and kiss, I thought back to the way my parents would always argue, and how April and I spent hours under the bed covering our ears. How full of fear we often were as we lay in bed at night listening to them yell at each other—the sound of glass breaking from the other side of the house. As Pavarotti played in the background and Violetta brought out the prosciutto garnished with buds of black pepper, onions, and tomatoes, I thought how much prettier and calmer this picture was. We never had appetizers while listening to opera at home, but telling Violetta how wonderful the prosciutto was and humming along to the music made me feel like I was betraying my mom. Even though my feelings for her were complicated and went from love to hate in a single instant, I was my mother's daughter, and I would stand by her during this divorce, especially since she seemed so uncharacteristically emotional.

One night, I even caught her looking through old photo albums, secretly admitting that she would miss my dad. After all, he had been in her life for nineteen years, and they had traveled all over the world together: London, Nairobi, Phnom Penh, Hong Kong, and Marrakesh while he was filming commercials. She even brought out a five-page love letter that he wrote a few years earlier; he expressed how he needed my mother to fill his emptiness and declared that no one could ever replace her. But there she was—replaced!

Not only had my mom been replaced, but when we looked around our living room, we noticed that a whole part of her life and our family life was not there. Packing up all his belongings a couple weeks earlier, my dad had taken not only his massive collection of shirts, but also many of the artifacts and memorabilia that had hung on our walls, including the hand-carved African masks and spears from the Maasai tribes of Kenya, from when my parents went on a photographic safari. My mom dreamily reminisced about how my dad, with the help of their private tour guide, charmed one of the elder tribesmen into accepting one of his cameras in exchange for the shields and spears. As a sign of Maasai gratitude and hospitality, my parents were invited into the communal hut—built from mud, grass, sticks, and cow dung—to eat a traditional meal of raw milk, cow's blood, meat, and tea. My mom said she did not usually like tea, and the idea of raw milk and cow's blood turned her stomach, but being respectful, she drank both. After drinking the blood, the sweet tea was unusually delicious.

The tea was made in a big saucepan over a wood fire. When the water boiled, the tea was dropped into the water and mixed with milk and many spices. After several minutes, it was carefully strained into old clay mugs and sweetened with a pinch of sugar. As my mom drank the tea, she and my dad watched the sunset. The cardamom, ginger, and cinnamon were calming, and the meat, consumed later, was flavorful and smoky-tasting from the fire. My mom said it was her favorite meal ever, and knowing my mother's attitude toward food, I knew this meant a lot.

Since my mom had come back from touring with my sister, she seemed nicer, more nurturing, even motherly. For years, she let me run around the city unattended. But now she needed to know where I was every minute—even forbidding me to go out clubbing past midnight, which is the time I usually left the house. I wanted to tell her it was too late, she couldn't control me or tell me what to do. I was grown, and she was just as responsible as my dad for this divorce. But I couldn't really tell either of my parents how I felt. They each wanted me to take their side, and I felt stuck in the middle of their conflict, their turmoil, and their anger at each other.

When I looked at my sister trying on Violetta's exercise pants that my dad bought her in every color from her favorite boutique in Milan, I saw no conflict, no tug-of-war, no division of loyalty—just a little girl enjoying new foods, making a new friend, and trying on some fashionable clothing, as the two of them did grand pliés in the kitchen. *"Perfecto, perfecto!"* Violetta kept shouting as April kept doing the ballet moves—position one, two, and three.

I felt guilty for being upset. It was good that April liked Violetta, and that the situation brought her no discomfort. Sitting down to dinner, watching Violetta, my dad, and April sprinkle Parmigiano-Reggiano on their carpaccio, talking about the origin of the oil that was deep, dark, and green because it came from Italy, and talking about Violetta and my dad's next vacation, on which they promised they would include April, I felt more alone than ever. I realized I did not know my dad, or my sister, and of course, I had just met Violetta. I wondered if they saw how uncomfortable I was, as I politely smiled, telling Violetta how delicious the veal with tuna sauce was. Actually, it was probably the most incredible thing I'd ever eaten, which made the situation even more confusing.

I knew I could learn a lot from Violetta about cooking, Italian ingredients, and the ways different people ate in different regions of Italy. But she was not looking to be my mom, my stepmom, or even my cooking teacher. She was looking to create her own world with my dad. I could also tell she liked April more than me. April looked like my dad with olive skin and a perfectly turned-up button nose. She even had his quick wit and sense of humor—luckily she did not inherit his problem with his weight—which was now back up to almost three hundred pounds.

April did not need anything from Violetta or my dad. She and Violetta were able to bond instantly and enjoy each other's company with no expectations. April never seemed to care that my dad missed every single parent-teacher conference, attended only a couple of her opening nights, and called her a only few times a month.

I envied April not only for her talent as an actress and a singer, but for the way she adapted to new situations, and her lack of expectations. As much as I didn't want to care, there was still a part of me that needed both of my parents to love and accept me.

Taking a breath, I remembered how free I had become over the last couple of years. Now, like my mom, I loved low-cut shirts, platform shoes, and the nightlife. I was no longer the little girl she had left behind who wanted to stay home, clean the house, and be relied on for babysitting and chores. I had my own life. I was popular and had found a whole underground subculture of artists, photographers, and misfits like me, where I was accepted and understood. I'd even had a photography exhibit at the International Center of Photography where I showcased my black-and-white pictures of homeless people, accompanied by poems about who they were and what they had dreamed of being when they were teenagers.

My home life was never going to be the fantasy I often played out in my mind—my life was only going to be as good as I made it. After that night, my dad and I never cooked together again. Violetta took care of my dad in a way that I could not. While he occasionally shared his new diets, I never lived with him again. My mom had full custody of me and April, and she became very involved in my day-to-day life, until my sister was cast in the off-Broadway show *Really Rosie*, then the film version of *Annie*, and later the hit show *Charles in Charge* with Scott Baio. I studied for my SATs, filled out college applications, and eventually received early admission to the Newhouse School of Public Communications at Syracuse University, where I would study film and photography.

I had often believed that if I tried hard enough, I could keep my family together. If I tried hard enough, I could meet their needs, their longing, their hopes, and then, one day, in turn, my longings would be met. But the truth is, like oil and water, some ingredients are not meant to be combined. In the words of my grandmother Beauty, "A good relationship, like a good recipe, requires balance—three cups of wisdom to every one cup of sugar."

I was ready to create the recipe of my life, mixing in new ingredients, tasting and adjusting, finding the right balance to discover what nourished me. And no matter where this experimenting would lead, I knew I would always have Beauty guiding my way.

Violetta's Vitello Tonnato

FOR THE MEAT:

 2 pounds boned veal, cut from the rump
 ½ tin of salted anchovies, drained and thinly sliced
 1 garlic clove, thinly cut
 2 bay leaves
 1 small carrot, peeled and quartered
 6 black peppercorns
 2 celery sticks, quartered
 8 ounces dry white wine

FOR THE SAUCE:

 2 large eggs
 1 garlic clove, peeled
 1 teaspoon salt (plus additional to taste)
 10 ounces extra virgin olive oil
 2 dessert teaspoons white wine vinegar
 7 ounces best-quality tuna, packed in oil, drained
 5 anchovy fillets, packed in olive oil, drained
 Juice of a lemon
 Salt and pepper, to taste

FOR THE GARNISH:

 2 tablespoons capers, drained, for garnish
 Lemon slices for garnish
 A few sprigs of parsley

Remove the fat from the veal. Make several incisions in the meat. Take 2 of the anchovy filets and cut into pieces. Insert the anchovies and garlic into the veal. Roll up the meat and secure with string. Put the meat in a bowl with the bay leaves, carrots, peppercorns, and celery, and pour the wine over it. Cover and marinate in the refrigerator for 2 hours.

Preheat oven to 325 degrees. Remove the meat from the marinade and place in a roasting pan and cook for 1 hour and 15 minutes. While the meat is cooking, make the sauce.

Break the eggs into a food processor, and add the garlic and 1 teaspoon of salt. Then pour in the oil slowly and mix. After all the oil has been added, stir in the vinegar and blend. Add the tuna and the anchovies and blend till smooth. Then add a tablespoon of the lemon juice, and salt and pepper to taste. Then chill. When the veal is done, take it out of the oven to cool. Slice it thinly. Spoon the sauce over the sliced meat and garnish with capers, lemon slices, and parsley. Cover with plastic wrap and chill overnight in the refrigerator before serving.

Real Italian Tiramisu

6 egg yolks
½ cup sugar
10 ounces Italian mascarpone cheese
4 egg whites
2 tablespoons sweet marsala wine or dark rum
24 ladyfingers
12 ounces Italian espresso or extra-strong coffee, brewed and cooled
3 ounces dark semisweet chocolate, shaved

In a large bowl, whisk the egg yolks and half the sugar until pale and doubled in volume. It should take about 4 minutes. Whip in the mascarpone, a little at a time. In another bowl, beat the egg whites and remaining sugar until stiff, glossy peaks form. Fold the egg whites into the mascarpone mixture. In another bowl combine the rum and cooled coffee. Dip the ladyfingers quickly into the coffee and arrange a layer of them at the bottom of a 9 x 13-inch pan. Do not over soak the ladyfingers in the coffee; otherwise your tiramisu will be soggy.

Spread ⅓ of the mascarpone mixture on top of the ladyfingers and sprinkle with shaved chocolate.

Top with another layer of dipped ladyfingers and then more cheese and chocolate. It's like building lasagna. Then one more layer of ladyfingers, cheese, and chocolate. Cover with plastic and chill overnight.

Note: *Violetta said the difference between American and Italian tiramisu was that "real Italians whip the egg whites into the cheese instead of using whipped cream. Also this tiramisu is not overly sweet."*

African Chai Tea

2½ cups water
2 teaspoons black tea leaves
½ teaspoon cardamom
2 cinnamon sticks
¼ cup sugar (you can use a little less if you don't like a sweet tea)
1½ cups milk of choice

Simmer the water, black tea leaves, cardamom, cinnamon sticks, and sugar for 15 minutes on a medium heat. Add the milk and heat for another 2 minutes. Strain and serve.

Epilogue

My Dad's Cancer

....

Healing Mushroom Miso Soup,
Mushroom Latkes, Beet Chips

....

Right before my son's second birthday, my dad called me. That in itself was unusual because it was Wednesday, and my dad only phoned on the first Sunday of the month or holidays. It was neither. As soon as I picked up the phone, he said, "It's bad, really bad!"

I thought his blood pressure, which was often in the danger zone, had gone through the roof, or his weight had ballooned again, or he had broken up with Violetta.

"Cancer, lung cancer," he said. "The prognosis is not good. I'm going to die."

I was totally taken aback. Although my dad was never the picture of health and had chain-smoked for years, I always assumed he would be around forever. I didn't know what to say. I was trying to be positive, telling him I knew he would be fine. But I didn't really know anything about his diagnosis. I could not even fathom it was real. He told me he had been coughing up blood for weeks, filling his handkerchief with red mucus, but he assumed that it was bronchitis He walked into the ER with the anticipation of getting a strong antibiotic and maybe some throat lozenges, but walked out with a stage three cancer diagnosis after the CT scan showed a grapefruit-sized tumor on the upper ventricle of his lung.

The room began to spin as my dad gave me a summary of the events of the past week. My son was curled up on my lap. I had just been trying to get him to fall asleep when my dad phoned. Rocking back and forth on the glider nursing chair that my dad had bought me when Dylan was born, I tried to muster up something witty or encouraging to say. But I was tongue-tied, and everything I said was just coming out wrong. And my dad, always an ad man, was not much for emotional conversations.

"You know there is an upside to this," my dad said.

I was hoping he was going to say something like when you get sick, it makes you realize that family is the most important thing, or he really wanted to spend more time with me and Dylan. Maybe he'd come into the city and go to the playground with us, or to an amusement park, or maybe have a regular weekend date at the Museum of Natural History. Maybe he would invite us to the Connecticut home he had moved to with Violetta when he retired, and we could have weekly family dinners. For that one brief second, I forgot my dad was sick and allowed myself to be swept up in that little-girl fantasy, where I felt safe with my dad's love and the promise that he was going to be a more present grandfather than he'd been a father. I had spent years waiting for my dad to say he loved me, was proud of me, was looking forward to spending time with me. Maybe he now longed to be closer as well.

"The good news is that one of the side effects of chemotherapy, which I will be starting next week, is weight loss. You win some, you lose some."

I didn't know how to respond, so I just chuckled. My dad was always happiest when his one-liners made you laugh.

"Did you get a second opinion, did you think of seeing a doctor with a more integrated approach? My neighbor Clara told me her father cured himself from cancer by meditating."

"It is what it is. My dad died of cancer, my brother Melvin had cancer, and now I have cancer."

"But Uncle Melvin is alive. If he fought it, so can you."

"Maybe. But I am not hopeful. Like the saying goes, 'You only go around once in life.' I've gone around at least twice."

After we hung up the phone, I called my sister, who was always much more logical, less emotional.

"Daddy just called; he says he has cancer and is going to die." It was only when I said the words out loud to my sister that the tears began to pour down my face.

"Daddy used to say he was dying when he had a cold. Lots of people survive cancer."

My sister, now a lawyer and married with a child of her own, was no longer an actress. She had gotten a law degree after attending Brown University for college. She was now taking time off to raise her son Sean, who was six, and living in LA with her husband, who was also a lawyer.

"I am going to call Daddy, and I will try to fly to New York next week. In the meantime, try to distract yourself until we have some real details. There is nothing we can do until we have some hard facts."

She was right. After I hung up with her, I called Beauty. She urged me to get out of my stuffy apartment and get a little fresh air. "Maybe take a walk to the health food store," she suggested.

"Read some books about foods that help cancer." I listened to her advice and transferred my sleeping child into the stroller, and off we went. The health food store had always been a magical place for me. I could find peace among the vitamins and bins of grains, perhaps the way Holly Golightly was able to find strength at Tiffany, or a religious person finds solace at temple or church. Once I was among the self-help books and vibrant green vegetables, the possibilities seemed endless. With Dylan in the stroller beside me, I looked through book after book on anti-cancer regimens that would help my dad live. I wanted my son to have the chance to get to know his grandfather. How was he going to get to know him if he was going to die?

While my dad was not great at being around, when he was around he could make me laugh harder than anyone else that I had ever met, and he was really, really smart. He knew how to make a room come to life with his charm and humor and was the most awesome Scrabble player I'd ever met. He knew almost every word in the dictionary, and when I was studying for my SATs and would call him—"I bet you don't know the meaning of this one"—he always did. I knew there was so much I did not know about my father, so many unanswered questions about his childhood, his relatives. I wanted to know why he was so private, what made him need to keep up such a protective wall that never allowed him to be comfortable with feelings, but mostly I wanted my son to know him, as I had never met my dad's father, who died of cancer before I was born.

The nutritionist at the vitamin counter was extremely knowledgeable on the subject—advising me to send my dad books about macrobiotics, juicing, vitamin therapy, the Gerson Diet, coffee enemas, raw foods, acupuncture, food combining, apple cider vinegar, and the power of positive thinking. I was feeling calmer, knowing there were so many ways to possibly heal yourself from cancer. The vitamin man said, "Sometimes cancer is not a death sentence but a wake-up call. While there is a lot we can't control, there is much we can control—the first being what we feed our body." He explained that when a person eats anything processed, he is not only eating dead food, where the enzymes have been destroyed, but also adding preservatives and toxins, which are very destructive to the body. "This may not be significant for a normal, healthy person, but for the cancer patient, eliminating anything with preservatives is a matter of life or death! The liver needs to detoxify, destroy, and metabolize all foreign substances from the body." He proceeded to draw a little diagram of the cells with swords. "When you have cancer, the bad calls are trying to destroy you. You must fight back with diet and a spiritual practice."

I was ready to help my dad fight.

Before I sent the books and notes to my father, I highlighted the pages I thought were the most enlightening and Xeroxed a bunch of recipes. The store was a local hangout for healers, holistic practitioners, and health junkies like me. Every day, I went there for both a power smoothie and some good conversations with other moms. While we usually spoke about things like should we or should we not vaccinate, should we give our kids cow's milk or soy milk, what was the best snack to tote in our Maclaren stroller, today I asked all the nursing moms in the cafe upstairs if they had any experience with cancer. Everyone seemed to have a story or a remedy. I received recipes for a miso mushroom broth guaranteed to rev up the immune system, a ginger tea to help with nausea from chemotherapy, a raw potato puree for suppressing the growth of cancer cells, and a carrot juice recipe to shrink tumors. I also grabbed a brochure on the power of noni juice to alkalize the body.

I was so excited to send my dad the books and recipes and even more excited when he called me the next day after he received the express package. Even though my dad was not a self-help kind of guy, something in those books and papers resonated within him. While days before he had felt defeated, believing that his diagnosis was a death sentence, now he seemed pretty upbeat. In addition to seeing his regular family doctor, who had sent him to the local oncologist at the Stamford Hospital, he began researching other doctors—even aggressively pursuing an oncologist at Sloan Kettering who he said wouldn't initially return his phone calls. He'd begun pitching high-profile doctors and creating a treatment plan with the same strategy he used when he was pitching new business and designing a marketing campaign for a product.

"Getting in to see one of these top doctors is like getting into a four-star restaurant on Saturday night without reservations. You can't believe how many favors I had to pull to meet with the different doctors who will be a part of my healing team."

My dad was now on a quest to beat cancer and survive. Instead of obsessing about his disease, he focused his energies on researching his survival. My dad had lived on white rice, liquid diets, and low-carb, high-protein, high-fat, and low-fat regimens. Now he was determined to tackle his illness with the same pure conviction and focus with which he approached every new diet or ad campaign. It was no longer about cancer; it became about trying new foods—goji berries, mushrooms, wheatgrass, blue-green algae, and fermented foods—that would put his body at ease and help combat disease. If there was one thing that excited my dad, it was trying new foods. As a lifetime yo-yo dieter, he was always looking for that miracle plan, that miracle food, that miracle spice, that miracle recipe, but this time he truly needed a miracle—and taste and calories were secondary to nutritional benefits.

My dad went through months of chemotherapy and radiation in order to shrink the mass enough so that he could have surgery to remove the tumor. He also experimented with all kinds of new food preparations. He sautéed, steamed, pureed, broiled, and juiced. He was open to all my ideas and recipes. He often called me. "Should I broil the mushrooms or toss them in a soup? Do I juice the vegetables or steam them? Do I really need to give up all desserts?"

To support his immune system, he also followed a strict elimination cleanse of no dairy, meat, alcohol, coffee, or sugar, and added gallons of vegetable juices, fish, and lots of healing broths. He also added several vitamin supplements, a tincture made out of a mushroom extract, and ten crushed apricot kernels per meal, and began doing Reiki. "Every time I perform Reiki on myself, I really feel the heat penetrating my body. I use the energy practice on myself when I am lying on medical tables, getting blood drawn, or getting chemotherapy. I also use it when I'm craving a Subway sandwich or Big Mac. Whenever I pass one of those drive-thrus, I stare them down—*It's you or me*. I choose me, and keep driving."

This anti-cancer regimen definitely took a lot of work, and the foods were a stretch from the Jewish food my dad grew up on or even the extreme diets he had subjected himself to on his endless quest to lose weight. As he made the anti-cancer soup with shitake, portabella, and maitake mushrooms, he remembered how his mother, my Bubbe Mary, cooked for him when he was in a coma, and how she said it was the smells from her kitchen that brought him back to life. Bubbe was gone, but he remembered her mushroom barley soup, and how the thick broth revived him. "Soup is good food," she always said. He agreed—turning it into a famous tag line for Campbell's home-style brand. Like his mom, he was now learning to cook with purpose.

Researching and learning about alternative therapies and cooking his own healing remedies gave him a new purpose and zest for living. In fact, he never lost his appetite during his chemo treatments, or felt sick or nauseous, which his doctors said was highly unusual. Rather than surrendering to the disease or putting himself only in the hands of Western doctors, he developed his own routine that empowered him and brought him strength. His days mostly revolved around cooking, shopping, acupuncture, and his weekly chemotherapy treatments. He said he kept waiting for some awful side effect, but he had none.

He did, however, have to get a buzz cut since he was losing a lot of hair. When he arrived at his chemo, he always was in good spirits, dressed in bright colors and equipped with a Woody Allen movie that he would watch during the treatment. My dad said it always bummed him out when he entered the waiting room and saw everyone wearing sweatpants and baseball hats. And when my sister bought him an LA Lakers' hat, he said putting that on and covering his head would make him feel like he was giving in. He would wait until he was well and had a clean bill of health to wear it. He didn't mind his crew cut and found a sense of peace in his routine. My dad had a big support team that consisted of not only me, my sister, and his girlfriend Violetta; but even my mother, who had been angry at him for years, got on board, sending him a special mattress made out of magnets to pull the toxins out of his body and finding him the strongest grade of medicinal mushrooms, which she located in LA, where she was now living to be closer to my sister.

When the results came back that the mass in my father's lung had shrunk enough to be operable, my whole family made a plan to have a big dinner the night before the surgery. My dad insisted he would abandon the healthy eating for one night, and no one was allowed to say the C word. No one questioned his decisions. My uncle Melvin flew in from Chicago. April flew in from Los Angeles. My dad booked a hotel room at the Plaza Athénée on East Sixty-Fourth Street, which was walking distance from both the restaurant Il Vagabondo, where we were going to dine, and Sloan Kettering Hospital, where the operation was going to take place. And I, who lived across town from the restaurant, just needed a taxi.

The dinner was a celebration of sauce, cheese, and the wonders of deep-fried food. During dinner, there was no talk about my dad's surgery the next day, no talk about what would happen next, just lots of food and several desserts. When the tartufo, the rum cake, and the spumoni ice cream appeared, my sister kicked me. "Not a word!" she pleaded. I kept quiet, making my dad happy by trying every dessert that went around the table. Like his mother, he believed there was a certain unspoken love in being surrounded by lots of big portions of food and mouths too busy to talk. Violetta did not even mention that this was not real Italian food.

At the hospital the next day, my dad made jokes before going into surgery, about carving a turkey and about his mobster roommate. "I think he is part of some famous crime family. Who knows what he has stashed under that green hospital gown." But before he was wheeled away, he squeezed my hands. "You know you have been a good daughter, right?" Lying there on that gurney covered with the lightweight white blanket was the most vulnerable I had ever seen my dad. But before I had the chance to say anything back, the nurse wheeled him away through the flapping doors, and then, just like that, he was gone.

It would be hours before we would know the results of the surgery. My father requested that instead of waiting in the cafeteria, where they had awful food, that April, Violetta, and I could make a quick run to Andre's Hungarian Bakery on Second Avenue for apple strudel. He said having a strudel waiting for him would bring him *mazel*—luck in Hebrew.

Whether it was the strudel with the flaky crust waiting for him, the gallons of carrot juice, or the hundreds of bowls of the mushroom miso broth, my dad came through the surgery like a champ.

During those months when he hovered between life and death, we had a connection. It was not like something in a Hallmark commercial, but we were able to bond over the excitement of talking about food and sharing healthy recipes—my two favorite things. While my dad was still the funny guy and I was still the emotional girl, we both could agree that when you cook a pot of mushroom soup just the right way, miracles can happen.

Twelve years have passed since my dad received a clean bill of health. Just before Thanksgiving, he had another health scare— a minor heart attack. He called me as I was preparing turkey for my family. "Guess what, I'm not eating turkey this year," he said. "I just found a new book with the vegan diet that President Clinton is following. Are you vegan?" he asked.

"No," I replied. "I eat a variety of food, fruits and veggies, some grass-fed meat, and wild fish." He was no longer listening, too excited to share his new diet adventure. . . .

Healing Mushroom Miso Soup

Yield: 8 servings

1 (2–3 inch) piece fresh organic gingerroot, peeled and coarsely chopped
½ organic onion, chopped
1 tablespoon ghee
6 garlic cloves, chopped
1 cup sliced mixed raw mushrooms—shiitake, portabella, maitake
64 ounces of vegetable broth
1 cup organic dried shiitake mushrooms
½ pound tofu, diced
¼ cup organic miso paste (There are many types of miso to choose
   from. I like sweet white miso—this is a paste, not a powder—and
   you can add a little more if you like a strong miso flavor.)
1 head roasted garlic cloves, peeled and mashed
2 organic carrots, chopped
1 teaspoon of salt (preferably a truffle salt or good-quality Himalayan
   salt) or more to taste

In a stockpot, sauté the ginger and onion in the ghee over medium heat until the onion just begins to sweat. Add the raw garlic and raw mushrooms and cook until browned. Then add the broth to the pot and bring to a slow boil. Add the dried mushrooms, carrots, and tofu and then lower the heat, cover, and simmer for 30 minutes, or until the shiitakes are fully reconstituted.

While the pot of mushrooms is simmering, ladle about 6 ounces of the broth into a separate bowl and add the miso paste to it, whisking until the paste is dissolved. Next, add the mashed roasted garlic to this mixture. Once thoroughly combined, add the garlic-miso mixture back into the pot. Add salt to taste, stir well, and enjoy all the healing properties of this magic broth.

Note: *Miso is a traditional Japanese fermented soy or rice paste. Its healing power is often compared to chicken soup, especially when paired with immune boosters like garlic, ginger, onion, and shiitake mushrooms.*

Mushroom Latkes

3 tablespoons olive oil
1 cup diced onions
10 ounces mushrooms of choice, chopped
¼ cup red or yellow peppers
2 eggs, beaten (plus additional, as needed, for thinning)
½ cup chopped pecans
Salt and pepper, to taste
½ cup whole wheat flour (plus additional, as needed, for thickening)

Heat 1 tablespoon of the oil in a large nonstick skillet over medium heat. Add the onions and stir until soft. Add a little more oil and add the mushrooms and peppers. After about 10 minutes transfer to a plate and set aside. In a large bowl combine the beaten eggs, the pecans, and a touch of salt and pepper. Add in the cooled mushrooms and the flour. Stir together. Add the remaining oil to a clean skillet and allow it to warm but not smoke. Ladle in about a quarter of the batter. Allow to brown on the edges before flipping. Cook a few minutes on each side. Continue with the rest of the batter.

Note: *If the pancakes seem a little runny, add a touch more flour; if they seem a little dense, you can add a little more egg.*

Beet Chips

Yield: 4 servings

2 beets, peeled and sliced thin
Olive oil
Salt and pepper, to taste

Preheat oven to 375 degress. Toss the sliced beets in a bowl with olive oil and salt and pepper. Place on a baking sheet and bake until soft and crispy, about 20 minutes.

Note: *You can also do this with sweet potatoes, kale, or eggplant. For kale, the cooking time is about 10 minutes.*

Author's Note

....

Beauty's Salmon Patties

....

A t the insistence of my daughter, who was born three years after my dad's cancer scare, I am adding one more recipe, for Beauty's famous salmon patties. This was the first recipe my grandmother taught me to cook, and it was the first recipe she taught my son Dylan and my daughter Sofia to cook. It was also the dish I served at her shiva in Los Angeles, where my mom had put together the most wonderful gathering in celebration of my grandmother's life.

My grandmother had moved to California the year before she died. Always the life of the party, she made many friends and had quite the active social life. The night before her stroke, she was at a party with my mom till 3 a.m. dancing, telling jokes, and giving love advice to all the young people. Beauty never acted old, was never sick, and never stopped laughing. She often made whole audiences laugh at a theater; she would laugh so hard and so long that the audience would begin laughing with her. Knowing I would never hear Beauty's laugh again or taste her delicious food, I tried not to cry. All Beauty ever wanted for me was to be happy and to share my stories and her recipes.

When the traditional Jewish ritual was over, I made sure everyone left with a recipe card for Beauty's salmon patties. That way a little bit of Beauty and the traditions that were so important to her would continue to live on.

Beauty

You will be the light in my heart that is always there.
You will be the voice that whispers someone cares.
You will be the spirit that carries me through the fright.
And the encouragements that will help me turn dark to
* light.*
You are in my kitchen when I cook and the inspiration for
* this book.*
I hope you hear me talking to you each day, as your voice
* has helped me to lead the way.*
When I was little, you called me your little beauty; and in
* turn, I named you.*
You touched everyone you ever met. Your spirit and fancy
* hats no one will ever forget.*
You danced and smiled till the end; I hope Papa is waiting
* for you when you ascend.*
You called me your hero but you were mine. You are the
* light inside that makes me shine.*

I love you
Dawn — (your little beauty)

Beauty's Salmon Patties

Yield: 16 patties

Oil, for frying
18 ounces canned wild salmon in water
2 eggs, beaten
1 cup finely chopped onion or ½ cup onion and ½ cup green or red
    pepper
1 cup tomato sauce
1 cup bread crumbs

Preheat oven to 350 degrees. Lightly oil a baking sheet. Drain the
liquid from the salmon and put the fish into a large bowl. Mash
with the back of a fork until the fish is in small flakes. Add the
eggs, onion, tomato sauce, and bread crumbs. Mix well and form
into patties. Fry the patties till brown. As soon as they are brown,
move them to the prepared baking sheet and bake for 15 to 20 minutes. Flip carefully with a spatula. Cook another 5 to 10 minutes.

Swap Chart

Many of the recipes in this book are in their traditional versions, as they were passed down from family and friends. As I do not want any recipe to be off limits, I am including the below chart of swaps. Whether you are gluten free, dairy free, nut free, egg free, or sugar free, there is an easy solution.*

Cooking with my grandmother Beauty, and then cooking for the ones I loved, created lasting memories. Use the recipes in this book as a blueprint to create your own family traditions. It is not so much what you cook, or how often you cook, but the bond that happens when you connect with the ones you love in the kitchen.

I look forward to connecting with you, hearing your stories and seeing your food photos, and answering your questions.

Love from my kitchen to yours,

Dawn

---

* I am not endorsing any specific ingredients or substitutions. I am just providing a brief list that I have found helpful when working with clients with various food sensitivities. Use the table as a guideline, as different ingredients may change both the taste and texture.

BREAD CRUMBS

Matzo Meal is a 1:1 swap in latkes and salmon patties—making it a perfect swap for Passover cooking.

BUTTER

Unrefined coconut oil, mashed bananas, applesauce, pumpkin puree, yogurt, Earth Balance, ghee, grapeseed oil, and margarine—these are all a 1:1 swap.

Mashed avocado is also a 1:1 swap. It works best in chocolate recipes. To start, try using half avocado and half butter, and if you like the results, you can add more avocado and less butter.

Prunes make a great butter substitute as well. Combine ¾ cup prunes with ¼ cup of boiling water and puree. This is a 1:1 swap.

CHEESE

Soy cheese, almond cheese

CHOCOLATE

Carob chips, cacao nibs

CORNSTARCH

Arrowroot: 1 tablespoon of arrowroot for every 2 tablespoons of cornstarch

CREAM CHEESE

Tofu cream cheese, ricotta cheese, cashew cheese (Soak cashews overnight. Drain and dry. Combine cashews and ¼ cup of water in a high-speed blender.)

EGGS

Ener-G Egg Replacer (follow directions on box)

1 tablespoon of flaxseeds whipped with 3 tablespoons of warm water. Let it sit in the fridge for ten minutes before using. Equals 1 egg.

2 egg whites: swap for 1 whole egg.

Chia seeds (Combine 1 tablespoon of chia seeds with 3 tablespoons of water and let sit for fifteen minutes. Then stir. The mixture substitutes for 1 egg.)

¼ cup of blended tofu equals 1 egg

¼ cup of regular yogurt or soy yogurt equals 1 egg

½ banana, pureed, equals 1 egg

¼ cup of applesauce plus 1 teaspoon of baking powder equals 1 egg

½ cup of buttermilk equals 1 egg

2 teaspoons of arrowroot equal 1 egg

GROUND BEEF

Ground dark meat turkey, ground lamb, ground dark meat chicken, and ground soy meat, tempeh

HONEY

Maple syrup, brown rice syrup, yacon syrup, raw honey, agave nectar, black strap molasses, sorghum syrup, evaporated cane juice, coconut nectar. These are a 1:1 swap.

Raisin puree (soak 2 cups of raisins in water overnight in a sealed container and then puree in a food processor.) Use 1 cup of the puree for 1 cup of a liquid sweetener.

Date puree (soak 1 cup of rinsed dates in 1 cup of water overnight in a sealed container and then puree in a food processor.) Use 1 cup of the puree for 1 cup of a liquid sweetener.

MILK

Soymilk, almond milk, rice milk, hemp milk, coconut milk, oat milk. The above all swap in equal ratios to dairy milk. These are a 1:1 swap.

NOODLES

Matzo can replace noodles in kugel and lasagna during Passover.

PEANUT BUTTER

Almond butter, cashew butter, sunflower butter, soy nut butter. These are a 1:1 swap.

SOUR CREAM

Full-fat yogurt, Tofutti sour cream

SOY SAUCE

Low-sodium soy sauce, tamari, Bragg's amino acids

WHITE FLOUR

Spelt flour, Bob's Red Mill gluten-free flour, Pamela's all-purpose baking powder, and sprouted flours are all a 1:1 swap.

Oat flour is a 1:1 swap, but add an additional 1 teaspoon of baking powder to make it less dense.

Black beans and garbanzo beans swap out great in brownies. It is a 1:1 swap—just drain, rinse, dry, and puree.

Almond butter and peanut butter can swap for flour in baking cookies. It is a 1:1 swap.

Whole-wheat flour: 7/8 cup whole wheat to 1 cup of white flour.

Teff flour, brown rice flour, buckwheat flour, millet flour, hemp flour, soy flour, barley flour, corn meal, almond flour, coconut flour, and quinoa flour can be used as a substitute for white flour, but these are not equal swaps and amounts needed will vary depending on the other ingredients in the recipe.

WHITE PASTA

Brown rice pasta, whole wheat pasta, soba noodles, lentil pasta, mung bean pasta, quinoa pasta. Zucchini pasta made from raw zucchini spirals, spaghetti squash, and kelp noodles. These are all a 1:1 swap.

WHITE RICE

Brown rice, quinoa, farro, couscous, pearl barley, bulgur, millet. These are a 1:1 swap but cooking time varies with each grain.

WHITE SUGAR

Coconut sugar, palm sugar, Sucanat, brown sugar, date sugar. These are all 1:1 swaps.

Stevia: 2 tablespoons of stevia is a swap for 1 cup of sugar.

Xylitol: a 1:1 swap for white sugar, but shorten the baking time by 5 minutes.

YOGURT

Low-fat, soy, coconut, goat's milk

Acknowledgments

So many people inspired this story. To my agent, Lynn Jones Johnston, for convincing me my story was more than a collection of recipes. To Tara Parker-Pope at the *New York Times* Well Blog for taking a chance on me. You changed my life, and I am forever grateful. Also a big shout-out to Toby Bilanow, Andrew Scrivani, Karen Barrow, and everybody at Well for making my blogs look so beautiful, and my food look so delicious.

And a big, big thank-you to my editor, Denise Silvestro, for making this book and my dreams a reality. You are my angel. And to her assistant, Allison Janice; publisher Leslie Gelbman; Pamela Barricklow; Diana Franco; and to all the dedicated people at Berkley Publishing who took part in making this book. I am truly indebted.

To my mom; my dad; my sister, April; my grandmothers, Beauty and Bubbe Mary; my cousin Linda; my Aunt Jeannie; and my friends who allowed me to share their stories. Thank you for coloring my world.

Tracy Behar, Shelly Desai, Stephan Morrow, Charlie Sadoff, Pam Graf, Elana Goodridge, Joseph Lin, Erik Marengo, Brett Jeffryes, Catherine Ventura, you were there from the beginning. Thank you for listening, reading, and believing in me. And Jenny Isenstark, may you rest in peace.

Chef Toni's Kitchen, Chef Crystal at It's Delicious, Denise

Gunkel, Dion Rhodes, Michelle Farkus, and my kids, Dylan and Sofia—thank you for testing and retesting my recipes.

And thank you, thank you, Mom, for being my biggest cheerleader throughout this project!!!!!

And Dad: without you, I would never have found my true calling. From one foodie to another, I love you.

About Dawn Lerman, MA, CHHC, LCAT

I am a board-certified nutrition expert and contributor to the *New York Times* Well Blog, as well as the founder of Magnificent Mommies, a company specializing in personal, corporate, and school-based education.

My interest in healthy eating began at an early age, as I watched my obese father struggle with yo-yo dieting and fluctuating weight. I became fascinated with the correlation between what we eat and how we feel. Fueling my passion was my mentor, my grandmother Beauty, who inspired me as a child to learn how to cook and taught me about the power of healing through fresh ingredients.

Growing up, I was also involved in show business, first as an actress, then as a producer and writer. I coauthored the popular book *The Twelve Step Plan to Becoming an Actor in L.A.*, which became a regional bestseller.

In my thirties, when my son was two years old, I realized that inspiring other moms to make healthier food choices for their children and teaching them to cook was more than a hobby—it was my true passion. During this same period, my father was diagnosed with lung cancer, and I started investigating the correlation between diet and healing. This gave me the incentive to return to school and earn my degree as a health practitioner.

I am now recognized as a nutrition expert, counseling clients on weight loss, diabetes, high blood pressure, ADHD, and other diet-related conditions. I lecture at schools and corporations as well as contribute to local and national media outlets. I am the mother of two children, Dylan and Sofia. We live in New York City.